COMMONSENSE
COOKERY BOOK

BOOK 2

THE COMMONSENSE COOKERY BOOK

BOOK 2

REVISED EDITION

**Revised By Molly Breaden
Member, Cookery Teachers'
Association**

Angus & Robertson Publishers

Angus & Robertson Publishers

London . Sydney . Melbourne . Singapore

Manila

First published by Angus & Robertson Publishers, Australia, as
The Advanced Commonsense Cookery Book, 1948
Reprinted 1948, 1951, 1952, 1955, 1958, 1959, 1962, 1963, 1966, 1968, 1970, 1971.
Revised edition (as Commonsense Cookery Book, Book 2) 1978
Reprinted 1979
© N.S.W. Cookery Teachers' Association 1948, 1978

National Library of Australia
Cataloguing-in-publication data.

New South Wales Cookery Teachers' Association.
  The commonsense cookery book, book 2.

  Index.
  First published as The advanced commonsense
  cookery book, Sydney: N.S.W. Public Schools
  Cookery Teachers Association, 1948.
  ISBN 0 207 13664 5.

  1. Cookery. I. Title.

641.5

Printed in Hong Kong

CONTENTS

TABLE OF MEASURES

CUP AND SPOON MEASUREMENTS

The cup used in these recipes is the Australian standard metric holding 250 ml. Fill cup to measuring line only, not right to the brim. It is preferable to pour dry ingredients (flour, cornflour) from the packet, rather than to spoon them in. Ingredients are not pressed down unless the instruction is given.

SPOON MEASUREMENTS AND EQUIVALENTS

The tablespoon used in these recipes is the Australian standard metric tablespoon, holding 20 ml. The teaspoon holds 5 ml. It is not possible to give a general equivalent to the dessertspoon as modern spoons of this type vary considerably. In addition, the measurement is not recognized outside England and Australia.

Caution: American recipes featured in many recipe books always use tablespoons and teaspoons. Their teaspoon holds 5 ml but their tablespoon holds only 15 ml, which means that this measurement is not correct for Australian recipes.

A spoon measurement is *always level*. Dry materials such as flour should be smoothed off lightly with the back of a knife. Pressure exerted when levelling the contents of a spoon can cause packing of the granules, sometimes leading to increase in weight. Fats are levelled very firmly as light handling leaves air spaces and reduces the weight. Liquids should come just below the edge of the spoon. They should not spill over when the spoon is lifted.

There is usually a discrepancy between a cup/weight measurement and its division into spoons. This is so slight when reduced to one spoonful that it does not affect a recipe. It is not advisable, however, to measure more than 60 grams (2 ounces) by spoon.

CONVERSION TABLES

Weights

Pounds to Kilograms		
	exact measure	accepted measure
1	0.454	.5
2	0.91	1
3	1.36	1.5
4	1.81	2
5	2.27	2.5
6	2.72	3
7	3.18	3.5
8	3.63	4
9	4.08	4.5
10	4.54	5

TABLE OF MEASURES 3

Ounces to Grams		
	exact measure	accepted measure
1	28.35	30
2	56.70	60
3	85.05	90
4	113.40	125
5	141.75	155
6	170.10	185
7	198.45	220
8	226.80	250
9	255.15	280
10	283.50	315
11	311.85	345
12	340.20	375
13	368.55	410
14	396.90	440
15	425.25	470
16	453.59	500

Ounces to Spoons and Cups

t = teaspoon, T = tablespoon, C = cup

Food	1 oz	4 oz	8 oz
Almonds, ground	¼ C	1¼ C	2¼ C
whole	¼ C	¾ C	1½ C
Apricots, dried		1 C	1¾ C
Breadcrumbs, soft	½ C	2 C	4¼ C
dry	¼ C	1 C	2 C
Biscuit crumbs	¼ C	1¼ C	2¼ C
Butter, soft pliable	6 t	½ C	1 C
Cheese, grated cheddar	¼ C	1 C	2 C
parmesan	¼ C	1 C	2¼ C
Cherries, glace	2 T	¾ C	1½ C
Cocoa	¼ C	1¼ C	2¼ C
Coconut, desiccated	1/3 C	1 1/3 C	22/3C
Cornflour, custard powder	3 T	1 C	2 C
Currants	2 T	¾ C	1 2/3 C
Dates, whole		¾ C	1½ C
chopped	2 T	¾ C	1 2/3 C
Flour	¼ C	1 C	2 C
wholemeal		1 C	1¾ C
Gelatine	2 T		
Glucose liquid, golden syrup, honey	1 T	1/3 C	2/3 C
Haricot beans, split peas, lentils	2 T	2/3 C	1¼ C
Macaroni, small		¾ C	1 2/3 C
Milk powder, full cream	¼ C	1¼ C	2¼ C
skim	1/3 C	1½ C	3¼ C
Mixed fruit		¾ C	1½ C
Nuts, chopped	¼ C	1 C	2 C
halved walnuts		1¼ C	2½ C
whole peanuts		¾ C	1½ C
Peel	2 T	¾ C	1½ C
Prunes, without seeds		2/3 C	1¼ C
Raisins		¾ C	1½ C
Rice	2 T	¾ C	1½ C
Sugar, granulated	6 t	¼ C	1 C
castor	5 t	½ C	1¼ C
icing	2 T	¾ C	1½ C
soft brown	2 T	¾ C	1½ C

Sultanas	2 T	¾ C	1½ C
Yeast, dried	3 T	1 C	1¾ C
compressed	6 t	½ C	

Length Measurements

inches	mm	cm
1/16	2	
⅛	3	
¼	5	
½	10	1
¾	20	2
1	25	2.5
2	50	5
2½	62	6
3		8
4		10
6		15
7		18
8		20
9		23
10		25
12		30
14		35
16		40
18		45
20		50

Temperatures

100 degrees Celsius (boiling point) = 212 degrees Fahrenheit
0 degrees Celsius (freezing point) = 32 degrees Fahrenheit

Celsius (C.) into Fahrenheit (F.)

deg. C.	deg. F.	deg. C.	deg. F.
120	248	200	392
130	266	210	410
140	284	220	428
150	302	230	446
160	320	240	464
170	338	250	482
180	356	260	500
190	374		

Fahrenheit into Celsius

deg. F.	deg. C.	deg. F.	deg. C.
250	121	400	205
275	135	425	219
300	149	450	233
325	163	475	246
350	177	500	260
375	191		

For oven temperatures degrees Celsius approximately equals half of degrees Fahrenheit.

	warm		moderate		hot			very hot	
°C	150	160	180	190	200	220	230	250	260
°F	300	325	350	375	400	425	450	475	500

DICTIONARY OF TERMS USED IN ADVANCED COOKERY

Allemand — A white reduced veloute sauce (one of the four foundation sauces) enriched with cream and yolk of egg.

Angelica — A plant with tender tubular branches preserved and crystallized and used for garnishing.

Aspic — A clear savoury jelly used for moulds and as a garnish.

Au Jus — Any dish served in its natural juices.

Au Maigre — Any dish from which meat or meat extracts are excluded and which therefore may be served on fast days.

Au Naturel — A term applied to plain food cooked simply, also to anything served in its raw state such as oysters.

Baba — A light yeast fruited cake, or dessert soaked with syrup.

Bain-Marie — A double container, the lower of which holds boiling water. Sauces or other food can be kept hot in the top compartment without impairing their quality or consistency.

Bechamel — A cream-enriched white sauce recognized as one of the four foundation sauces.

Beignets — Fritters.

Bisque — Soup made of crayfish, chicken, game or fish.

Bouillon — A plain, clear soup made from shin of beef or veal.

Brioche — Very light yeast dough rich with eggs and butter, baked in muffin tins or cup moulds

Canapes — Small pieces of bread (plain, fried or toasted) used as a foundation for savouries.

Caviare — Pickled sturgeon roe.

Compote — A fruit stew cooked in a thick syrup, wine sometimes being added.

Condiments — Acid or salty or highly flavoured seasonings or spices.

Consomme — A clear soup.

Croquettes — Finely chopped cooked meat, fish, poultry, vegetables or nuts, bound with a panada, shaped and dipped in egg and breadcrumbs and wet fried. Two-thirds meat to one-third panada gives a soft, creamy mixture.

Croutes — Shapes of fried or baked bread, small or large, upon which entrees or hors-d'oeuvres are served.

Croutons — Small cubes of bread.

Cuisine — Kitchen cookery.

Eclair — Small finger-shaped choux pastry filled with cream or custard and iced.

Farinaceous — Foods containing or rich in starch, usually the flour or meal of wheat, corn, nuts or starchy roots.

Fleur — A shape of rich short crust, usually baked in a ring.

Flummery — A name given to a cold sweet for dessert; smooth fruit flavoured and jelly-like.

Fritter — Any article of food, sweet or savoury, dipped in batter or thin paste and deep fried.

Frosting — A white finish for cakes, based on stiffly beaten egg white.

Galantine — White meat or poultry boned, stuffed, cooked in liquid, pressed, glazed with aspic and served cold.

Garlic — A bulb resembling onion with a pungent taste, divided into many sections called cloves. Used so that it cannot be individually detected even though supplying the special flavour desired.

Garnish — To decorate a dish with edibles of ornamental appearance, to whet the appetite and create an attractive finish.

Gateau — A round, square or oval rich buttery cake or dough, decorated and served as a dessert.

Gherkin — A small green cucumber pickled with salt or vinegar, served as an hors-d'oeuvre and used for salads and sauce as well as for decorative purposes.

Giblets — Parts of poultry (neck, gizzard, liver, heart), used for soups, broths or pies.

Glace — Anything with a smooth or glossy surface such as a meat glaze, sauce or gelatine.

Hors-d'Oeuvres — Small cold or hot savoury dishes served as appetizers.

Horseradish — The fleshy root of a plant with a hot, pungent flavour, used fresh or dried for flavouring savoury sauces.

Julienne — A name given to vegetables cut into match-like lengths and to a vegetable clear soup garnished with julienne shreds.

Kedgeree — A dish of Indian origin, consisting of cooked fish and rice with hard-boiled egg and cream. A slight curry flavour.

Lentils — Seeds of a leguminous plant rich in vegetable protein. There are two varieties — red and brown.

Macaroni — A wheaten paste prepared from flour rich in gluten. *Paste lunghe* — shaped into various lengths and thicknesses, e.g. vermicelli, spaghetti. *Paste tagliate* — decorative shapes, e.g. shells, stars, letters.

Macaroons — A kind of sweet biscuit made of almonds, sugar and egg whites.

Macedoine — A mixture of various kinds of vegetables or fruits cut into small, even shaped discs.

Mousse — French term indicating frothy or foamy light-textured sweet/savoury dishes.

Nougat — A sweetmeat containing sugar and nuts.

Panada — A very thick white sauce used for binding croquettes etc.

Potage — Thick soup.

Quenelles — Delicate forcemeat balls made of fish, poultry or meat, dipped in egg and breadcrumbs and fried. Used as a garnish or may be served as a separate course. Often cooked in stock or water.

Ragout — A rich dark stew of meat or game.

Ramekins — Small quantities of savoury mixture with a sauce foundation, baked and served in special crockery or paper moulds.

Rissoles — Mixtures of finely chopped red or white meats bound with flour, egg, potatoes or breadcrumbs, made into various shapes and fried.

Rusks — Slices of cake or bread twice baked until dry and crisp.

Sauce — A liquid seasoning, savoury or sweet, served and eaten with food to improve appearance and flavour. The four rich foundation sauces are bechamel, veloute, allemande and espagnole.

Scallop — Shellfish.

Souffle — A light sweet or savoury dish well risen or puffed up with a stiffly-beaten egg white foundation. Cooked gently in a steamer or oven.

Tartare — A cold sauce made of egg yolks, oil, mustard, capers and gherkins, served with fried fish or cold meats or used as a dressing for salads.

Timbales — Mixtures of creamy white meat or fish cooked in dome-shaped moulds. The mould is often lined with macaroni, rice or short crust.

Veloute — A rich white sauce made from chicken stock and cream.

Vol-au-vent — A round or oval case of puff pastry filled with a savoury or sweet mixture.

COLD STORAGE IN THE HOME

REFRIGERATOR

The main purpose of a refrigerator is the short-term storage of food, which allows of many economies, for food can be kept until it is required. The housewife need not go shopping every day, and left-over dishes will keep safely, while many dishes can be prepared from food that would otherwise be thrown away. The food must be cooled before it is put into the refrigerator. Remember that free air circulation is essential. Cover all foods which do not have their own protective covering, except eggs, which are best kept in a rack or open bowl to ensure complete ventilation. Remember that wrapping and newspaper acts as an insulation preventing the proper penetration of cold. This should always be removed and replaced by thin plastic such as Glad Wrap available in bag or strip. Remember also that newspaper used for wrapping has been obtained from unknown sources, and could contaminate food.

Vegetables: These should be thoroughly washed and trimmed if necessary, and wrapped in suitable covering material. Salads in particular should always be stored in a special container to retain the moisture they need. What is known as a crisper is ideal for this because it has a cover. Good wrapping material or bags may be used instead of a crisper if liked. Small amounts of food can be put into screw-topped jars, and covered dishes or bowls may be securely fastened with cellophane covering, waxed paper, or plastic food wrapping.

Butter, Cream, Cheese and Milk: Dairy foods should be kept covered in their specially prepared wrappings. There is such a high percentage of fat in them that it will quickly absorb the flavour from any other food in the refrigerator.

Meat: Fresh meat, stored for daily use, in a separate section does not need to be wrapped, but the container should not be overloaded. Wash and dry the container before each supply of fresh meat goes in. Enough for four days should be the limit. Cooked meat must be cold then wrapped in suitable material or placed in a plastic container with tight fitting lid. Cover the cut surface of left-over joints with greaseproof paper before wrapping in plastic material.

Fruit: Bananas should not be stored in the refrigerator. All other fruit should be wrapped before it is placed on the refrigerator shelves, and berry fruit must be kept in covered jars or trays. Fruit remains in the same stage of ripeness when kept like this, especially the soft fruits such as berries, peaches, apricots, and plums. Pawpaws or rockmelons (cantaloupes) should be chilled before use, but they should either be wrapped whole in greaseproof paper and plastic wrapping or when cut put into large screw-top jars, otherwise the odour would affect other foods. Most modern refrigerators provide sufficient humidity space for fruit as well as vegetables.

Defrosting: Defrosting of the refrigerator is necessary when there is about a quarter of an inch of frost on the freezing coils. Turn the dial to the DEFROST position and remove foodstuffs and ice trays. When all frost has melted, remove and wash the shelves and wipe the interior of the cabinet with a clean soft cloth wrung out in warm water in which a little bicarbonate of soda, borax, ammonia, pure vanilla, or detergent has been dissolved. This should be done each time the refrigerator is defrosted, but never use soap. If you are going away, be sure to defrost and clean the refrigerator just before you leave. The refrigerator doors should be *left open.* If the refrigerator has automatic defrost it is essential that contents are checked and interior washed regularly.

HOME FREEZER

A home freezer has capabilities distinctly different from a refrigerator and offers new facilities and convenience for each owner to discover and enjoy.

Good food preservation requires a knowledge of the causes of spoilage and deterioration and the changes which may occur in food before and during the preserving processes. Ways to prevent or retard changes and spoilage are used to provide a satisfactory product. Deterioration may be caused in freezing by:

(i) desiccation, the loss of moisture-vapour from the food. It causes discolouration, often called "freezer-burn"; and

(ii) oxidation, when oxygen is absorbed into the product. When air is present it causes rancidity of fats and tainted flavours in food.

Desiccation and oxidation can occur simultaneously in foods at temperatures below freezing point 0°C. This kind of deterioration can be reduced to a minimum by proper packaging of food; containers made from moisture-vapour-proof materials, from which air can be removed, are best.

Benefits

A carefully-planned and well-stocked home freezer provides a variety of foods ready for selection when planning meals.

Home freezing is a safe method of preservation when carried out correctly, using quality foods prepared under hygienic conditions.

Home freezing retains a high proportion of the nutritive value of foods. Indeed, fruit and vegetables picked at their prime from the home garden and immediately quick-frozen, are superior in nutritive value when used months later to the so-called "fresh" fruit and vegetables sold through many retail channels.

Home freezing retains the original appetizing flavour, texture and appearance of food more closely than other preserving methods.

Money is saved when home-grown or home-produced foods are preserved in the home freezer. Added economy is possible by purchasing foods in bulk, or in season.

A home freezer makes available a wide variety of foods regardless of season. When foods are scarce and expensive, supplies from the home freezer can be used.

The number of crops grown each year can be reduced to one main crop of each product required, such as beans, carrots and broccoli. The most suitable variety for a particular locality can always be grown.

A whole animal carcass can be jointed, prepared, and stored at one time if freezer capacity is sufficient.

Less time and fewer journeys are needed for shopping, because larger quantities of food can be preserved at one time by freezing.

A concentration of labour and time must be made available for the preparation of foods in comparatively large quantities. Food for freezing can be prepared in time set aside for this purpose, or during less busy periods. A plan of work or re-arrangement of the work timetable is often helpful.

The major expense in the home freezing of foods is the cost of the freezer itself, but its many advantages more than compensate for the initial cost.

Types of Home Freezers

There are two main types of freezers for domestic use, the upright type and the chest type. Combination models of refrigerator with freezer are also available.

CHEST-TYPE FREEZER

Chest-type freezers have a lid opening. This type is slightly less expensive to run than other types because very little cold air spills out when the freezer is opened, and little warm, moist air enters.

More food can be packed into chest-type freezers as there are less space-divisions. Baskets provided in most models enable foods to be appropriately grouped. Defrosting and rotating of foods can be difficult if the owner of the freezer cannot easily reach the bottom of it. The chest-type freezer requires more floor space and overhead clearance than the upright type.

UPRIGHT-TYPE FREEZER

Upright-type freezers have a door opening and are fitted with shelves. Some or all of the shelves are surrounded by pipes through which the refrigerant circulates; this speeds the freezing of foods placed on the shelves. Foods are easily grouped and rotated on shelves. Latest models are fitted with sliding basket shelves which make storing, rotating and selecting food a very simple process.

Upright freezers sometimes frost-up more quickly than chest types because of easier passage of air in and out when the door is opened.

COMBINATION REFRIGERATOR-FREEZERS

Combination refrigerator-freezers are insulated cabinets cooled by refrigeration, but divided into two separated parts with separate doors.

The interior temperature of the refrigerator section is normally maintained between 2°C (35°F) and 5°C (40°F). This temperature is only suitable for holding fresh foods for a few days. The temperature in the frozen food section should be -20°C (0°F) or lower.

In some combination models, one thermostat controls temperature of both refrigerator and freezer section. The refrigerator temperature can be varied, but the freezer temperature may fluctuate with it. This is highly undesirable. In other combination models, the temperature of the freezer section is set to remain constant, even when defrosting the refrigerator section.

When purchase of combination models is considered, it is essential to find out to what temperature the freezer can be set, and if this temperature is constant. The temperature in the freezer can be checked with a freeze thermometer.

If the freezer is unsatisfactory, all reliable manufacturers are happy to investigate complaints and if possible, remedy any fault.

REFRIGERATORS WITH FROZEN STORAGE SPACE

Most modern refrigerators have space for frozen food storage. This is usually marked with a dividing door inside and separate to the main door.

Generally, unless specially designed otherwise, temperature in the frozen storage space fluctuates widely between the highest and lowest thermostat setting. In some models temperature in the frozen storage space can be reduced to -20°C (0°F), and so is suitable for storing frozen foods but not always suitable for freezing.

Before purchasing a home freezer find out what temperature the manufacturer guarantees the frozen storage space will maintain. It is important to find out before purchase the capabilities of any freezer, or refrigerator, or combination model. A manufacturer cannot make any one model serve purposes other than those for which it has been designed. Before starting to use it, read all information supplied with the machine. Machines have been well tested for all kinds of use.

Emergencies

Allow only experts to check the mechanism of your freezer when something goes wrong. Do not attempt to correct the trouble yourself.

Before sending for the service man check the following points:

- Is the main switch on?
- Is the electric plug loose or pulled out?
- Is the thermostat turned off?
- Has the fuse blown out?
- Is there a power blackout in the area?

A well-stocked freezer will keep contents safely frozen for about 24 hours in the event of a power failure, provided the freezer is kept tightly closed.

Dry ice may be used during a power failure, and when placed in the freezer with the frozen foods will keep them frozen in good condition for much longer than 24 hours.

THAWED FOOD

Food which becomes accidentally thawed must not be refrozen. It should be used within 24 hours if kept at refrigerator temperature 2°C (35°F) to 5°C (40°F). If this is not possible the food should be discarded or cooked and then frozen in this condition.

Planning

Plan the contents of the freezer several months in advance. Keep a record of the food stored with the date it was put in the freezer; this enables proper rotation of stocks. Remember to cross off the list those foods which are removed from the freezer. This list is a record which enables you to plan the freezer contents.

The main points to consider when planning are:
- Freezer capacity.
- Size and needs of the household.
- The appropriate seasons, or time of abundance of various foods.
- Quantity and type of foods produced in the home, garden or on the property.
- Time required and help available to prepare the foods for freezing.
- Rotation of frozen food stocks.

Selection of Foods

Select only those foods which are of good quality and optimum maturity; freezing does not improve the quality of a poor product.

All foods should be prepared and frozen when fresh, that is shortly after harvesting, soon after killing or immediately after preparation of cooked food.

Preparation of Foods

Prepare foods and freeze as quickly as possible. Fruits and vegetables will taste better and be more nutritious if prepared and frozen immediately after harvesting.

Pack all foods in moisture-vapour-proof materials in the quantities expected to be used at one time — for example, one package can comprise a family-size serving for one meal.

Packing the Freezer

Put food into the freezer only when the package is cold. Place packages to be frozen in the coldest area of the freezer. This is close to the sections in which the refrigerant circulates, usually the side walls of a chest model, and some of or all the shelves of an upright model. Leave a small space between packages; this speeds the freezing process.

Never freeze at one time more than the quantity advised by the manufacturer because large amounts of food will raise the temperature in the cabinet. If no advice is given, up to 5 kg at one time is satisfactory. Refrigerate excess food prepared for freezing.

The temperature of the first load of food should be reduced to -20°C (0°F) before it is transferred from the quick-freezing area to the storage section. Add the next load to the quick-freezing area, and repeat the process described.

Make full use of the freezer. Keep it filled with a variety of foods to obtain greatest efficiency and economy.

Make sure that the interior temperature of your freezer remains at -20°C (0°F) or lower, in order to store your frozen foods with the greatest degree of safety for the maximum possible time.

Store food no longer than the recommended maximum time; food kept frozen longer than this time may lose flavour or develop off-flavours. Milk sauces, non-egg custards, cream-pie fillings, gravy and mayonnaise tend to separate out and have a curdled appearance. Some sandwich fillings, for example, lettuce, tomato, jam may seep into the bread and make it soft.

The flavour of imitation vanilla deteriorates in low temperatures, so always use pure vanilla for flavouring foods to be frozen. Spice-type flavourings, for example, salt, chilli, pepper and onions lose their flavour after one to two months, so it is best to season food when it is reheated.

Fruits and vegetables unsuitable for freezing include potatoes, lettuce, cucumbers, celery, spinach, cabbage, watermelon, pears, rockmelon, pawpaw, tomatoes and bananas.

Care of the Freezer

FROSTING AND DEFROSTING

Frost accumulates on the inner surfaces of many freezers. When it becomes more than 6 mm thick it should be removed by scraping with a wooden or plastic scraper. Prevent an accumulation of loose ice in the bottom of the freezer by collecting the frost on sheets of paper placed over packages in the freezer.

Complete defrosting should be necessary only once or twice a year. Defrosting is necessary if a package has become damaged in the freezer and has caused an unpleasant odour or a tacky mess.

METHOD OF DEFROSTING

Complete defrosting takes about 30 to 45 minutes. Choose a time when the weather is cool and the freezer contains less food than usual.

The following steps should be taken to defrost a home freezer:

- Turn off power, work quickly.
- Remove food from freezer and either stack in the refrigerator, or wrap well in thick newspaper and blankets. Alternatively, packages may be kept cold by packing them with dry ice or a salt and ice mixture.
- Scrape off the frost, using a plastic or wooden scraper.
- Wash inside surfaces with warm water containing 1 tablespoon bicarbonate of soda to 4½ litres of water. Do not use hot water because a sudden change of temperature may damage the freezing coils.
- When all traces of ice are removed mop up all surplus water.
- Dry thoroughly with a clean towel.

- Turn on the power and replace contents.
- Close freezer and keep closed until the original low temperature is again reached.

Packaging and Wrapping

The packaging material should keep moisture in and air out of the package to prevent desiccation or freezer-burn. The material should prevent the development of off-flavours in food, or the transference of flavours between foods, and the tainting of air in the freezer. It should hold convenient quantities and prevent spillage, which leads to loss of food, loss of storage space, and an untidy, dirty freezer.

PACKAGING MATERIALS AND CONTAINERS

These materials must be moisture- and vapour-proof, unaffected by the food either before or during freezing and the storage or during thawing; and must not be spoiled by temperatures below -20°C (0°F). The material should not contaminate the food, for example by odour or taste, and it must enable the package to be sealed tightly with a minimum of air remaining. It should be strong enough to avoid tearing by irregularly-shaped food, for example poultry. Packages and containers vary according to the type of food to be frozen and stored. Some containers are rigid with a tight-fitting lid, for foods in liquid or semi-liquid form, for example fruit in syrup. Others may be flexible, for meat, poultry and fish.

Filling, sealing and opening operations should be speedy, and packages should be easy to handle. Unusual or unevenly-shaped containers and packages take up more space than necessary compared to cube or rounded shapes. Some containers are made to stack compactly to save space. The size of containers should be suitable for various quantities of foods, depending on the size of the family.

Transparent, opaque or coloured packages make recognition of foods easy, for example green containers could indicate vegetable contents. Containers should be identified by stick-on labels or marked with a felt pen. Comparatively inexpensive flexible bags, discarded after use, are preferable to rigid, hard-to-clean containers.

MEAL PLANNING

Thoughtful cooks plan meals well in advance, to allow for variety and to save time in shopping and preparation of food. Those living in isolated parts must plan over a longer period.

It is as well to plan for the entire day's meals rather than for each meal, so that the foods are well balanced. The dinner menu should be considered first, then the breakfast and luncheon menus. For dinner, the choice may vary from the very simple menu to the more elaborate:

1

Meat
3 vegetables
Dessert
Beverage

2

Soup
Meat
3 vegetables
Dessert
Beverage

3

Soup
Meat
2 vegetables
Salad and dressing
Dessert
Beverage

4

Fruit, fish, or savoury
    cocktail
Soup
Meat
3 vegetables
Dessert
Beverage

5

Fruit, fish or savoury
    cocktail
Soup
Fish
Meat
3 vegetables
Dessert
Coffee
Biscuits and cheese
Nuts, sweetmeats

It is best to decide on the meat first, then on the vegetables, which should be fully in season if possible. Next choose the soup and the dessert. Remember that choice cuts of meat are usually expensive; the cheaper cuts are just as nutritious, and can be made appetizing if cooked in a way that will make them tender. For instance, the tougher cuts of steak cooked in a casserole or minced and made into a baked meat loaf make a tender and savoury dish. You will find it necessary to make frequent use of certain fruits and vegetables while they are fully in season. Avoid always cooking them the same way; different methods will help you to avoid monotony.

Most wise housekeepers budget their income and set aside a sum for expenditure on food. Try to keep within that sum when you are planning the menus. If possible, serve fish and liver at least once a week. Avoid having pastry desserts at the same meal as roast meats; such a meal would be too rich in fat. Give plenty of bulky foods such as green vegetables, fruits and cereals. Too much sweet food should not be included, as this causes fermentation, and usually has little nutritive value. Combine crisp foods with soft foods. Food soups should be served if there is not sufficient protein in the main course. Thin and clear soups make a stimulating first course. Purees and cream soups can provide supplementary or additional food value where needed. Served with cracker biscuits — plain or cheese flavoured — or crisp toast, soup makes quite a substantial lunch or tea.

In choosing desserts, remember that a light dessert is best following a hearty meal, and vice versa. The dessert is just as much a part of the meal as any of the other courses, and it should round off the meal satisfactorily. During summer, particularly, avoid any excess of starchy foods, sweets and fat. Summer is the time for fruits and salad vegetables and these should appear on the table every day.

Four Simple Dinner Menus

1

Salmon or tuna mayonnaise
    served on salad vegetables
    with dressing
Ice cream and fruit salad
    with custard sauce

2

Roast seasoned lamb and
    vegetables in season
Lemon chiffon pie with
    custard or ice cream

3

Chilled fruit juice
Grilled steak
Green salad
Potatoes and grilled
    tomatoes
Ice cream with fruit,
    chocolate or caramel
    topping

4

Grapefruit segments or
    other fruit in season
Meat loaf and apple sauce
Mashed potatoes
Spinach and tomato halves
Baked custard and
    preserved or canned fruit

Four More Elaborate Dinner Menus

1

Roast seasoned chicken,
   bacon rolls, baked jacket
   potatoes with sour cream,
   green peas and carrots
Apple crumb or charlotte
   and ice cream
Coffee
Cheese biscuits

2

Cream of tomato soup
Fillet of fish and tartare sauce
Seasoned veal with
   vegetables in season
Caramel cream cups and
   ice cream
Coffee
Cheese straws

3

Chilled pineapple juice
Salmon mornay
Lamb croquettes and
   savoury sauce with
   vegetables in season
Jellied peaches with cream
Coffee
Cheese straws

4

Celery creme soup
Curried prawns
Chicken, tossed salad,
   potato salad
Apricot chiffon pie
Coffee
Cheese biscuits

DINNER FOR TWO

The business-person's task of planning for the main meal of
the day needs considerable thought and organization so that
there is variety in methods of cooking and in foods served.
He or she should try to:

Plan meals a week in advance, avoiding too much
repetition.

Plan to suit the food markets.

Plan within the income and food allowance.

Plan for contrast in colour, texture and flavour.

A starchy food may be potatoes, macaroni, spaghetti or
rice.

Plan to serve new recipes occasionally.

Plan the dessert course so that it really rounds off the meal.
Have a substantial dessert after a light main course, and a
light dessert after a substantial main course.

Remember that a good cook always tastes food as he or she
prepares it, and adds additional flavouring if necessary, also
testing for tenderness before serving.

A great deal of early preparation may be done if it is
possible to store foods in a refrigerator or freezer.

Salad dressing can be made in quantity; so can stock for
soups, and even sauces such as curry sauce, tomato sauce, or
vegetable sauce. These sauces will be a great help when you
wish to reheat left-over meat, poultry or fish or make a curry
or potato pie. Ice cream, custards, stewed fruits and jellies
may be prepared in advance.

For the busy cook the simplest and quickest method of
cooking is grilling. The best cuts of meat will be needed as a
rule, for there is nothing in the process of grilling that will
make the meat tender. However, meat-tenderizing powder can
be used on the less expensive cuts.

The cuts of meats and the other foods suitable for grilling
are:

Lamb: Cutlets, short loin chops, rib chops

Beef steaks: Sirloin, porterhouse (T-bone), fillet, rump

Other foods: Sausages, fish bacon, chicken

To accompany grills, try the following: Core and cut into

thick rings some ripe pears, apples or pineapple, brush with melted butter or margarine, dip in brown sugar and grill or cook in a buttered pan over the griller.

Four Menus Featuring Grills

1

Cream of tomato soup
A mixed grill with green
   salad
Stewed fruit and marsh-
   mallow rice
Coffee

2

Onion soup or other tin
   soup
Grilled steak and horse-
   radish sauce with
   vegetables (including potatoes)
Fresh fruit
Coffee

3

Oyster or cream soup
Grilled fish, potato chips
   and salad
Hot apple sponge and
   cream sauce
Coffee

4

Fresh fruit cocktail
Grilled beef patties
   with grilled pineapple
   rings, chipped potatoes
   and vegetables
   in season
Ice cream with
   chocolate sauce
Coffee

CATERING FOR HOLIDAYS

For meals in a holiday house choose recipes which require little preparation and take a comparatively short time to cook. Try to take with you, to start with, cooked foods such as a cold pumped leg of lamb (if nicely cooked this is almost as good as a ham), or corned beef, also a savoury sausage, a large boiled fruit cake, a nut loaf or two, homemade biscuits and jams, canned beetroot, corn, cucumber and tomato. For days spent out of doors, to save work and preparation, take sliced loaves or crusty rolls, tinned meats, butter, etc., and make your sandwiches on the spot. In addition to these, have fresh fruits, salad vegetables, cake, syrup drinks and a thermos for hot drinks.

Some preparation for the evening meal should be done early in the day so that when the weary surfers or hikers return there won't be too much to do.

CHRISTMAS MEALS

Christmas menus should include all the traditional flavours and colours. Plan ahead so that you will not be working all the time on the day itself, but will have time to join in the festivities. The cook trying to keep pace at this season of the year can easily become overworked and tired out. The wise ones will start organizing about the end of November. First make a list of foods required. It is essential to have good recipes for the cake, pudding, and mince pies. The cake, mincemeat and pudding should be made beforehand, but in this warm climate not too long in advance.

When you know just how many people you will be catering for, order the bird or meat well ahead and stock up with goods such as ginger, candied fruits, cake decorations, brandy or rum. Decorations must be considered: Christmassy paper napkins, table covers, wrapping papers and coloured strings and streamers. Try to introduce some original decorations of your own making. The room should be as bright and gay as possible. The linen, silver and glassware must all be in readiness. Fruit may be used for a centrepiece, but in

Australia what could be better than our own Christmas flowers and Christmas bush as floral decorations?

You may decide to serve cocktails or chilled soups, tomato or fruit juices in the lounge-room or living-room, accompanied by dainty savoury morsels such as plain thin wafer biscuits, devilled biscuits, olives, salted nuts, tasty cheese, small pickled onions, celery curls.

This is a time of family reunions and the gathering of friends, so the planning is not only for Christmas menus but for party gatherings also. It is always wise to have ready the "cut and come again" cold joint of ham, poultry, mock ham, or corned beef. A store of homemade biscuits will be useful at this season; use a good foundation recipe and vary the shape, colouring and flavour. Of course you must also have a Christmas cake.

Now a word about the Australian Christmas menu. Year after year experts advise that a cold meal is desirable in such a climate, but the traditional meal continues to be very popular. The two cold and two hot menus may help you to decide.

Four Christmas Menus

Australian Christmas Menu 1

Iced fruit cocktail
Iced asparagus soup
Cold chicken or turkey and
    ham with tomato with
    cucumber and green salad
Jellied Christmas pudding
Mince pies
Coffee
Cheese biscuits
Nuts and fruits

Traditional Menu 1

Oyster cocktail
Clear soup
Roast turkey or chicken and
    accompaniments
Baked potatoes, green peas
    and diced carrots
Christmas pudding with hard
    sauce
Muscatels and devilled
    almonds
Coffee
Cheese straws

Australian Christmas Menu 2

Oyster cocktail
Cold chicken, turkey, ham or
    pumped sliced leg of lamb
    or moulded chicken
Tossed salad and mayon-
    naise and potato salad
Mince pies with ice cream
Iced fruit cup
Coffee
Cheese crisps
Nuts and fruits
Bonbons

Traditional Menu 2

Iced pawpaw
Roast duck and apple sauce
    with vegetables in season
Christmas pudding with
    brandy sauce
Ice cream and chocolate sauce
Nuts, raisins, fruit
Coffee

Careful preparation is the secret of a happy day, so plan everything before Christmas eve, and on the eve do as much preparation for Christmas day as possible, getting sauces, stuffing, etc., ready. Make out a timetable for the day itself (this will certainly be a help to the inexperienced).

Here is an example of a simple Christmas meal and the timetable:

Simple Christmas Menu

Roast seasoned chicken with crisped smoked bacon and bread sauce
Roast potatoes and pumpkin and green vegetables
Christmas pudding and custard sauce
Mince pies
Fruits
Coffee

Timetable

On Christmas eve:

Make the stuffing for the fowl and prepare the bird; leave it covered in refrigerator.
Make a giblet stock for the gravy.
Make and bake the mince pies.
Have pudding made in advance.
Prepare the crumbs for the bread sauce.

On Christmas day:

9.30 a.m.   Check the pudding cloth. Replace the greased paper and foil on steamed pudding. Put the pudding into steam in boiling water, check frequently so that it does not boil dry.

10.30 a.m.   Place the prepared, seasoned poultry in a baking dish containing 2 tablespoons melted butter, cover with greased paper, foil, or oven film. Put into moderate oven.

10.35 a.m.	Prepare the vegetables. Make the bread sauce and the sauce for the pudding, cover and keep warm. Place the potatoes and the pumpkin in the baking dish in the oven. Set the table, check the nibbles, drinks and garnishes, de-rind the bacon and place on a dry baking tray. Set out the pies and fruits on silver or glass dishes. Put all the serving dishes and dinner plates to warm. Relax with family and friends, but don't forget to check the food quite often.
12.15 p.m.	Put the bacon into the oven. Remove the poultry and vegetables from the baking dish, drain and lift on to heated serving plates. Reduce oven heat, return the vegetables to oven. Keep bird hot. Put the green vegetables on to boil. Make the gravy, pour in to a hot jug. Re-heat the bread, sauce, put into a hot bowl. Remove the pudding from the boiling water. Turn on to a large heated plate, keep warm. Pour the sauce in to a glass jug and keep warm. Have ½ cup brandy ready to warm and ignite when the pudding is served. Drain the green vegetables, add butter. Arrange the bacon around the chicken with garnishes.
1.00 p.m.	Serve the meal.

WEDDING BREAKFASTS

With a little planning, a simple wedding breakfast may be arranged in the home provided the number of guests is limited to suit the space available. The "breakfast" may be a buffet or a sit-down meal. Preparation should begin at least three days ahead. All orders should be checked, then re-checked, one week before, and left with tradesmen to allow for special selection and any unusual items. Choose flowers of good, lasting quality so that they may be arranged the night before or very early in the morning. The hostess should allow herself at least three hours to relax and dress.

The wedding cake should take pride of place, and should be set in front of the bridal couple.

Four wedding breakfast menus

Buffet Wedding Breakfast 1

Hors-d'oeuvres
Fish croquettes
Cold poultry and ham with
    salads
Decorative stuffed eggs
Small buttered rolls
Diced pineapple, mint
    and cherries
Individual frozen sweets
Wedding cake
Coffee
Fruit punch

Buffet Wedding Breakfast 2

Cocktails and savouries and
    savoury dips
Small fried fillets of fish
Choux pastry savouries
Spaghetti bolognaise
Chicken supreme
Buttered macaroni
Stuffed eggs
Trifles
Ice cream cake and
    chocolate sauce
Wedding cake
Coffee
Fruit Cup

Sit-down Wedding Breakfast 1

Savouries
Hors-d'oeuvres
Fruit cocktail in frosted
    glasses
Fried fillets of fish with
    tartare sauce
Chicken or lamb a la king
    with potato balls and green
    salad, parsley butter
Fruit salad and ice cream
    or arctic pie
Wedding cake
Coffee
Fruit punch

Sit-down Wedding Breakfast 2

Oyster or prawn cocktail
Fillets of whiting in wine
    sauce
Roast turkey and vegetables
Individual chiffon pies and
    ice cream
Wedding cake
Coffee
Fruit punch

BUFFET DINNERS OR TEAS

A popular way of entertaining that allows the housewife to entertain a greater number of people than a sit-down meal is a buffet dinner or a buffet high tea. The following dishes are suitable, because they can be eaten easily with a fork or in the fingers: savoury dips, hot or cold; macaroni or spaghetti with rich savoury meat sauces; curry and rice; croquettes (lamb, chicken or turkey); curried prawns; savoury stuffed tomatoes; scalloped chicken or fish; fish mornay; small fried fillets of fish and tartare sauce; oyster patties; sausage rolls or savoury puffs or boats; savoury patties; sandwiches with thick and interesting fillings; chicken and ham pieces cut small and served with salad; cocktail frankfurts and tomato sauce; potato crisps; fruit salad and ice cream; meringues (as individual pavlova cakes); party cakes and pies; coffee; fruit punch; cheese straws and biscuits; confections. Recipes for most of these will be found in this book or its companion *The Commonsense Cookery Book, Book 1.*

PLANNING ENTERTAINMENT IN YOUR HOME

A successful party need not mean weeks of preparation or reckless spending. Some of the best parties are given on a budget. A warm, welcoming atmosphere, simple, well-prepared food, and a host and hostess who can spend time with their guests are the essentials.

Here are points to keep in mind when planning a party:

Start with the guest list and plan the party according to those invited. Some prefer dinner parties and others like gatherings where they can meet new people.

Invite only as many guests as you can comfortably accommodate. Check that you have sufficient glasses, china and cutlery and set all out ready for use.

Send out invitations early and make clear the type of party. Give date, time, duration, your name and address and, for a written invitation, an R.S.V.P. or telephone number for acceptance or refusal. If inviting people for the first time give directions on finding your address.

Be explicit about the dress you expect your guests to wear.

Keep a party book with a record of menus to save repetition at future parties.

Be sure as host or hostess to greet guests at the door. Also see them off when leaving.

For a dinner or buffet party make a detailed list of the food to be served, including garnishes. Put it in a prominent place in the kitchen where you can refer to it as you work.

Make a complete shopping list for the party and buy everything the day before or earlier.

Menus should not be elaborate but dishes should be prepared and served with special care. If trying something new have a ''rehearsal'' a few days before.

Buffet meals are easiest for large crowds. Serve foods that can be eaten with a ''Splayd'' — the implement designed to serve as both knife and fork.

For formal dining decide beforehand where guests are to sit.

Set aside a room or hanging space for guests' coats and have plenty of hangers available.

Provide plenty of utility ashtrays placed conveniently around the house.

Remember that the simplest party planned on the spur of the moment can be just as enjoyable as an elaborate one organized weeks ahead.

The formal party requires more elaborate dishes, the best glasses and tableware and a party air in the house created by flowers, soft lighting and special table settings.

To match informality at a party, simple food should be served. It can be just as enjoyable as a four-course formal meal that has taken hours to get ready and cost the earth.

As the hostess's duty is to see that all her guests feel welcome and are enjoying themselves, she should choose a menu that will leave her plenty of time to spend with them.

Make sure guests know whether the party is to be formal or informal.

Choose the right type of refreshments for the party.

How to Budget Your Party

Budgeting for a party means balancing the cost against the number of guests invited, choosing and preparing food that will supply the right number of servings, working out amounts of drinks and generally organizing all arrangements to suit the party situation.

Menu planning is much easier if you know the amounts of food to allow. Here are some quantities to help work out amounts:

A large unsliced sandwich loaf cuts into 36 slices which will make 18 full sandwiches and cut into 72 small ones.

250 g butter, softened and beaten with a little warm milk, is enough for that quantity of bread.

For a buffet one 5 kg ham, 6 No. 15 chickens, one 6 kg turkey, 3 kg shredded cabbage for slaw, 5 kg potatoes for potato salad, will make up into sufficient serves for 40.

For an afternoon party or kitchen tea allow four small sandwiches and four savouries each; three or four small cakes or tartlets, petits fours, meringues, etc.; one helping fruit salad, ice cream or mousse for each guest.

For 70 small sausage rolls allow 500 g puff pastry and 750 g sausage mince for filling.

A 6-egg pavlova with fruit and cream serves 12-14 people.

A cream sponge cuts into eight large slices.

3 kg bladebone or chuck steak with 6 tablespoons curry powder and other flavourings will make curry for 18-20.

3 kg chicken pieces with 4 tablespoons curry powder will make curry for 18-20.

Allow 1/3 cup rice measured before cooking for each serving.

Spaghetti with a good sauce is an excellent party dish that doesn't cost much. 500 g spaghetti and appropriate sauce will serve 6-8 persons.

HOW TO SELECT WINES

Consult the wine retailer or licensed grocer who will have a wide selection for your approval. As a general rule, whites are ready to drink when purchased, while most reds improve with keeping. To begin with, until you discover which wines you will prefer to "lay down" in your own cellar, it is a wise practice to select, as a "starter" collection, a bottle each of appetizer, sparkling and dessert wines, and two or three bottles of red and white table wines.

Appetizer Wines: Sherry (dry, medium or sweet); vermouth (dry or sweet).

White Table Wines: Chablis,* hock, riesling* and white burgundy, all "dry" (unsweet); pearl and moselle, in-between wines, slightly sweet; sauternes,* graves,* spatlese,* light, semi-sweet.

Red Table Wines: Rose,* light and delicate; claret and burgundy, fuller-bodied, more hearty.

Sparkling Wines: Champagne and sparkling moselle, both white, ranging from "dry" to sweet; sparkling hock and sparkling burgundy, both semi-sweet; sparkling pearl wines, white and slightly sweet.

Dessert Wines: Port, muscat, madeira, frontignac* and tokay,* all rich, full-bodied wines.

*Pronounced Shably, Reezling, So-tern, Grarves, Spat-leesa, Ro-zay, Fron-tee-nack, Toe-kay.

APPETIZERS

This chapter includes many small, savoury dishes ideal for serving before dinner, with drinks, or as a first course. Most of the recipes given here are for dishes which may be eaten with the fingers — savoury dips, small hors-d'oeuvres with a base of pastry, and so on. A few interesting first courses such as fondue and marinated zucchini are also given, though of course you will find many other dishes suitable for use as a first course in other chapters of this book.

HORS-D'OEUVRES

Hors-d'oeuvres are small, savoury dishes with a piquant flavour, served as appetizers at the commencement of dinner. They may be served on a small plate or in paper cases if desired. Garnish with parsley.

Foundations

Hors-d'oeuvres are often made on a foundation of bread, toast, croutes (small bread shapes fried, toasted or baked), pastry (short crust, rough puff, flaky, puff, or choux) or biscuits (plain, salted, cheese, poppy or sesame seed).

Suitable Foods

Some suitable foods for making hors-d'oeuvres are: oysters, anchovies, herrings, small fish, tongue, ham, olives, lettuce and salad vegetables, pate de foie gras, caviare, prunes, cream cheese, rockmelon, grapefruit, pineapple, avocado.

Olives: There are several types of olives: (i) French olives — small and dark green; (ii) Italian olives — larger than French olives, yellowish-green; (iii) Spanish olives — larger than French olives, yellowish-green; (iv) black or ripe olives — softer flesh.

Pickled olives may be (i) added to meat dishes to improve the flavour; (ii) served alone as an appetizer, or as a garnish for hors-d'oeuvres; (iii) handed round between courses to freshen the palate and stimulate the appetite.

Olives must be kept covered with pickling liquid, otherwise they will ferment. The container should be kept tightly sealed.

To remove the stone from an olive:

Take a sharp, pointed knife.

Loosen the skin at the bottom.

Hold the knife in a slanting position.

Cut well against the stone.

Loosen the skin gently at the top.

Remove the stone.

Caviare: Caviare consists of the hard, salted roe of the sturgeon. The taste for it is generally an acquired one. The roe is first washed in vinegar and then salted, and may be served either plain or dressed. If plain, the roe is mixed with lemon juice and cayenne and served on toasted or fried bread or plain bread and butter. Finely chopped shallot with lemon juice, oil, and a little finely chopped parsley can also be added sparingly. Always use a wooden spoon for mixing caviare; a metal spoon impairs the flavour.

Flavoured Butters

Garlic: 2 cloves of garlic, well rushed, to 250 g butter.

Herb: 1 teaspoon finely minced fresh herbs, e.g. dill, thyme, basil, savoury, parsley, chervil, horseradish, mustard, chives, paprika and nutmeg.

Start with ½ cup soft, creamy butter, taste, then adjust, using more butter or more herbs. A little lemon juice will help to intensify some of these flavours. When ready, store in containers with tight lids and keep refrigerated.

When using flavoured salts, dried herbs and spices, begin with a small quantity then adjust to suit taste.

Savoury Dips, Toppings and Fillings

These mixtures are most useful when entertaining small or large numbers of guests as they can be made in advance and stored in the refrigerator or freezer.

If the consistency is kept fairly thick the mixtures may be used as toppings and fillings for small hors-d'oeuvres. Garnishes such as sliced stuffed olives, caviare, sieved egg yolk, onion rings, slices of black olives, devilled almond slivers, tiny prawns, anchovies or shrimps enhance the appearance of the hors-d'oeuvres. Use tiny cocktail cutters to cut shapes from slices of cooked carrot, beetroot, gherkins, potato and turnip, thin strips of red and green capsicum, fresh or canned.

The mixtures also make excellent fillings for sandwiches (triangle, strip, rainbow, ribbon or loaf), pinwheels or hollowed-out bread sticks, and of course may be made slightly thinner, and served as dips with raw vegetables, savoury biscuits or potato crisps.

Suitable Foods: Seafood — anchovies, smoked salmon, caviare, red salmon, tuna, sardines, lobster, crab, prawns, smoked oysters.

Cheese — cottage, cream, cheddar, Swiss, Italian, blue vein, smoked.

Meats — chicken, turkey, ham, cold meats, bacon, pressed tongue, chicken livers, sausages, pork, ham, salami, liverwurst, beef, ground beef.

Eggs.

Vegetables and fruit — onions, fresh or pickled, shallots, chives, canned artichoke hearts, celery, gherkins, pineapple, avocado, asparagus, corn, herbs, fresh and dried, parsley.

Condiments of all classes.

Binding Agents: Mayonnaise, thick salad dressing, thick white sauce or thick gravy, whipped cream, packet sauces, stock cubes, packet soup, canned soup, cup-o'-soup, all make interesting flavour variations, either individually or combined, one to complement the other.

Preparation: Vitamize ingredients whenever possible, otherwise chop all into even smaller pieces. Pounding with a pestle in a mortar gives smooth, even distribution of flavours. When heating or reheating, use foods with low fat content or remove as much fat as possible before or during cooking. These savoury foods are intended to stimulate the appetite, not dull it.

SOUTH AMERICAN DIP

2 large ripe avocados, mashed
1 tablespoon minced onion
1 clove garlic, crushed
¼ teaspoon salt
1/3 cup heavy mayonnaise
6 rashers crisp cooked bacon, crumbled

Combine avocado, onion, garlic, seasonings and mayonnaise with half bacon. Cover the top completely with bacon and chopped parsley to help keep good green colour.

ONION DIP

Combine 1 carton sour cream with 1 packet French onion soup, mix well. Chill at least overnight.

BLUE CHEESE SPREAD OR DIP

1 cup blue cheese, crumbled
1 × 125 g packet cream cheese
2 tablespoons sour cream
2 tablespoons salad dressing

Combine ingredients, beat well, sprinkle with chopped parsley.
For dipping use biscuits, potato crisps, celery or carrot sticks.

SMOKED OYSTER DIP

2 cans smoked oysters, well drained
10 stuffed olives
1 small packet cream cheese
2 teaspoons lemon juice
½ cup heavy mayonnaise

Chop well-drained oysters and olives. Blend cheese and mayonnaise, stir in other ingredients. Sprinkle with chopped parsley.

BEEF DIP FILLING SPREAD (HOT OR COLD)

4 rashers lean bacon, chopped small
1 onion chopped or minced
250 g ground round or topside steak
1 teaspoon dry mustard
1 teaspoon nutmeg
Freshly ground black pepper
2 tablespoons flour
1 beef cube
300 ml water

Cook bacon in saucepan until fat is quite clear, add onion and cook 5 minutes. Do not brown. Stir in the beef, mustard, nutmeg, freshly ground black pepper. Stir over heat, cook 15 minutes. Stir in flour and beef cube. Mix well, add water while stirring. Bring to the boil and simmer 10 minutes. Garnish with chopped chives.

CURRY FLAVOURED BEEF DIP FILLING SPREAD

Make as for Beef Dip Filling Spread above but omit mustard and nutmeg. Add 2 teaspoons curry powder to fried bacon and onion. Stir in 1 tablespoon plum jam, 1 tablespoon sultanas with meat. Serve with toast fingers, biscuits or potato chips for dipping, fill short pastry cases or small choux pastry puffs, or spread on bread.

HAM DIP

½ cup mayonnaise
1 tablespoon worcestershire sauce
⅛ teaspoon ground cloves
⅛ teaspoon nutmeg
2 tablespoons finely chopped onion
1 cup chopped ham

Blend first 5 ingredients thoroughly and fold in chopped ham.

CHICKEN DIP

Make as Ham Dip (p. 43), using chicken in place of ham. Fold in also ¼ cup chopped stuffed olives.

MOCK CHICKEN

¼ cup butter
1 cup Kraft cheese, grated
1 small onion, grated
1 small teaspoon mixed herbs
1 peeled tomato
Chopped parsley
1 beaten egg

Combine everything except egg in double pan and cook 10 minutes. Just before it is cooked add egg. Finish cooking. Cool. Store in refrigerator.

Finger Foods

DEVILLED ALMONDS

1¼ cups almonds
1½ tablespoons butter
Olive oil
Salt and cayenne

Place almonds in a saucepan, cover with water and bring to the boil. Drain, skin and dry. Heat butter and a little oil in a small pan. Put almonds into pan and cook until lightly browned all over, stirring occasionally. Lift out and drain on paper. Sprinkle with salt and cayenne, shaking up in paper to make certain almonds are completely covered.

SALTED ALMONDS OR PEANUTS

1¼ cups almonds or peanuts
1 tablespoon butter
Salt

Blanch and dry nuts. Heat butter in small pan and add nuts. Cook until evenly browned, stirring constantly. Drain on paper and sprinkle with salt. Serve in small dishes.

SAVOURY SHAPES

250 g good short crust (made with 2 cups flour)

Make pastry into small cones, boats or tart shapes, and bake. Use with one of the following fillings, or one of the mixtures given in the section Savoury Dips, Toppings and Fillings (p 41).

Ham and Gherkin Filling:

1 cup panada sauce (p. 115). Mix with 60 g minced ham, 1 gherkin, 1 hard-boiled egg, ¼ teaspoon mustard, and a pinch of cayenne. Fill pastry with mixture and garnish with lettuce leaves and celery ticks filled with cheese.

Anchovy Filling:

1 cup panada sauce (p. 115). Mix with 2 teaspoons anchovy sauce or paste and pepper and salt to taste. Fill pastry and garnish with lattice made of strips of gherkin or an olive. Serve with lettuce or curled celery.

Crab Filling:

1 cup panada sauce (p. 115). Mix with 1 small tin crab, pepper and lemon juice to taste, chopped parsley if desired. Fill pastry and reheat if desired.

Brain and Walnut Filling:

1 cup panada sauce (p. 115). Add chopped brain and walnut. Add chopped parsley, pepper and salt. Fill pastry with mixture. Garnish with sprigs of parsley.

Oyster Filling:

1 cup panada sauce (p. 115). Mix with 12 chopped oysters. Flavour with 1 teaspoon lemon juice and a pinch of cayenne. Place 2 teaspoons of this mixture in each pastry boat, cone or

tart. Reheat in oven and garnish with slices of lemon and sprigs of parsley before serving.

Prawn Filling:

1 cup panada sauce (p. 115). Mix with 1 cup shelled and chopped prawns. Flavour with 1 teaspoon lemon juice and a pinch of cayenne. Partly fill pastry shapes with mixture. Reheat in oven and garnish with shelled prawns, slices of lemon, and sprigs of parsley.

Cheese Filling:

1 cup panada sauce (p. 115). Stir in 2 tablespoons grated cheese and pinch cayenne. Place in a forcing bag and fill pastry shapes. Reheat if desired and garnish with curled celery.

STUFFED LARGE GREEN OLIVES

Croutes of fried or toasted bread
Olives
Chopped parsley

Paste:

1 hard-boiled egg yolk
1 teaspoon chutney
2 tablespoons soft butter
1 tablespoon anchovy fillets
Salt and cayenne

Make croutes. Stone olives. Make paste of egg yolk passed through a sieve, butter, salt, cayenne, chutney, and anchovy fillets. Fill olives with paste. Decorate with roses of creamed butter and chopped parsley.

OLIVES A LA MADRAS

9 Spanish olives
2 hard-boiled eggs
½ teaspoon chutney
2 teaspoons anchovy paste

2 tablespoons soft butter
Salt and cayenne
Rounds of fried bread about 4 cm in diameter
Anchovy fillets
Parsley

Stone olives. Vitamize or pound together olives, egg yolks, chutney, paste, and butter. Season with salt and cayenne. Rub mixture through a sieve. Spread some of the mixture on each croute. Sprinkle some finely chopped white of egg on each and a curl of anchovy fillet garnished with parsley.

MUSHROOMS ON TOAST

250 g mushrooms
4 teaspoons butter
2 rashers bacon
Salt and pepper
2 teaspoons flour
2 tablespoons cream
1 squeeze lemon juice
2 teaspoons chopped parsley
Toast rounds

Wash and trim mushrooms, dry, and chop. Melt butter in saucepan, add mushrooms, chopped bacon, salt, pepper. Cook till tender. Mix flour into cream. Add to mushrooms and stir until smooth. Add lemon juice and chopped parsley. Stir and boil two minutes.

STUFFED MUSHROOMS 1

2 teaspoons butter
2 teaspoons chopped ham
1 tablespoon chopped parsley and shallot
Salt and pepper
Grated lemon rind
1 tablespoon fine breadcrumbs
1 chicken stock cube
½ doz medium mushrooms
Small toast rounds
Parsley

Melt butter in saucepan and stir in chopped ham, parsley, and shallot, salt, pepper, lemon rind, breadcrumbs and stock cube. Heat five minutes. Prepare mushrooms by peeling, washing, drying, and removing stalks. Arrange with stalk side up on a greased baking dish and put a little mixture on each. Cover with a greased paper or foil. Bake in a moderately hot oven 20 minutes. Place each mushroom on a small round of buttered toast. Garnish with sprigs of parsley.

STUFFED MUSHROOMS 2

12 medium cap mushrooms
½ cup drained crab meat
1 tablespoon butter
¼ cup finely chopped celery
2 tablespoons mayonnaise
1 teaspoon lemon juice
2 tablespoons dry breadcrumbs tossed in
    1 teaspoon melted butter
White pepper
Parsley for garnish

Wash, dry and trim mushrooms. Remove stalks and chop them leaving caps whole. Remove any bones from crab, cut up finely. Cook chopped stalks in butter until tender, stir in remainder of ingredients, fill into mushrooms. Place on greased tray in preheated oven (204°C, 400°F) for 10 minutes. Garnish with parsley. Serve on toast rounds or in little short crust pastry cases.

CREAMED CHICKEN

1 cup melted butter sauce
½ cup mayonnaise (optional)
Salt and pepper
Squeeze lemon juice
Chopped parsley
1½ cups finely diced chicken
Chives

Blend sauce and mayonnaise until quite smooth. Add salt, pepper, lemon juice and parsley. Mix in chicken. Chill. Serve garnished with chopped chives as a dip; or in pastry cases.

CAPSICUM SLICES

3 capsicums (2 red, 1 green)
1 tomato
1 tablespoon butter
1 tablespoon flour
¾ cup milk or cream
2 hard-boiled eggs
1 tablespoon chopped chives
Chopped olives
2 tablespoons grated cheese
Salt and pepper
Lettuce

Wash capsicums and stand in cold salted water. Chop very finely flesh of peeled and seeded tomato. Melt butter in saucepan, add flour, and cook 1 minute. Add milk or cream and stir till mixture boils and thickens. Add chopped eggs, chives, olives, tomato pulp, grated cheese, and salt and pepper to taste. Drain and dry capsicums and remove centres. Fill with mixture and freeze or press. Cut into 3 mm slices and serve on lettuce leaves, placing red and green alternately.

PRUNE SAVOURIES

15 large dessert prunes
2 tablespoons cream cheese
¼ cup butter
2 teaspoons finely chopped parsley
1 teaspoon lemon juice
Salt and cayenne
15 rounds toast or fried bread 4 cm diameter

Stone each prune by cutting into four petals. Fill centre with cream cheese. Make Maitre d-Hotel Butter by creaming butter, adding parsley, then blending in lemon juice, salt and cayenne. Arrange prunes on fried bread or toast. Place Maitre d'Hotel Butter in forcing bag and decorate prunes.

PRUNES WRAPPED IN BACON

15 prunes
5 rashers of bacon cut in 3 pieces
Parsley
Toothpicks

Remove stones from prunes. Roll each in piece of bacon. Spread out on absorbent paper on oven tray. Cook at 232ºC (450°F) until bacon fat is quite clear. Serve very hot, on bed of fried parsley.

STUFFED EGGS

Hard-boiled eggs
Mayonnaise
Chives

Parsley
Paprika

Halve lengthwise hard-boiled eggs, remove yolks, reserve
whites. Press yolks through a fine sieve, mix them with half
of their volume of mayonnaise, very finely chopped chives
and parsley. Fill egg white with the yolk mixture, using bag
and rose pipe. Garnish with mayonnaise sprinkled with
paprika, or coat with aspic and sprinkle with tarragon.

EGG AND ANCHOVY SAVOURY

1 egg
2 teaspoons anchovy sauce
2 teaspoons butter
1 tablespoon milk
Cayenne
Lemon juice (optional)
Fingers of toast, savoury biscuits, or fried croutes
Some strips of capsicum, gherkin, or olives

Beat egg and add anchovy sauce, butter, milk, cayenne and
lemon juice (optional). Cook very gently until set. Heap on
fingers of toast, savoury biscuits, or fried croutes. Garnish
with sliced capsicum, gherkin or olives.

SARDINE MAYONNAISE SAVOURY

1 large tin sardines
Lemon juice
Salt and cayenne
Small savoury biscuits
Small lettuce cups
¼ cup mayonnaise
Some gherkins or olives

Trim sardines and remove bones, mash well with lemon juice,
salt, and cayenne. Butter biscuits, place a lettuce leaf on each
and add sardine mixture to centre. Mask with mayonnaise.
Garnish with strips of gherkin or olive.

HADDOCK AND CHEESE SAVOURIES

90 g cooked haddock
2 tablespoons butter
¼ cup grated cheese
Cayenne
1 egg yolk
2 tablespoons milk
250 g puff pastry

Mash haddock finely. Add butter, cheese, cayenne, half the
egg yolk and the milk. Make pastry, or buy ready made, and
roll out 1 cm thick. Cut into 5 cm rounds. Put a little haddock
mixture in centre of each round. Moisten edges and gather up
to form a triangle, pinching together. Brush over with other
half of egg yolk. Sprinkle with cheese. Bake in oven 10
minutes. Serve hot or cold.

LOBSTER CANAPES

3 tablespoons lobster or crab,
    canned or frozen
3 tablespoons cream
Salt
Cayenne
Butter or oil
½ doz rounds bread
Olives or gherkins
Lemon
Small lobster claws (optional)

Chop lobster into small pieces. Mix with cream and add salt
and cayenne. Heat butter or oil, and wet fry bread a golden
brown. Spread bread with lobster paste and decorate with
chopped olives or gherkins. Garnish with slices of lemon and
small lobster claws.

CANAPE MUSCOVITE

Toast
Smoked salmon
Caviare
Anchovies
Cress or parsley

Cover toast with sliced smoked salmon and spread with caviare. Cross thin pieces of anchovy over centre, garnish with cress or parsley.

CANAPE FAVOURITE

Toast
Swiss cheese
Ox tongue
Sour pickles

Cover toast with slice of Swiss cheese and cover this with slice of ox tongue. Garnish with sour pickles.

FIRST COURSES

CHEESE FONDUE

1 loaf crusty white bread
1 clove garlic
150 g emmental cheese
300 ml white wine
1 teaspoon flour
1 tablespoon kirsch
Salt and pepper

Use a chafing dish or fondue pan. Cut bread into bite-size

cubes. Rub pan with crushed clove of garlic then put in thinly sliced cheese. Add wine slowly, stirring all the time, and bring slowly to the boil. Make a smooth paste of flour and kirsch and pour drop by drop into cheese. Stir well, flavour with pepper and salt. Reduce heat until only just simmering. Take a cube of bread on long-handled fork, plunge it into hot fondue and quickly turn the thready cheese around bread.

PRAWNS IN RAMEKINS

1½ tablespoons butter
1½ tablespoons flour
250 ml hot stock
2 teaspoons tomato sauce
2 egg yolks
Salt and cayenne
Grated onion
2 teaspoons cream
500 g prawns
6 teaspoons lemon juice
Breadcrumbs

Heat butter, add flour, and stir till smooth. Add stock and tomato sauce and stir till boiling. Cook 3 minutes. Remove from fire and allow to cool slightly. Add egg yolks, salt, cayenne and grated onion to taste. Lastly add cream. Reheat gently over a low fire. Add prawns. When well heated remove from fire and carefully add lemon juice. Place mixture into 1 large or 4 small buttered ramekins, sprinkle top lightly with breadcrumbs, add a tiny piece of butter, and brown lightly under hot griller.

CUCUMBER SALAD

2 cucumbers, peeled and sliced into thin rounds
Salt
2/3 cup yoghurt

1 onion, finely sliced
Pepper
Paprika

Sprinkle cucumber slices with salt. Allow to stand a few minutes then drain. Mix with yoghurt and onion slices. Sprinkle with pepper and garnish with paprika in a pattern on top of salad. Serve chilled.

ORIENTAL YOGHURT SALAD

2 cucumbers, peeled and sliced into thin rounds
1 cup yoghurt
Salt and pepper to taste
½ teaspoon turmeric
2 teaspoons grated onion
2 teaspoons chopped dill pickles
2 teaspoons chopped chives

Prepare cucumbers, sprinkle well with salt, allow to stand a few minutes, drain. Make a dressing of yoghurt, additional salt, pepper and turmeric (add more if desired), onion and pickles. Put cucumber slices into dressing, chill. Serve in crisp lettuce cups, garnish with chives.

TANGY CARROT BOWL

6 large carrots, grated (3 cups)
1 teaspoon lemon juice
Celery salt
1 cup yoghurt
Watercress or celery curls

Sprinkle carrots with lemon juice. Add celery salt to yoghurt, reserving 2 tablespoons yoghurt for later garnishing. Fold yoghurt into carrots lightly and pile in centre of shallow glass bowl. Garnish with a ring of celery curls or watercress, top with remaining yoghurt.

MARINATED ZUCCHINI

¼ cup sour cream
½ cup cottage cheese
2 teaspoons lemon juice
½ teaspoon garlic salt
¼ teaspoon salt
1½ cups sliced, cooked zucchini
2 tomatoes, peeled and diced
¼ cup diced green pepper
Lettuce

Blend sour cream, cottage cheese, lemon juice and garlic salt. Add salt, zucchini, tomatoes and green pepper and serve in lettuce-lined bowl.

TOMATO CUCUMBER FANS

6 large, oval-shaped, firm, ripe tomatoes
1 medium cucumber
1 cup cottage cheese
1 tablespoon grated onion
¼ teaspoon seasoned salt
⅛ teaspoon peper
Paprika

Scald and peel tomatoes. Chill. Cut tomatoes two-thirds of way down in 4 sections, gently spread apart to resemble a fan, fill centre cut with a scored slice of unpeeled cucumber. Combine cottage cheese, grated onion, salt and pepper. Spoon cottage cheese mixture between each of other sections, dust with paprika. Serve with Bacon Cream Dressing.

BACON CREAM DRESSING

4 bacon slices
1 cup sour cream
1 tablespoon red wine vinegar

½ tablespoon lemon juice
1 teaspoon grated onion
½ teaspoon salt

Grill bacon slowly until crisp. Remove from griller. Chop finely and put aside. Let bacon drippings cool, but not congeal. Add sour cream, red wine, vinegar, lemon juice, onion, salt and bacon. Mix well. Chill thoroughly. Serve with Tomato Cucumber Fans (p. 56).

MILANO SALAD

Crisp lettuce leaves
1 large avocado, sliced
4 medium tomatoes, peeled and sliced
3 small zucchini, finely grated (unpeeled)
1 cup sour cream

Arrange lettuce in 4 small salad bowls. Place small slices of avocado in a circle at outer edge. Make inner circle of sliced tomatoes. Heap grated zucchini in centre, top with a large spoonful of sour cream.

EASTERN YOGHURT SALAD

1 cup yoghurt
1 clove garlic, crushed
Fresh mint leaves, chopped
2 cucumbers, peeled and thinly sliced
Salt and pepper
3 red radishes, sliced

Mix yoghurt and garlic. Stir in chopped mint leaves. Add cucumber slices, salt and pepper to mixture. Garnish sides of serving dish with radish slices.

CUCUMBER SOUP

2 large green cucumbers
5 cups buttermilk
1 tablespoon chopped green onions
1 teaspoon salt
¼ cup finely chopped parsley
½ teaspoon monosodium glutamate
Pepper

Wash and peel cucumber, cut in half, remove seeds. Grate or chop very finely. Combine cucumber with other ingredients. Cover and chill about 4 hours. Mix again. Check seasoning. Serve in chilled cups, garnished with slice of unpeeled, fluted cucumber and sprig of parsley. Serve with cheese or salt-flavoured biscuits.

ASPARAGUS SOUP

1 large can asparagus pieces or cuts
1 medium onion
1 medium stalk celery
3 stalks parsley
Salt
1 litre white stock or liquid from asparagus
    + water and soup cube
1 tablespoon butter
1 tablespoon flour
300 ml thin cream
Cayenne pepper (very little)
Croutons

Drain asparagus and make up stock with liquid, if desired. Peel and dice onion, chop washed celery, place in heavy saucepan with parsley, salt and stock. Boil gently until vegetables are quite soft. Add asparagus cuts, reserving some of the better-shaped pieces for garnish, if desired, and reheat. Put all through a sieve to make smooth puree. Melt butter, add flour, stir until smooth. Add cream and seasonings, boil 2 minutes.

Combine cream mixture with vegetable puree. Reheat but do not boil. Serve with croutons garnished with reserved asparagus pieces.

Variations

For asparagus substitute:

500 g peeled and sliced Jerusalem artichokes, boiled until tender *or*

500 g fresh green peas, boiled; include the youngest pods; use mint instead of parsley *or*

500 g washed, chopped, sauteed mushrooms *or*

500 g peeled and sliced swede turnip, boiled, *or*

500 g peeled and sliced potatoes, boiled, *or*

1 cup diced carrot, boiled, *or*

1 cup diced pumpkin, boiled, *or*

1 small cauliflower, retain and boil some of the flowerets for garnish.

POTATO SOUP

500 g potatoes
1 onion
2 thick stalks celery
1 parsnip
½ turnip
2 level tablespoons butter
7 cups cold water
3 cups milk
2 level teaspoons sugar
2 level teaspoons salt
1½ level tablespoons plain flour
Chopped parsley.

Wash and dry vegetables, peel them and cut up roughly. Heat butter in a saucepan, add vegetables and steam for a few minutes. Add water and cook slowly till tender. Rub through a sieve or vitamize. Return to saucepan, add milk, sugar, and salt, and thicken with blended flour. Cook for 5 minutes, stirring all the time. Serve sprinkled with chopped parsley, and fried or baked croutons.

CABBAGE SOUP

1 small cabbage
1 tablespoon bacon dripping or lard
1 tablespoon flour
Salt
Fresh black pepper
6 cups beef or chicken stock
5 bacon bones (rib)
5 continental sausages or frankfurts

Wash cabbage, remove all stalks and hard centres of leaves, shred finely. Cook in dripping until limp, stir in flour and seasonings. Add stock and bacon bones and simmer 1 hour. Boil sausage separately 5 minutes. Drain. Cut into slices and add to soup just before serving. Serve with hot garlic bread or thin slices caraway seed rye bread.

FRENCH ONION SOUP

6 large onions, peeled and sliced thinly
2 tablespoons butter
1 tablespoon olive oil
6 cups beef stock
Salt and pepper
1/3 cup dry sherry or port
½ cup diced gruyere or Danish samsoe cheese
6 slices buttered, toasted French bread 2 cm thick
1 cup mixed grated gruyere and parmesan cheeses
1 tablespoon melted butter

In large, heavy saucepan, saute onions in butter and oil until golden colour and limp. Cover and gently simmer for 15 minutes. Pour on beef stock, cover, cook slowly 30 minutes. Add seasonings, taste and adjust. Pour soup and wine into an ovenproof earthenware casserole, cover and heat in moderate oven 30 minutes. Remove from oven. Sprinkle with diced cheese. Cover with even layer of toasted French bread, sprinkle with grated cheese. Drip melted butter overall.

Return to hot oven for 10 minutes uncovered. Place under griller or hot oven-top to brown cheese. Serve immediately in hot earthenware bowls.

Note: If necessary, toast and grated cheese may be prepared and grilled before placing on top of soup.

VICHYSSOISE

3 medium leeks, sliced finely
1 medium onion, sliced finely
2 tablespoons butter
4 medium potatoes, sliced
5 cups chicken stock
Salt
Fresh black pepper
300 ml cream
½ bunch watercress, washed, dried and chopped
¼ teaspoon nutmeg
Chives

Cook leeks and onion in butter until transparent. Add potatoes, stock and seasoning. Simmer until vegetables are very soft. Pass through sieve. Stir in cream and watercress. This can be served hot but is quite delicious chilled and served garnished with chopped chives.

GIBLET BROTH

2 sets of giblets and chicken legs
6 cups water
1 teaspoon salt
3 stalks parsley
⅛ teaspoon ground nutmeg
1 onion
2 tablespoons sago
Chopped chives

Wash giblets and legs well. Cut up and place in saucepan with water, salt, parsley and nutmeg. Bring slowly to boil. Peel and dice onion, add to pan, cover and simmer 2 hours. Strain off

meat and bones. Add sago which has been washed and soaked
for 10 minutes. Stir and boil gently 15 minutes. Garnish with
chopped chives. Serve with cracker biscuits.

Note: This stock is a good base for gravy served with baked
or barbecued chicken.

CHICKEN BROTH

Make as Giblet Broth (p. 61) but use chicken carcase, wingtips,
necks and feet instead of giblets. Add diced carrot and 1 stick
celery. Use 3 tablespoons rice instead of sago. Remove all
bones.

OXTAIL SOUP

1 large oxtail
12 cups water
Seasoned flour
2 tablespoons butter or bacon dripping
125 g diced lean bacon
2 medium onions
2 medium carrots
1 small turnip
1 large stick celery
1 bouquet garni
2 cloves
Generous amount freshly ground black pepper
Salt
1 tablespoon cornflour
¼ cup dry sherry

Cut oxtail into joints, place in water, bring to boil then remove
meat from stock. Put stock aside. Roll joints in seasoned
flour, fry in heated fat until brown. Add bacon and
vegetables. Stir and cook 5 minutes. Add stock and
flavourings. Cover and simmer 3-4 hours. Remove large
pieces of meat and chill soup. Remove set fat and reheat. Mix

cornflour and sherry to smooth paste, stir into just boiling soup and cook 5 minutes. Garnish generously with chopped parsley. Serve with hot garlic bread.

CORN CHOWDER

1 large can golden corn or 2 cups
   cooked golden corn
1½ cups cooked diced potatoes
2 or 3 thick rashers bacon (optional)
½ cup minced onion
1 cup chopped celery
3 level tablespoons plain flour
1 litre scalded milk
1½ level teaspoons salt
¼ level teaspoon pepper
2 tablespoons chopped parsley

Dice and lightly fry bacon, then add onion and celery, cooking till lightly browned and tender (if not using bacon, fry onion and celery in 30 g butter). Stir in flour, mixing well. Gradually add milk and cook slowly till thick, stirring all the time. Add corn, potatoes, salt and pepper. Heat thoroughly, then stir in parsley. Serve piping hot in small low bowls.

FISH

Oysters

Signs of freshness in an oyster are (i) that the shell is difficult to open, and (ii) that there is no unpleasant odour.

Preparation: To prepare, scrub the shell thoroughly, then open by holding firmly with the thick part towards the palm of the hand, and forcing a strong oyster knife between the shells near the back, cutting the strong muscle which holds the shell together. Drop the oyster and liquor into a strainer over a bowl — the liquor can be used in the making of soup or sauce.

It is possibly more convenient to buy the required number of oysters on the shell, as late as possible on the day of use. For soups, sauces and made-up dishes buy oysters in bottles or cans. Frozen crumbed oysters, scallops and prawns are readily available. Using frozen crab and lobster meat and shelled prawns obviates wastage and reduces preparation time to a minimum.

OYSTERS AU NATUREL

Oysters au naturel should be served in the shell on a plate of cracked ice, garnished with slices of lemon and sprigs of parsley, and accompanied by slices or rolls of brown bread and butter.

Sea mussels are a good substitute for oysters. The horny beard must be removed and discarded.

SCALLOPED OYSTERS

300 ml medium-thick white sauce
Lemon juice
220-230 g can oysters or 2 bottles oysters
Fine breadcrumbs
Butter
Lemon slices
Parsley

Grease 3 or 4 scallop dishes. Make 300 ml medium-thick white
sauce by the melted butter method, using 2 level tablespoons
butter, 3 level tablespoons plain flour, 300 ml milk, flavoured
with salt and paper. Add a squeeze of lemon juice to sauce,
then add prepared oysters. Put mixture into scallop dishes,
sprinkle with breadcrumbs and dot with butter. Bake in a
moderate oven until golden brown, or brown under a hot
griller. Garnish with slices of lemon and sprigs of parsley.
Serve with crisp toast.

OYSTER PATTIES

500 g puff pastry or 24 ready-made patty cases
½ cup oyster liquor
½ cup milk
2 peppercorns
Few drops anchovy sauce
2 tablespoons butter
3 tablespoons flour
2 tablespoons cream
2 bottles or 220-230 g can oysters
1 lemon
Parsley

Roll pastry out 5 mm thick and cut out with a plain 50 mm
round cutter dipped in boiling water. Cut half way through
rounds with a small cutter. Bake in a hot oven 15 to 20
minutes. Bring oyster liquor, little lemon rind, milk and

flavourings to the boil and simmer gently, covered, 3 minutes. Strain.

Melt butter in pan, stir in flour, then oyster liquor, stirring constantly. Remove from fire and add cream. Add oysters to sauce. Remove centres from patties, fill with oyster mixture and garnish with slices of lemon and sprigs of parsley.

Lobster

In lobsters the largest pieces of white succulent meat are found in the big claws and tail. To cook fresh lobster, boil in salted water for 10 minutes per 1 kg lobster. Uncooked lobsters are greenish-black in colour and turn red when cooked.

Pick up lobster at the back, place head first into boiling, salted water to cover (1 tablespoon salt to each litre of water). (If preferred, the spinal cord may be cut before boiling by inserting a sharp, narrow knife between head and tail.) Count five when water begins to boil again. If overcooked, meat will be tough and stringy. Remove and cool at room temperature, then wipe over shell with a little oil.

Place lobster on its back on a large flat chopping board, and cut open from end to end using a strong, sharp, long-bladed knife. Begin at head, press claws back to keep body flat. Remove the strong vein which runs from head to tail, also the small bag or sac at the back of the head. Both the green and coral parts are edible. Pry the body meat loose with a fork. Remove. Crack the claws with mallet or hammer. Remove meat.

LOBSTER OR CRAB MORNAY

½ lobster or 250 g frozen crab
2 hard-boiled eggs
Salt and cayenne
Lemon juice
1 tablespoon butter
300 ml thick white sauce

2 teaspoons anchovy sauce
1 tablespoon cream
Lemon
Parsley

Take lobster from shell and cut into small pieces. Shell eggs, put 1 yolk aside for garnishing. Chop whites and other yolk finely. Place in a basin with salt, cayenne and lemon juice. Place butter, white sauce, anchovy sauce, lobster, egg whites and yolk in saucepan, and stir till well heated. Remove from stove and add cream. Place on toast or fill lobster shell and grate the remaining yolk over all. Place on a dish and garnish with lobster claws, slices of lemon and sprigs of parsley.

LOBSTER CUTLETS

250 g lobster or crab
2 tablespoons butter
2 tablespoons flour
3 eggs
¾ cup milk or water
2 tablespoons cream
Salt and cayenne
1 lemon
Anchovy sauce
Breadcrumbs
Frying fat
8 small pieces lobster claws
Lemon
Parsley

Chop lobster into very small pieces, and add soft sections from the head. Melt butter in small saucepan, stir in flour, and cook well. Add milk or water and stir till boiling. Add eggs, beaten, cream, salt, cayenne, ½ teaspoon lemon juice, anchovy sauce and lobster. Cook 1 minute. Spread on plate and allow to become cold. Cut 8 portions, place on floured board and make into a cutlet shape with a knife. Beat 1 egg. Dip shapes into beaten egg and then into breadcrumbs. Deep fry, then drain. Place a small piece of claw into end of each cutlet. Serve garnished with slices of lemon, fried parsley and remaining egg, hard-boiled and chopped.

LOBSTER NEWBURG

600 ml cream or evaporated milk
3 tablespoons flour
2 egg yolks
3 tablespoons butter
3 tablespoons dry sherry
3 cups lobster meat in bite-size pieces
Pepper
Salt

Blend the flour with 2 tablespoons cream, add egg yolks, mix well. Heat remaining cream, pour on to flour mixture and stir. Return to saucepan on low heat. Stir in butter, sherry, then lobster. Continue stirring for 3 minutes. Have prepared shells ready with layer of parsley rice in base. Fill in mixture. Place under hot grill to brown. Serve very hot with lemon and hot crisp potato slices.

CRAB CUTLETS

Make as for Lobster Cutlets (   ), substituting crab for lobster.

ABALONE

This is a single-shelled fish which clings to rocks with a broad muscular foot. The nacre-lined shell is in the shape of an ear. The edible white flesh needs special preparation:
    Remove fish from shell, cut off frilly edge then scrub until white. Beat flat with a wooden mallet or rolling pin to break fibres and soften. (The fish may be bought ready prepared.) Cut to size required.
    (i) Cover with seasoned flour, fry in oil or bacon fat until light brown. Make brown bacon gravy, simmer abalone for 30 minutes. Serve with parsley, lemon and boiled rice.

(ii) Place in buttered casserole with ½ cup of water, cover and simmer 20 minutes, add ½ cup dry white wine, 250 g button mushrooms and simmer 15 minutes. Just before serving, stir in 60 ml cream and 1 tablespoon chopped parsley. Served with boiled potato.

AVOCADOS WITH PRAWNS

6 tablespoons oil
2 tablespoons vinegar or lemon juice
1 clove garlic, crushed
Salt and pepper
Few drops hot pepper sauce
  (optional)
250 g shelled small prawns, deveined
2 ripe avocados, chilled

Pour oil into a bowl and gradually beat in vinegar, then add garlic. Season to taste with salt, pepper and pepper sauce, if used. Add prawns, cover and leave at least 1 hour. To serve, cut avocados in halves, remove seeds and fill cavities with prawn mixture.

Note: For a creamy sauce, stir 2 tablespoons sour cream or mayonnaise into prawn mixture before serving. A combination of seafoods (prawns, lobster, crab) may be used instead of prawns alone.

PRAWN DILL CREAM

2 tablespoons butter
1½ tablespoons plain flour
½ teaspoon salt
Pinch cayenne pepper
1 cup cream or evaporated milk
1 teaspoon ground dill
250 g shelled prawns
½ cup toasted slivered almonds

Melt butter, stir in flour and cook 2 to 3 minutes, stirring. Add seasonings, then blend in cream. Add dill and stir mixture until it boils and thickens. Add prepared prawns. Heat through and serve in individual dishes. Garnish with toasted almonds.

ISLAND PRAWN CURRY

3 tablespoons butter or clarified butter
2 large onions, chopped
1 clove garlic, crushed
2 cm bruised green root ginger
4 level teaspoons curry powder
1 level teaspoon salt
Pepper
2 tomatoes, peeled and chopped
1 small cucumber, peeled and diced
2 cups coconut milk
1 kg prawns, shelled
1 tablespoon lemon juice
Fluffy boiled rice

Heat the butter and saute the onion, garlic and ginger till tender. Remove ginger and discard. Stir in the curry powder, salt, pepper and tomatoes, and fry 3 minutes. Add the cucumber and coconut milk and stir until almost boiling. Add prawns and lemon juice and heat through. Serve with fluffy boiled rice.

COQUILLES SAINT-JACQUES

½ cup water
¼ cup sauterne
½ teaspoon salt
2 drops tabasco sauce
500 g fresh or frozen scallops
2 tablespoons butter
1 small onion, minced
2 tablespoons flour

1 small clove garlic, crushed
1 teaspoon chopped parsley
1 egg yolk, beaten
1 cup white breadcrumbs fried in butter
2 tablespoons parmesan cheese, grated

Combine water, wine, salt, tabasco and washed scallops in saucepan. Just simmer 5 minutes. Remove. Reserve liquid. Cut scallops into quarters. Melt butter in same pan, saute onion 5 minutes but do not brown. Stir in flour until smooth. Add liquid, stir until thickened, add garlic and parsley. Cook 5 minutes. Remove from heat, stir in beaten egg yolk. Add scallops. Reheat gently for a few minutes. Have 6 scallop shells or suitable heat-resistant dishes greased ready, spoon in mixture, cover with crumbs and cheese. Bake in hot oven until brown, or place under griller for a few minutes. If served as a main course add unmashed boiled potatoes tossed in parsley butter, chopped green beans and carrot rings tossed in melted brown sugar, butter and vinegar.

Note: If scallops are boiled in liquid they shrink and become hard.

SALMON RING

220 g can good red salmon or tuna
Salt and pepper to taste
2 tablespoons lemon juice
1 tablespoon grated onion
1 tablespoon chopped parsley
2 cups melted butter sauce
5 eggs
Fine breadcrumbs
Prepared mustard
Gherkin fans

Drain salmon and remove skin and bones. Flake the fish with a fork. Season with salt and peper, add lemon juice, onion and parsley. Mix well. Make 2 cups thick melted butter sauce with butter, flour and milk. Beat 3 eggs until light, add to salmon with two-thirds of the sauce, with seasoning to taste. Grease a ring-mould and sprinkle thickly with fine dry breadcrumbs. Fill mould with salmon mixture, set it in a pan of hot water and bake for about 50 minutes in a moderate oven. Hard-boil remaining 2 eggs and put aside. When salmon ring is cooked, loosen round edges with a spatula, turn mould over a hot dish and allow it to stand a few minutes. Lift off mould. Fill centre of ring with sliced hard-boiled eggs combined with the remainder of sauce which has been flavoured with a little prepared mustard. Garnish with slices of hard-boiled eggs and gherkin fans.

SALMON AU GRATIN

1 cup breadcrumbs
½ cup dry cheese, grated
Grated nutmeg
Salt and cayenne
425 g tin salmon
½ cup melted butter sauce
1 tablespoon lemon juice
Butter

Combine breadcrumbs and cheese, nutmeg, salt and cayenne in a bowl. In another bowl combine sauce, salmon and lemon juice. Grease a piedish and coat well with seasoned breadcrumbs. Alternate layers of salmon mixture and crumb mixture, till all the ingredients are used up, having cheese and breadcrumbs for the top layer.

Top with little pieces of butter and bake in a moderate oven 15 to 20 minutes. Garnish with lemon wedges and parsley.

SALMON CAKES

4 large potatoes
425 g tin salmon
1 tablespoon chopped parsley
Good squeeze lemon juice
1 teaspoon salt
Cayenne

1 egg
Egg and breadcrumbs
Frying fat
Parsley sauce

Boil and mash potatoes. Strain liquor from salmon, put into a bowl and break flesh with a fork. Remove bones. Add potatoes, parsley, lemon juice, salt and cayenne and enough beaten egg to bind (too much makes it impossible to handle mixture). Make into round shapes, dip into beaten egg and then into breadcrumbs. Deep fry, drain and serve hot with tossed salad on the side or boiled carrots and zucchini in butter sauce.

FISH PIE

425 g can salmon or other cooked or
   canned fish
1 cup cooked rice
½ cup thick sour cream
½ teaspoon anchovy sauce
Squeeze lemon juice
Salt and cayenne
Mashed potatoes
Beaten egg or milk
Butter

Remove small bones from salmon or other fish, mix with rice, cream, anchovy sauce, lemon juice, and salt and cayenne to taste. Put mixture into greased piedish. Cover with mashed potatoes and brush with beaten egg or milk. Dot with butter. Bake in a moderate oven till brown. Serve with green and other vegetables.

FILLETS OF FISH IN CASSEROLE

4 fish fillets
1 lemon
1 cup melted butter sauce
Chopped parsley

Wash fillets, drop into boiling salted water, turn off heat and allow to stand for 20 minutes. Take fillets one at a time from water, removing skin and bones. Place fillets in a casserole dish. Sprinkle with juice of half a lemon. Add melted butter sauce. Cover. Bake in a slow oven 20 minutes. Garnish with slices of lemon and sprigs of parsley.

Note: Smoked fish may be used, if desired.

BAKED FISH WITH CHEESE SAUCE

1 kg flathead or bream
Lemon juice
Salt and pepper
Small pieces butter
6 stuffed olives
Parsley

Sauce:

2 tablespoons butter
2 tablespoons flour
2 cups milk
½ cup grated cheese
1 egg yolk
Salt and pepper

Wash and dry fish and cut into 6 pieces. Arrange on greased dish, add lemon juice, sprinkle with salt and pepper and place small pieces of butter on top. Cover with greased paper.

Bake in a moderate oven 15 minutes or till flesh leaves the bone easily. Lift on to heated entree dish and garnish with slices of stuffed olives and parsley. For sauce, melt butter, add flour and cook over heat 1 minute, stirring constantly. Add milk, stir till boiling and cook 3 minutes. Remove from heat, add finely grated cheese, beaten egg yolk and salt and pepper. Return to heat and cook 2 minutes without boiling. Serve fish hot accompanied by sauce in a sauce bowl.

FISH CUTLETS

2 tablespoons mashed potato
1 cup cold flaked cooked fish
2 tablespoons thick white sauce
⅛ teaspoon salt
Pepper
Squeeze lemon juice
1 teaspoon chopped parsley
2 teaspoons flour
1 egg
3 tablespoons fine white breadcrumbs
Frying fat
Potato straws

Mix together potato, fish, sauce, salt, pepper, lemon juice and chopped parsley. Form into cutlet shapes on a floured board. Dip cutlets into beaten egg, then into breadcrumbs. Press breadcrumbs on firmly with a large knife. A second coating of egg and breadcrumbs is an improvement. Fry in hot fat till golden brown on both sides, then drain. Use potato straws to represent cutlet bones.

Serve hot, garnished with sprigs of parsley and slices of lemon.

GRILLED FISH

Fillets of or 1 small whole whiting, bream or garfish
1 lemon
Butter or oil
1 tablespoon Maitre d'Hotel Butter (p. 50, Prune Savouries.)

Prepare fish. Sprinkle with juice of half a lemon and brush with melted butter or oil. Place under heated griller and grill 8 to 10 minutes, turning twice carefully. Place on hot serving plate. Place Maitre d'Hotel Butter on top. Garnish with slices of lemon.

CREAMY COD KEDGEREE

500 g smoked fish
3 tablespoons butter
2 large onions, chopped
2 level tablespoons curry powder
3 level tablespoons flour
2 cups milk
2 hard-boiled eggs, chopped
2 large tomatoes, peeled and chopped
Juice of ½ lemon
Salt and pepper
2 level teaspoons sugar
Fluffy boiled rice
Chopped parsley

Place fish in cold water, bring to the boil and drain. After repeating this process, flake fish and remove bones. Melt butter in a large saucepan and fry the onion and curry powder for 3 minutes. Remove from heat and blend in the flour and milk. Return to heat, bring to the boil, stirring constantly. Add the fish, eggs, tomato, lemon juice, salt, pepper and sugar. Gently reheat. Serve in a border of fluffy boiled rice, sprinkled with chopped parsley.

FISH MOULDS

2 tablespoons butter
4 tablespoons milk
½ cup breadcrumbs
¾ cup cold cooked fish, preferably fresh, not canned
1 egg, separated
3 tablespoons capers
1 teaspoon worcestershire sauce
Salt and pepper
Lemon wedges
Parsley

Heat butter and milk in saucepan. Pour on to breadcrumbs in a bowl and allow to soak for a few minutes. Remove skin and bones from fish, flake finely, and add to breadcrumb mixture. Beat in egg yolk, 1 tablespoon chopped capers, worcestershire sauce, and salt and pepper to taste. Fold in stiffly beaten egg white. Turn mixture into small buttered moulds and cover with buttered paper. Place in large saucepan containing a little water and steam gently until set (about 20 minutes). Do not allow to boil dry. Turn out and garnish with remaining capers, lemon wedges and parsley. Serve with creamed potatotes, carrots and beans.

BAKED FISH SOUFFLE

1 tablespoon butter
2 tablespoons milk
1 cup mashed potato
2 eggs, separated
1 cup cooked flaked fish, or boned salmon
1 teaspoon chopped parsley
Salt and cayenne
Lemon juice

Butter a souffle mould or china piedish. Heat butter and milk in saucepan, add mashed potato and beat till thoroughly hot, smooth and light. Add egg yolks, beating in well, then flaked fish, parsley, salt, cayenne and a squeeze of lemon juice. Stir in stiffly beaten egg whites, mixing very lightly, and pour into prepared piedish. Bake in a moderate oven for about 30-40 minutes (till well risen and golden brown). Serve immediately.

FISH A LA ROUNAISE

4 wide flat fish fillets
2 tablespoons butter
2 tablespoons flour
1 cup fish stock
125 g shelled prawns or lobster
Salt and cayenne
Lemon juice
2 tablespoons cream
Oil or butter
Chopped parsley or pistachio nuts
Lemon slices

Skin fillets of fish, wash and dry. Make a sauce with butter,
flour, and fish stock. Add to it lobster or prawns cut into small
pieces, salt, cayenne, lemon juice to taste, and cream. Spread
fillets with some of the prawn or lobster mixture. Brush with
oil or butter, roll up and tie with white thread, or use toothpicks. Place on greased dish and bake in a moderate oven till
tender. Place on a warm dish, remove threads or picks, and
cover with remaining white sauce. Garnish with parsley or
pistachio nuts and slices of lemon.

PAN FRIED FISH

Fillets of or 1 small whole whiting, bream or garfish
1 lemon
Flour
Salt and pepper
Butter
1 tablespoon Maitre d'Hotel Butter (p. 50, Prune Savouries.)

Prepare fish. Sprinkle with juice of half a lemon and dust with
flour seasoned to taste with salt and pepper. Melt sufficient
butter to just cover the base of a heavy pan. Heat until
foaming. Add fish, white side down, if fillets, and cook
quickly turning once. When cooked, place on hot serving
plate. Place Maitre d'Hotel Butter on top. Garnish with slices
of lemon.

SOUSED FISH

1 kg bream or flathead fillets or end cutlets
   jewfish or snapper
1 large onion
5 peppercorns
5 cloves
1 chili
1 teaspoon salt
1 teaspoon brown sugar
450 ml vinegar
1 lettuce
2 tomatoes
6 shallots
6 celery curls
6 radish roses

Wash and dry fish and cut into slices. Prepare and slice onion.
Place fish slices in a steel, enamel or glass baking dish, and
cover with sliced onion. Add peppercorns, cloves, chili, salt
and brown sugar, then the vinegar, and cover with greased
paper. Bake in a moderately hot oven 30 minutes. Let fish
stand in liquor till set. Lift fish out carefully and place in
centre of serving dish. Strain liquor over fish. Garnish with
lettuce leaves, tomato wedges, shallots, celery curls and
radish roses.

MEAT AND POULTRY

ARABIAN PORK CHOPS

6 lean leg pork chops
Flour
Salt and pepper
2 tablespoons fat
1½ cups cooked rice
3 tomatoes
2 onions
1 lemon
3 cups water or stock
3 apples
2 tablespoons sugar
Parsley

Trim chops, dip in a little flour seasoned with salt and pepper, and fry in hot fat till seared and brown. Place chops in a casserole, cover with cooked rice, sliced tomatoes and onions, and two thin slices of lemon. Add water or stock, cover, and place in a moderate oven to cook gently for about 1 hour or until quite tender. About 30 minutes before the meat is cooked, add sliced, cored apple rings, sugared and sprinkled with grated lemon rind. Cook till tender. Garnish with parsley and serve hot.

BURGUNDY BEEF ROLLS

750 g round steak, about 10 mm thick
Salt and pepper
½ cup cooked rice

2 medium onions (1 chopped, 1 sliced)
2 teaspoons chopped parsley
2 teaspoons anchovy sauce
Plain flour seasoned with salt and pepper
2 tablespoons fat
1¼ cups stock
2/3 cup burgundy
2 teaspoons white or tarragon vinegar

Cut steak into pieces about 100 x 80 mm and sprinkle with salt and pepper. In a bowl mix together rice, chopped onion, parsley and anchovy sauce. Place portion of this filling on each piece of steak, reserving a little. Roll up and tie with string or fasten with skewers. (This is a soft filling, so roll carefully to keep as much in as possible.) Dip each roll in seasoned flour, firming flour on, particularly at the ends of each roll. Brown rolls in hot fat, then add sliced onion and cook till brown. Place rolls and onion in an ovenproof dish, add remainder of rice filling (this helps to thicken the gravy) and pour on stock, burgundy and vinegar. Cover and cook in a moderate oven for approximately 2 hours. Serve with jacket potatoes, green peas, cauliflower and white sauce.

BEEF RUMP

Butter or oil
2 kg piece of beef rump
1 small bottle beer
2 tablespoons mushroom ketchup
Onion stuck with 3 cloves
½ teaspoon powdered mace
4 tablespoons vinegar
Bouquet garni
Little cayenne pepper
Salt

Heat a little butter or oil in a large, very heavy saucepan. Add the meat, fat side down. Brown each surface well at moderate heat. This should take about 1 hour. Remove any excess fat and add beer, ketchup, onion and seasonings. Stew gently over low heat 2 hours. Do not hurry this, or meat will become coarse and stringy. Place meat on hot serving plate in oven. Strain and thicken gravy. Carve meat, re-arrange on plate. Pour on gravy. Serve with plain boiled potatoes, buttered zucchini or baby squash and sauerkraut.

BEEF STROGANOFF

1 onion
½ cup butter or margarine
250 g mushrooms
500 g fillet steak
Salt and pepper
½ cup sour cream (or fresh cream soured with lemon juice)

Fry chopped onion in half the butter, fry mushrooms in remainder. Cut steak into thin strips, fry in the onion-flavoured butter; season well. Add warmed cream, heat together gently, then add mushrooms and serve at once on boiled rice.

Note: If steak is chilled until quite firm, very thin slices can be cut.

LIVER, BACON AND TOMATOES EN CASSEROLE

500 g liver
Salt and pepper
4 bacon rashers
1 cup prepared seasoning
4 large tomatoes (peeled)

Prepare liver, cut into thin slices, season and place in a casserole with alternate layers of bacon and seasoning. Place a thick layer of sliced tomatoes on top. Bake in a moderate oven for 1 hour.

MINTED MUTTON

2 kg leg of mutton, boned if possible
Flour

Salt
Pepper
300 ml mint sauce
Bouquet garni

Trim meat and if necessary tie into shape. Rub surface with flour, salt and pepper. Place in greased casserole and bake dry and uncovered for 40 minutes. Remove any excess fat, pour mint sauce over meat, add herbs. Cover and cook in moderate heat 1½ hours, basting and turning frequently. Remove meat to warm plate, skim fat away, remove herbs, thicken gravy a little. Serve with jacket potatoes and sour cream, mashed swede turnips and butter or lima beans.

STUFFED VEAL STEAKS

1 kg veal steak, 5 mm thick
6 bacon rashers
2 cups soft white breadcrumbs
¼ cup milk
1 beaten egg
250 g minced pork
1 onion, chopped finely
1 level teaspoonful salt
¼ level teaspoon pepper
¼ level teaspoon powdered sage
6 whole carrots
1¼ cups stock

Cut veal into individual servings and place each on half a bacon rasher. Make the seasoning by mixing all remaining ingredients except carrots and stock. Place a spoonful of seasoning on each piece of veal and roll up, fastening with a toothpick. Brown these rolls in hot fat. Pour off remaining fat, place in the casserole, add prepared whole carrots and stock, cover lightly, and bake in a moderate oven for 2 hours, uncovering for the last 20 minutes to crisp and brown the top.

VEAL AND PATE DECKS IN ONION SAUCE

2 cups sliced white onion
½ cup butter or margarine
2 cups chicken stock or consomme (canned)
2 tablespoons flour
¼ cup cream
2 teaspoons salt
⅛ teaspoon nutmeg
1/16 teaspoon ground white pepper
12 veal scallops pounded thin
185 g chicken or goose liver pate
6 large mushrooms
Chopped parsley or chives

Fry onions in all but 2 tablespoons of the butter until clear and
limp. Drain off fat. Add half chicken stock and cook until
quite tender. Put through seive or blender to make puree. Melt
2 tablespoons butter in a saucepan, remove from heat and
blend in flour. Add rest of chicken stock, stir over medium
low heat until thick and smooth. Add onion puree, cream, ¼
teaspoon salt, nutmeg and white pepper. Heat well. Sprinkle
the remaining salt on both sides of veal. Fry in 2 tablespoons
butter. Place 6 pieces of veal in base of large oven dish, cover
with layer of pate, then with remaining veal slices. The
mushrooms, which have been trimmed, washed and dried, are
lightly fried. Place one on each deck of meat round side up.
Pour sauce over and around. Reheat completely. Serve on
rounds of thin crisp toast. Garnish with chopped parsley and
chives. Serve with duchess potatoes, buttered broccoli and
carrot straws.

SEASONED ROAST VEAL ROLL

2 kg veal. Have butcher cut meat from ribs, or bone a
    forequarter spread as flat as possible
Lemon juice
Salt and pepper
½ teaspoon monosodium glutamate
Cornflour

2 rashers of bacon
Seasoning:
1 cup white breadcrumbs
2 eggs lightly beaten
1 rasher chopped bacon
2 tablespoons melted butter
1 clove garlic, crushed
1 teaspoon minced onion
1 tablespoon chopped parsley
1 small sprig rosemary, crushed
Salt
Pepper
2 tablespoons marsala

Sprinkle meat with lemon juice, salt, pepper and monosodium glutamate. Mix the seasoning ingredients well. Spread over the meat surface. Roll up neatly and firmly. Skewer and tie into shape. Rub surface with cornflour until well coated. Arrange in rather small dish in which some bacon fat has been heated. This helps meat keep its shape. Brown and turn for 1 hour at 175°C (350°F), then cover with bacon rashers, foil or film, and bake at 150°C (300°F) for 1½ hours. Remove meat and allow to settle in a warm place before removing ties. Leave skewers until carving. Skim off any fat. Make gravy, adding a little more lemon juice to taste. Serve with crisp baked potatoes, baby carrots, creamed corn and brussel sprouts.

SUCKLING PIG

1 suckling pig, about 2 weeks old
2 large onions
Butter
4 cups fine white breadcrumbs
Salt, pepper and cayenne to taste
1 teaspoon chopped sage
1 tablespoon minced parsley
1 small raw potato
Fat or oil
Plain flour
1 red apple

Wash the pig well inside and out and dry it. Chop onions and fry in 2 tablespoons butter until light brown. Add crumbs, salt, pepper, cayenne, sage and parsley and 4 tablespoons melted butter. Stuff the pig and sew up with strong white cotton. Bend the forelegs backwards and the hind legs forwards and fix with a skewer. Place a raw potato in the mouth and cover the ears with greased paper. Rub the pig all over with good fat or oil, then dust with plain flour. Wrap in two or three layers of well greased paper, and bake in a hot oven for 3 to 3½ hours, basting frequently. Half an hour before serving, remove paper, brush with melted butter, dust with flour, and brown. Remove potato, loosen head, split body right down the back to loosen bone and arrange on large serving dish in whole shape, surrounded by parsley, watercress and small whole red tomatoes or halved red apple cups filled with apple sauce. Place a nice red apple in the mouth. Serve with brown gravy, apple sauce, and vegetables in season. This is delicious cold with salads.

HAWAIIAN CHICKEN

1 packet Maggi creme of chicken soup
1 green capsicum
1 clove garlic
2 tablespoons oil
425 g can pineapple pieces
2 teaspoons soy sauce
2 cups cooked chicken, chopped
Toasted almonds (optional)

Make soup up with 2 cups water. Chop capsicum, saute with garlic in oil until soft. Adjust consistency of soup with pineapple juice, add half the pineapple pieces, chicken meat, capsicum and soy sauce. Heat, stirring occasionally. Serve over fluffy boiled rice. Garnish with toasted almonds and pineapple pieces and serve with boiled fresh or frozen green peas.

MILDURA BRAISE

1 tablespoon butter
3 small onions, cut in half
2 medium carrots, cut into pieces
2 small sticks celery, cut into pieces
750 g breast veal, cut into pieces
2 tablespoons seasoned flour
1½ cups vegetable or meat stock
1 tablespoon tomato paste
½ teaspoon grated lemon rind
½ teaspoon salt
Pinch pepper
¼ cup stoned chopped prunes
1 tablespoon dry sherry
2 tablespoons chopped walnuts

Melt the butter in a heavy saucepan and lightly fry the onions, carrots and celery. Remove and set aside. Toss veal pieces in the seasoned flour and fry until golden. Return vegetables to pan and add stock, tomato paste, lemon rind, salt and pepper. Bring to the boil, cover and simmer gently for ½ hour. Add the prunes and sherry and continue simmering for a further ½ hour or until meat is tender. Serve topped with chopped walnuts.

CHICKEN MARENGO

20 black olives
No. 12 roasting chicken
3 tablespoons oil
1 clove garlic
4 teaspoons tomato paste
½ cup dry white wine
½ cup clear chicken stock
2 large ripe tomatoes
12 champignons (button mushrooms)
1 teaspoon butter
1 teaspoon chopped parsley

Put olives to soak in warm water. Joint the chicken, fry golden brown in heated oil in heavy saucepan or casserole. Remove chicken, add sliced garlic. When this begins to brown, add tomato paste. Cook, stirring a little. When the paste darkens a little, add white wine and stock, and peeled, quartered tomatoes from which seeds have been removed. Add seasonings. Return chicken pieces to sauce as it comes to boil. Simmer gently 45 minutes. Fry mushrooms gently in butter. Remove olives from warm water and remove seeds. Add mushrooms and olives to chicken, continue simmering 15 minutes. Serve in deep dish, sprinkled with chopped parsley.

Note: For special effect when served at table, fold parsley in with olives and mushrooms, pour over 1 tablespoon warm brandy or dry sherry and flame.

CREAMED CHICKEN WITH BUTTERED ALMONDS

1 kg or 4 cups cooked chicken meat
4 tablespoons butter
6 tablespoons plain flour
Salt
Cayenne pepper
2 cups milk
1½ cups chicken stock
Juice ½ lemon
1 or 2 sliced gherkins
3 tablespoons mayonnaise
1 beaten egg
¾ cup tasty cheese
1 cup soft white breadcrumbs
¼ cup blanched almonds

Melt butter, add flour, salt and cayenne pepper. Return to heat and cook 1 minute. Add milk and stock and stir constantly until it boils and thickens. Add lemon juice, gherkins, mayonnaise, beaten egg, cheese and chicken meat.

Pour into a greased casserole dish and top with breadcrumbs and almonds, browned lightly in heated butter. Reheat completely to crisp the crumbs. Serve on heated plates, with crisp potatoes, carrot rings and lightly boiled string beans.

To prepare the almonds blanch and dry them. Heat 2 tablespoons butter in small pan, add crumbs and almonds. Turn frequently on moderate heat until lightly browned. Add extra salt and dash of cayenne pepper.

COQ AU VIN

No. 14 chicken (up to 1.5 kg)
Salt and pepper
2 tablespoons butter
½ cup diced bacon
12 button mushrooms or small can champignons
12 small or pearl onions
2 shallots
1 clove garlic
2 tablespoons flour
2 cups dry red wine
1 bouquet garni
Chopped parsley

Cut chicken into 8 pieces, 2 legs, 2 second joints, 2 wings, 2 breasts. Wash, dry and season each section with salt and pepper. Melt butter in wide, heavy saucepan or casserole. Brown the bacon lightly, remove from fat. Brown chicken pieces on both sides. Add mushrooms and onions, cover and cook gently until onions are just tender and very lightly browned. Pour off half the fat, add the shallots finely chopped, crushed garlic, and the flour. Stir until flour browns, mix in wine and sufficient water to come to top of chicken, with the herbs. Add bacon, cover container and simmer 40 minutes or until very tender. (If in a casserole cook in oven.) Skim off fat, remove bouquet garni, adjust seasonings, sprinkle lavishly with chopped parsley. Take casserole to table.

CHICKEN A LA KING

No. 10 cooked chicken, cut in pieces
4 tablespoons butter or ½ cup cream
Freshly ground black pepper
4 tablespoons flour
2½ cups chicken stock or chicken soup and milk
250 g mushrooms, washed, sliced, sauteed in butter
1 cup finely shredded red and green peppers, covered with
    boiling water 10 minutes and drained
1/16 teaspoon nutmeg, freshly ground
½ teaspoon salt
1 tablespoon sherry

Blend cream and flour until smooth or melt butter, mix in
flour until smooth. Cook, stirring, 1 minute. Add liquid,
stirring well, to make smooth creamy sauce. Boil 2 full
minutes. Add seasonings, chicken, mushrooms, peppers and
sherry. Reheat thoroughly. Turn mixture over. Do not stir.
Serve with or on parsley rice (add 2 tablespoons chopped
parsley to 3 cups of cooked rice).

CHICKEN AND PEACH SALAD

6 freestone peaches
1 tablespoon oil
¼ cup vinegar
2 cups seedless grapes
4 cups chopped cooked chicken
1 cup sliced celery
1 small onion, chopped
2/3 cup mayonnaise
½ level teaspoon lemon rind
2 drops tabasco sauce
Lettuce
Toasted slivered almonds

Peel, stone and slice peaches. Add oil, vinegar and grapes,
marinate for 2 hours. Combine next 6 ingredients. Add

peaches and marinade, mix lightly. Serve in lettuce cups
sprinkled with almonds.

JELLIED CHICKEN MOULD

2 tablespoons gelatine
½ cup hot water
1 large can cream of chicken soup
2 tablespoons mayonnaise
2 tablespoons lemon juice
Salt, pepper and celery salt to taste
2 cups diced, skinned, cooked chicken
¼ cup each of grated onion, chopped celery, chopped
    capsicum

Mould lining:
1 rounded teaspoon gelatine
¼ cup hot water
Lemon juice
5 slices cooked carrot
5 stuffed olives
2 hard-boiled eggs

Dissolve gelatine in hot water. Blend undiluted soup with
mayonnaise, lemon juice and seasonings. Stir in the dissolved
gelatine. When mixture is beginning to thicken fold in chicken,
onion, celery and capsicum. To line mould, dissolve 1 rounded
teaspoon gelatine in ¼ cup hot water and few drops lemon
juice. Cool well. Brush base and sides of mould liberally with
thickening mixture. Decorate with hard-boiled egg slices,
shaped carrot slices, and sliced stuffed olives. Spoon mixture
in carefully until well filled. Refrigerate until well set,
unmould, serve with salads.

VEGETABLES

ASPARAGUS AU FROMAGE CREME

1 cup cottage cheese
1½ tablespoons lemon juice
1½ tablespoons dry white wine
1 egg yolk
1 teaspoon salt
⅛ teaspoon cayenne pepper
¼ teaspoon dry mustard
1 large can asparagus spears or 1 bunch freshly prepared
    asparagus or 250 g frozen spears, boiled 6 minutes in
    lightly salted water

Force cheese through sieve, then mix or vitamize with lemon
juice, wine and egg yolk. Place in top of double boiler with
salt, pepper and mustard. Cook over hot water, stirring until
very well heated. Spoon over asparagus arranged on oval
heatproof dish. Garnish with finely chopped parsley. Serve as
entree or luncheon dish with crisp toast or wholemeal rolls
and butter.

AUBERGINE (EGGPLANT) SAVOURY

1 large aubergine
2-3 tablespoons oil
1 large green and 1 large red pepper
Little seasoned flour
1 clove garlic
3-4 firm ripe tomatoes
Extra salt
Freshly ground black pepper

Peel aubergine, cut into 10 mm slices. Spread in shallow dish,
sprinkle with salt, leave for 1 hour. Remove from the liquid
formed, dry and coat with seasoned flour. Fry gently in
heated oil, remove. Lightly cook shredded peppers, remove.
Peel and seed tomatoes, cook lightly, season with salt and
pepper. Arrange in alternate layers in oven dish. Top with
crumbs. Cook 15 minutes in a medium oven. If wanted as a
meatless dish, add thin slices of grated tasty cheese to each
layer. Finish with cheese and crumbs.

MUSHROOMS IN CREAM SAUCE

250 g mushrooms
½ cup butter
1 clove garlic
1 tablespoon finely chopped parsley
1-2 egg yolks
½ can evaporated milk

Trim, wash and slice mushrooms, drain. Heat butter in
frypan, add crushed garlic, parsley and mushrooms. Shake the
pan over low heat to mix. Continue until mushrooms are
tender. Whisk egg yolks and milk together. Pour on to
mushrooms. Allow to just thicken or set. Serve at once on
French toast, pancakes or hot potato crisps.

STUFFED GREEN CAPSICUM

2 uncooked pork sausages (continental)
½ cup white breadcrumbs
1 teaspoon chopped parsley
Salt and pepper
¼ teaspoon marjoram
¼ teaspoon thyme
1 tablespoon chopped shallot greens
2 tablespoons tomato sauce
1 tablespoon melted butter
1 large halved capsicum or two small ones

Remove sausage skins. Mix meat, crumbs, herbs, sauce and melted butter. Remove stalk and seeds of capsicum. Wash and dry. Immerse in boiling water for 5 minutes. Drain well. Fill with mixture and cook in covered, greased oven dish until tender. Serve with cauliflower au gratin, carrot straws, potato puffs.

Note: This mixture may be also rolled in blanched cabbage leaves. Cook the rolls in pork or chicken stock for 30 minutes in a medium oven. Minced or ground pork is obtainable from continental style butcher shops.

FRIED ZUCCHINI (Courgettes)

4-6 zucchini
½ teaspoon salt
1 tablespoon seasoned flour
Oil or bacon fat

Wash, dry and trim zucchini. Cut lengthwise in four or six pieces according to size, spread out and sprinkle with salt. Allow to stand 10 minutes. Press in kitchen cloth to dry. Do not crush. Coat with seasoned flour and deep fry until golden brown. While hot and crisp serve with vinaigrette sauce.

Vinaigrette Sauce:

5 tablespoons olive oil
Salt, pepper
1 teaspoon continental mustard, French or German
3 tablespoons vinegar
1 hard-boiled egg, very finely chopped
1 small onion, grated
1 tablespoon finely chopped parsley

Blend oil, salt, pepper and mustard, then carefully add vinegar and other ingredients. If vitamizer is available, place egg, onion, parsley, mustard and oil in first. Vitamize, then add vinegar slowly while vitamizing. Season.

Note: This sauce may also be used with chilled avocado, asparagus and baby corn.

GLOBE ARTICHOKES

Strip off the outer, tough leaves. Remove stalk close to base, trim, rub with lemon juice. Cut off the tip of each leaf with scissors. Remove inner part which is unpleasant to eat. Use thread to tie artichokes in shape while cooking in boiling salted water, to which has been added a little lemon juice or vinegar. Boil 15-20 minutes. Test base with fork. Drain well. Serve hot with Hollandaise sauce or plain melted butter. Serve cold with vinaigrette sauce.

JERUSALEM ARTICHOKES

Carefully wash 500 g artichokes, using a brush. Just cover with boiling, salted water and cook 20 minutes. Drain. If desired skins may be rubbed off. Make a melted butter sauce, masking consistency. Slice artichokes, arrange in oven dish, cover with sauce. Cover with breadcrumbs and dots of butter. Reheat until crumbs are crisp and browned.

JELLIED BEETROOT

4 medium beetroot
5 level teaspoons gelatine
2 cups cold water
1/3 cup vinegar
1½ level teaspoons brown sugar
1 level teaspoon salt
½ level teaspoon pepper

Cook beetroot in boiling salted water till tender, about 20 minutes. Allow to cool in water, peel and slice. Soften gelatine in cold water, dissolve over hot water. Add remaining ingredients and allow to thicken slightly. Pour over beetroot which has been placed into a wet mould. Allow to set. Unmould before serving.

POTATO RING

3 tablespoons sour cream
1 teaspoon plain flour
1 egg
1 cup hot, well-mashed potato
Salt, pepper

Blend cream, flour, egg yolk. Combine with mashed potato until smooth. Beat egg white until stiff and fold evenly through potato. Use large forcing bag, shape a shallow round or oval base on a well-greased oven tray, then build up the sides to form a case. Bake in medium to hot oven until lightly browned. Serve filled with any meat, fish or vegetable mixture on a base of parsley or watercress.

STUFFED BAKED POTATOES

3 large baking potatoes
½ cup avocado
1 tablespoon chopped chives
½ cup cream
2 teaspoons salt
⅛ teaspoon pepper
1 tablespoon milk
Paprika

Scrub and dry potatoes. Bake on oven shelf until quite tender (1½ hours in a moderate oven). Cut in half lengthwise, scoop out, mash well with avocado, chives, cream and seasonings until fluffy. Pile into potato shells (forcing bag may be used). Brush with milk, sprinkle with paprika. Return to oven, reheat 15 minutes. Serve with mixed vegetables.

BECHAMEL POTATOES

8 to 10 potatoes
3 rashers streaky bacon
1 tablespoon butter, margarine or bacon fat
1 large onion
2 tablespoons flour
2 cups milk
⅛ teaspoon nutmeg
Pepper, salt

Wash, peel and cook potatoes and cut into thick slices while
hot. Cover and keep hot. Cut bacon into small pieces, fry
lightly in heated fat, add chopped onion, stir, cook until onion
is clear. Stir in flour, cook 1 minute. Add milk gradually, stir
until boiling. Flavour with nutmeg, pepper and salt. Add
potatoes to sauce, cover and reheat. A good accompaniment
for pot roast, braised meats or fried thick sausages.

POTATO PIE

250 g potatoes
2 tablespoons flour
2 tablespoons milk
1 clove garlic, crushed
1 onion finely chopped
Marjoram to taste
Salt
Freshly ground black pepper
1 tablespoon butter

Peel, grate and drain the potatoes. Blend flour and milk, combine with potato, garlic, onion and seasonings. Place in a well-greased oven dish. Dot with butter. Bake in centre of hot oven 30 minutes.

RICE

In this section are recipes for cooking rice by steaming, boiling and frying; for rice pilau which when served with side dishes can form a complete meal; and for sweet dishes made with rice.

Long, medium and short grained rice is obtainable. Most people prefer to use the long grain rice for savoury cooking, although the medium grain is a good all-purpose rice for savoury or sweet dishes.

Add a good squeeze of lemon juice, or a slice or two of lemon to the rice when cooking; this will whiten and flavour the grains. For additional flavour, one or two small stock cubes can be crumbled into the water.

Boiled or steamed rice can have many flavourful additions lightly forked through, such as finely chopped chives, parsley or mint; grated carrot with finely chopped shallots; raisins, toasted halved or slivered almonds, diced cooked vegetables; chopped hard-boiled eggs. The choice is as wide as the imaginative cook cares to make it.

Rice triples its size during cooking; 1 cup of uncooked rice will swell to 3 cups when it is cooked. Allow approximately ¾ cup cooked rice for each main dish serving.

HOW TO REHEAT RICE

To save time in meal preparation, a quantity of rice can be cooked in advance. When cool, store in a plastic bag or covered bowl in the refrigerator. It is easy to reheat by any of the following methods:

Indian Method: Fill a large saucepan half full with water, bring to rapid boil. Add boiled rice, stir, leave in water not more than 4 seconds. Drain at once.

To Reheat with Steam: Place cooked rice in colander, stand over saucepan of simmering water. Cover colander with lid. Steam until rice is heated through.

Another method of steaming cooked rice is to pour just enough water into a saucepan to cover the base of pan. When boiling, add rice, cover, steam 5 minutes or until water is absorbed and rice is hot. The size of the saucepan will depend on the amount of rice to be reheated; use a large saucepan for a large amount of rice, so the steam can penetrate the grains.

To Reheat in the Oven: Spread rice in a shallow ovenproof dish, sprinkle with a little water or milk, dot with butter. Cover the dish with a lid or aluminium foil. Place in a moderate oven until heated through.

To Reheat in a Frypan: Melt a little butter in a frypan, add the rice. Stir with a fork until heated through.

FLUFFY BOILED RICE

8 cups water
2 teaspoons salt
1 cup rice

Put water into a large saucepan, bring to rapid boil, add salt. Then gradually, letting it dribble through your fingers so the water does not go off the boil, add rice. Boil rapidly, uncovered, 12 to 15 minutes. Cooking time depends on the type of rice used and also on the way you like your rice — tender, or still with a slight firmness left in the grain. Start testing at the end of 12 minutes. Lift a few grains from the pan with a fork and bite into the grain. When cooked to your liking, drain at once in a colander.

Note: Brown unpolished rice may be substituted. It takes longer to cook than white rice.

CHAWAL (Indian Rice)

8 cups cold water
250 g rice
2 teaspoons salt

Bring 7 cups water to the boil in a large saucepan. When
boiling briskly, add the rice. Stir a little and cook, uncovered,
until cooked (about 20 minutes). When it is cooked at the core,
add salt and remaining cup water to the boiling rice.
Immediately remove from heat and drain in colander.

STEAMED "PEARLY" RICE

Put required amount of well washed rice into saucepan, add
water to come 2 cm above level of rice. Add salt to flavour.
Bring water rapidly to the boil, then cover tightly, reduce heat
to lowest simmer and cook for further 20 minutes. For a
firmer grain, many cooks prefer to simmer the rice 15 minutes
only; then remove the pan from the heat and let it stand, still
tightly covered, for 5 to 10 minutes.

OVEN-STEAMED RICE

1 cup rice
Salt
2¾ cups boiling water

Place 1 cup rice into casserole dish, sprinkle lightly with salt.
Pour over 2¾ cups boiling water, cover tightly. Cook in
moderately hot over 20 to 25 minutes.

FRIED RICE

2 tablespoons butter
2 onions
1 clove garlic

2½ cups cooked rice
Dash paprika
Salt and pepper
1 tablespoon worcestershire sauce
250 g prawns
¾ cup ham
2 eggs
¼ cup toasted desiccated coconut
½ cup chopped peanuts

Heat butter in pan, add chopped onions and crushed garlic, saute until golden. Remove from pan. Add a little more butter to pan if necessary; add rice. Cook, turning often until golden brown. Sprinkle in paprika, salt and pepper to taste, and worcestershire sauce. Fold in the shelled prawns which have been cut into small pieces, chopped ham and sauteed onions and garlic. Leave in covered pan to keep warm. Beat eggs with 1 teaspoon water, make into thin omelette. Fry until well cooked, cut into thin strips. Garnish each serving of rice with omelette strips. Sprinkle on each plate some of the toasted coconut and chopped peanuts.

QUICK SPANISH RISOTTO

1 clove garlic, chopped
2 onions, chopped
2 green peppers, sliced
6 cups cooked long grain rice
2 tomatoes, sliced
500 g prawns, cooked, shelled and deveined
1 can whole kernel sweetcorn, drained
Butter for frying
Salt and pepper to taste

Saute garlic, onions and peppers in butter in frypan. Add rice and heat through. Add rest of ingredients and toss while heating.

BEEF STEAK CREOLE

Meat Sauce:

¼ cup butter
500 g minced steak
2 cloves garlic, crushed
2 teaspoons each oregano and basil
2 teaspoons salt
2 cans 425 g whole peeled tomatoes
1 tablespoon tomato paste

Cheese Sauce:

2 eggs
2 tablespoons flour
¾ cup milk
1 cup cheddar cheese, grated

Rice:

2 tablespoons butter
4 cups cooked rice
2 tablespoons parsley, chopped
1 cup matured cheddar cheese, grated

To make meat sauce, heat butter, brown meat. Add remaining ingredients. Simmer uncovered for ½ to ¾ hour until thick. Stir occasionally. Skim any fat from sauce. Keep warm. Make cheese sauce by beating eggs, flour and milk together, and adding cheese. Put aside. To make rice, melt butter in heavy saucepan. Toss rise and parsley in butter until well coated. Add cheese. Spoon half rice into a 23 cm square casserole, top with meat sauce then remaining rice. Pour cheese sauce over. Bake in moderate oven (175°C) for 30-35 minutes or until set and golden brown. Serve cut into squares.

LAMB KEBABS WITH BUTTERED ALMOND RICE

1½ kg boned leg of lamb
Juice of 2 lemons
1 clove garlic, crushed

1 teaspoon salt
Freshly ground pepper
2 green peppers, each cut into 6 squares
6 small white onions, cooked
12 small whole tomatoes
½ cup melted clarified butter

Trim fat and gristle from lamb. Cut into 4 cm cubes. Combine
lemon juice, garlic, salt and pepper to taste. Pour over lamb.
Stand several hours or overnight. Parboil peppers, drain. On 6
skewers thread 4 or 5 lamb cubes alternately with onions,
tomatoes and peppers. Brush with clarified butter and
remaining marinade. Grill about 5 cm from heat for about 10
minutes, turning to brown all sides. Brush with clarified butter
several times during cooking. Serve on a bed of Buttered
Almond Rice, with a tossed green salad.

Buttered Almond Rice:

½ cup melted butter
6 cups cooked long grain rice
Salt and pepper
1 cup currants
½ cup blanched slivered almonds

In frypan toss rice in butter till well coated. Add salt and
pepper to taste. Pour boiling water over currants to cover.
Stand 2 or 3 minutes. Drain well. Toss into rice with almonds.

ITALIAN RICE SALAD

1½ cups rice
12 black olives
6 slices smoked salami sausage
1 large tomato
½ cup sliced shallots
½ cup Italian dressing

Cook rice in boiling salted water until tender; drain and allow
to cool. Pit and slice olives, finely chop salami and tomato. In
a bowl, combine all ingredients with dressing. Refrigerate
before serving.

Heat butter in frypan, add chopped onion, chopped celery, parsley and diced ham, but do not allow to brown. Add rice, mix well together. Cook, stirring, until rice is a light brown colour. Add curry powder, season with salt and pepper, then add boiling stock nearly to cover the rice. Add peas, cover, and cook gently until rice is tender and has absorbed nearly all the liquid.

YELLOW PILAU

4 tablespoons butter
1 large onion
2 cloves garlic
2 cardamom seeds
4 cloves
2½ cm stick cinnamon
1 teaspoon ground allspice
2 cups rice
1 teaspoon turmeric
½ cup mixed fruit
¼ cup blanched almonds
Good pinch cayenne pepper
Salt to taste

Heat butter in frypan. Chop onion and garlic, add to frypan. Add cardamom, cloves, cinnamon, and allspice; fry until golden brown. Reduce heat, add rice, and fry 2 minutes, tossing rice lightly. Add turmeric stirred well into ½ cup boiling water. Add enough boiling water to cover the rice by 3 cm. Cover pan tightly, cook slowly until rice has absorbed all the water and is perfectly cooked and in separate grains. Lightly stir in mixed fruit, almonds and remaining butter. Season to taste. Mix well and serve hot with papadams and tomato chutney.

CURRIED RICE SALAD

1 cup long grain rice

1 onion
1 tablespoon vinegar
2 tablespoons oil
2 teaspoons curry powder
1 cup chopped celery
2 cups cooked green peas
1 cup French dressing

Cook rice in usual way, drain well. Mix together in basin the rice, chopped onion, vinegar, salad oil and curry powder. Stir in chopped celery, peas and dressing. Refrigerate well before serving.

CURRIED EGGS

1 tablespoon butter
2 onions
½ teaspoon turmeric
¼ teaspoon ground ginger
¼ teaspoon cinnamon
½ clove garlic
2 teaspoons cumin
Shake of cayenne pepper
or 1 level tablespoon curry powder
1 tablespoon flour
2 teaspoons black sauce
1 cup stock
Salt
4 hard-boiled eggs

Melt butter and lightly fry chopped onions. Crush the cumin seeds and tie them in a piece of muslin (so that they can be removed from the sauce before serving) then add the spices and crushed garlic, or the curry powder if it is being used, and the flour to the onions. Cook for a few minutes. Gradually add the stock and sauce, season and simmer 20 minutes. Cut the eggs in half and heat in the sauce for 10 minutes. Serve the curry surrounded by boiled rice and accompanied by mango chutney, diced tomatoes and papadams if available.

GREEN PEA PILAU

1 tablespoon butter
1 onion
1 stick celery
2 teaspoons chopped parsley
1/3 cup diced lean ham or bacon
2 cups rice
1 teaspoon curry powder
Salt and pepper
4 cups chicken stock
1 cup frozen peas

BEEF AND RICE PEPPERS

2 large green capsicums
500 g minced round steak
1 clove garlic, crushed
½ teaspoon pepper
¼ teaspoon salt
2 tablespoons butter
2 cups boiled, drained rice
¼ teaspoon oregano
4 slices tasty cheese

Halve capsicums lengthwise, remove cores and seeds. Cover with water in saucepan and simmer until they are just tender. Season beef with garlic, pepper and salt. Shape meat into a flat cake, saute in butter until browned on the outside but still quite rare inside. By now capsicums should be done. Remove from water, drain, place in shallow baking dish. Heat rice, stir in oregano. Break up meat, toss with rice. Stuff capsicums with mixture, top each with a slice of cheese. Grill until cheese is melted.

SALAD INDIENNE

4 cups cooked and cooled rice
1 red capsicum, chopped

1 cup sultanas
1 can crab meat, salmon, tuna or prawns
4 shallots, chopped
1 cup pineapple pieces, drained
1/3 cup oil
2 level teaspoons curry powder
¼ cup white vinegar
Dash hot chili sauce
Juice ½ lemon
Salt
Freshly ground black pepper
Salad vegetables
1 packet salted cashews

Mix rice, capsicum, sultanas, fish, shallots and pineapple in serving bowl and chill. Combine oil, curry powder, vinegar, sauce, lemon, salt and pepper in a screw-top jar. Shake vigorously and pour over rice. Toss well and serve with crisp salad vegetables and sprinkle with cashews.

RICE AND PRAWN SALAD

1 cup rice
Boiling salted water
250 g shelled prawns
1 small can minted peas
1 small can asparagus cuts
¾ cup diced green cucumber
½ cup sliced celery
Salt and pepper
1/3 cup French dressing

Cook rice in boiling salted water 12 minutes or until tender. Drain and rinse with cold water. Shell prawns; if small leave whole, chop large prawns. Place cold rice in bowl, add prawns, drained peas, drained asparagus, cucumber, celery, and salt and pepper. Pour over French dressing and toss lightly. Serve in lettuce cups with tomato wedges.

GREEN RICE

1 cup hot cooked rice
½ cup minced parsley
1 tablespoon butter

Stir parsley and butter into rice until evenly distributed.

HAM AND CHICKEN RICE SALAD

1 cup long grain rice
½ cup French dressing
1 tablespoon sultanas
2 tablespoons chopped walnuts
1 cup diced chicken
½ cup diced ham
1 green pepper

Cook rice in boiling salted water, drain. In bowl combine rice, French dressing, sultanas and chopped walnuts. Add chopped chicken, ham and green pepper to rice mixture. Mix well. Refrigerate before serving.

SWEET RICE DISHES

RICE BALLS

1 cup rice
2½ cups milk
2 cups water
½ cup sugar
½ teaspoon cinnamon
¼ teaspoon nutmeg
1 teaspoon vanilla
Desiccated coconut

Wash rice, put into frypan or heavy saucepan with milk, water, sugar, cinnamon and nutmeg. Bring to the boil, cover, simmer until rice is cooked and liquid absorbed (approximately 1 hour). Add vanilla and cook few minutes longer. Set aside to cool. Grease hands lightly with butter, roll rice into balls about the size of a ping-pong ball, then roll in coconut. Serve with whipped cream and black cherries.

SWEET GOLDEN RICE

1 cup rice
2½ cups water
Good pinch salt
¼ teaspoon turmeric
1 cup sugar
½ cup butter
2 cardamom seeds
2 whole cloves
Juice ½ lemon
½ cup nuts (cashews or almonds)
¼ cup raisins

Half-cook the rice in 1¾ cups boiling water with salt and turmeric (this colours the rice to a rich gold). Boil sugar in remaining ¾ cup water 2 minutes, stirring well to make a thin syrup. Melt butter in separate pan, fry cardamom seeds and cloves over low heat 10 minutes. Add syrup, boil for a minute, then add rice. Cook slowly, stirring gently until the syrup and butter have been absorbed and the rice is cooked. Add lemon juice, raisins and nuts. Turn into a casserole. Place in slow oven 10 minutes; cool. Serve with whipped cream or ice cream.

MARSHMALLOW RICE

1½ cups rice
2 cups skim milk
2 cups whole milk
1 pkt pink marshmallows
Grated rind and juice of 1 lemon
Nutmeg

Boil washed rice gently in skim milk until liquid is absorbed. Stir in whole milk, cook very slowly, stirring occasionally to prevent sticking. Cut marshmallows with floured scissors. Stir them with lemon into rice until marshmallows are almost melted. Pour into wet dish and sprinkle with nutmeg.

PINEAPPLE RICE CUSTARD

2 cups cooked rice from refrigerator
425 g can pineapple pieces
1 punnet strawberries, washed and sliced crossways
2 cups custard
1 cup whipped cream
¾ cup desiccated coconut

Combine rice, pineapple pieces (reserving a few pieces for decoration), half the strawberries, the custard and half the whipped cream. Place in serving bowl and refrigerate until set. Decorate with remaining pineapple pieces, strawberries and whipped cream. Sprinkle with coconut.

SAUCES

ESPAGNOLE SAUCE

Rich brown foundation sauce

2 tablespoons butter
1 medium onion, sliced
1 medium carrot, sliced thinly
3 tablespoons chopped lean bacon
1 bouquet garni
3 peppercorns
2 tablespoons flour
2 cups brown stock or 2 beef cubes and water
3 ripe medium tomatoes, chopped
3 tablespoons dry sherry

Melt the butter in a saucepan. Cook the onion, carrot, bacon, herbs and peppercorns until brown. Add flour, stir to remove any lumps and cook until brown. Add stock and tomatoes and stir until boiling. Cover and simmer gently for 30 minutes. Strain through fine wire strainer. Add sherry, reheat.

BECHAMEL SAUCE

2 tablespoons butter
1 tablespoon finely chopped onion
4 tablespoons flour
3 cups scalded milk
¼ teaspoon salt
3 white peppercorns
1 large stalk of parsley
1/16 teaspoon freshly ground nutmeg

Melt the butter and cook the onion until soft and still golden.
Remove from heat and add flour, mix well. Stir constantly
over heat until colour changes but does not brown. Remove
from heat and gradually add the milk, stir vigorously and cook
until mixture is thick and smooth. Add the salt, peppercorns,
parsley and nutmeg, cook very slowly, stirring frequently for
about 30 minutes or until there is two-thirds of the original
quantity. Strain through a fine wire strainer before serving   or
using.

WHITE SAUCE

1½ tablespoons butter or margarine
1½ tablespoons flour
Salt and pepper to taste
1 cup milk

Melt the butter in saucepan, do not brown. Remove from heat
and add flour, salt and pepper. Stir with wooden or plastic
spoon until smooth. Stir over low heat for 1 minute, do not
brown. Remove from heat and add milk. Return to heat, stir
until boiling, continue stirring and boiling 2 minutes.

Use this sauce with meat, fish or vegetables.

Add parsley, capers, cooked onions or celery, grated cheese.

For a thicker sauce use

2 tablespoons flour
2 tablespoons butter
1 cup milk
Salt and pepper to taste

Follow the same method

This sauce is used for masking such foods as boiled
cauliflower or steamed fish fillets which may be sprinkled
with cheese and/or breadcrumbs, dotted with butter and
browned lightly.
It is also used to bind or hold cooked foods together, e.g.
salmon, tuna, cooked diced chicken, oysters, scallops, lobster,

crab, mushrooms and cooked diced vegetables, when serving "fork" meals, when making fillings for savouries, pastry cases and chilled moulds.

PANADA

Very thick white sauce

3 tablespoons butter
3 tablespoons flour
Salt and pepper to taste
1 cup milk, warmed

Melt the butter and stir in the flour, salt and pepper until quite smooth. Stir and cook well for 1 minute. Remove from heat and add milk gradually, beating well after each addition until quite smooth. Stir rather vigorously over a medium heat. Once again remove from heat and beat well to smooth out uneven thickening.

This sauce is very thick and requires care and undivided attention during the cooking.
Use this sauce as a base for souffles, for croquettes and the filling for vol-au-vent.

BEARNAISE SAUCE

2 shallots, chopped
Ground pepper
150 ml white wine
Bouquet garni
125 g butter
4 egg yolks
½ teaspoon tarragon, chopped

Place the chopped shallots, ground pepper, wine and bouquet garni into a small heavy saucepan and boil gently until the quantity is reduced to 1 tablespoon. Add ½ tablespoon of water and strain into the top of a double saucepan. Add the butter. Do not let water in bottom of saucepan boil. Add beaten egg yolks a little at a time, stirring vigorously until the sauce thickens and becomes shiny. Serve with steak garnished with chopped tarragon.

VINAIGRETTE SAUCE

5 tablespoons olive oil
Salt and pepper to taste
1 teaspoon prepared mild mustard
3 tablespoons white vinegar
1 hard-boiled egg, chopped finely
1 tablespoon finely chopped parsley
1 onion, chopped very finely

Blend the oil, salt, pepper and mustard. Add vinegar a little at a time, beating well. Stir in the remaining ingredients. Stand for 1 hour before using. Serve with artichoke hearts, asparagus or diced avocados.

BARBECUE SAUCE (i)

1 cup soy sauce
1 cup tomato sauce
1 tablespoon dry mustard
½ cup dry white wine
½ cup honey
1 tablespoon sliced preserved hot ginger

Mix all ingredients in a stainless steel saucepan, allow to simmer 5 minutes, keep covered.

The meat may be marinated in the sauce before cooking and it can be used for basting during cooking.

BARBECUE SAUCE (ii)

¼ cup salad oil
1 large onion minced or chopped very finely
2 tablespoons malt vinegar

3 tablespoons lemon juice
1 cup water
1 teaspoon salt
1 teaspoon celery salt
2 tablespoons brown sugar
1 tablespoon prepared hot mustard

Heat the oil in a heavy saucepan, fry the onion until it is transparent, not coloured. Add all the other ingredients and simmer for 30 minutes. Good for basting poultry and lamb kebabs.

MUSTARD SAUCE

1 tablespoon butter
1 tablespoon sugar
2 tablespoons dry mustard
2 eggs
½ cup meat liquid (water used to cook meat)
1/3 cup malt vinegar

Combine butter, sugar and mustard with well beaten eggs. Slowly add liquid and vinegar. Cook in the top of a double saucepan stirring continuously until thickened. Do not allow the water in the bottom saucepan to boil as this sauce curdles easily. Serve with hot corned beef.

ORANGE AND RAISIN SAUCE

2 tablespoons cornflour
⅛ teaspoon salt
⅛ teaspoon nutmeg, freshly ground
1 cup water
1 teaspoon grated orange rind
¼ cup orange juice
2 tablespoons lemon juice
¼ cup raisins, chopped

Combine cornflour, salt and nutmeg with the cold water in a saucepan. Cook and stir until boiling and thick. Remove from heat and immediately stir in rind, juices and raisins. Use with duck, pork or lamb.

GOLDEN SAUCE

125 g butter, softened
125 g soft brown sugar
2 eggs, well beaten
150 ml brandy
⅛ teaspoon grated nutmeg

Beat the butter and sugar together to a soft cream. Add the egg gradually. Place cream in the top of a double saucepan over slowly simmering water, stir in the brandy a little at a time. Cook until thickened and perfectly blended. Flavour with nutmeg. Serve hot with steamed puddings or cold with bananas, or a mixture of banana, orange and apple.

MEAT SAUCE (for spaghetti)

2 tablespoons oil or bacon dripping
250 g finely minced topside or round steak (no fat)
125 g minced shoulder bacon
1 large can peeled tomatoes
1 small can (180 g) tomato paste
2 cloves garlic, minced
1 large onion, minced
¼ teaspoon each rosemary, basil and oregano
1 tablespoon chopped parsley
½ cup dry white wine
½ teaspoon salt
250 g mushrooms, cleaned and chopped

Heat the oil in a heavy saucepan. Add meat and stir with fork until browned. Add all other ingredients. Cover and simmer 45 minutes to 1 hour, stirring often. If thickening too much, add beef stock made with beef cubes or tomato puree. Can be frozen.

HARD SAUCE

To serve with hot Christmas pudding

250 g pure icing sugar or fine soft brown sugar
125 g unsalted butter
2 tablespoons brandy with 4 drops of vanilla

Sieve the icing sugar to remove all lumps. Cream the butter until soft. Gradually add the sugar until mixture is very pale and light. Add the liquid a little at a time, about 1 teaspoonful, and mix well. If liquid is added too quickly the mixture will separate. Chill, do not freeze. Cut into cubes or balls for serving.

SOUFFLES

The souffle is the lightest of sweet or savoury "puffed puddings". There is a cold or uncooked souffle or mousse which is not a real souffle but a gelatine mixture. A true souffle is based on a thick, well-cooked sauce called a panada. The liquid or added flavour decides the name. Eggs must be fresh and at room temperature. The yolks are added individually and beaten well. The whites should be whisked up well to stiff points (1 extra white is a good idea). When combining the egg whites with the mixture, first add 2 tablespoons and beat; this allows the remainder to be folded in evenly with a metal spoon.

Choose the baking container carefully. It should be of thick material with straight sides. Grease it all over lightly, then tie a piece of white paper or double thickness of greaseproof paper around the outside. This should stand 5-6 cm above the container. When steaming, use thick white paper or foil lined with greaseproof paper around the sides then cover the top with a larger round of the same.

Flavourings: Added foods should have a definite or distinctive flavour, and be reduced to a fine light texture. If anything cold or heavy is added the souffle will not rise properly.

SAVOURY SOUFFLES

Basic souffle mixture

3 tablespoons butter
4 tablespoons flour

½ cup each milk and cream or 1 cup milk
3-5 eggs

Cream butter and flour. Bring milk to boil, and gradually pour on to butter-flour mixture, stirring all the time. Beat well and cook slowly until very thick. Continue stirring. Remove from heat whilst beating well to make smooth. Add yolks one at a time, beat and heat until very smooth and pale yellow. Add the stiffly beaten whites and flavourings and bake in a moderately hot oven (175° - 190°C) for 40-45 minutes. If slower cooking is needed place container in tray of water. Serve in the dish in which it was baked after removing papers. Do not leave standing in cool air. The souffle must be served immediately, therefore all accompaniments and sauces must be ready to go to the table or on to the plates, which should be heated.

Savoury additions

1 or 2 cups grated cheese, dash cayenne and mustard
½ cup tomato puree combined with milk and cream
   to make 1 cup
½ tablespoon chopped chives
½ teaspoon fresh herbs
¾ cup of any of the following, cooked and shredded finely
   or pounded: bacon, crab, chicken, ham, lobster, mushroom,
   salmon or prawn.

CHEESE SOUFFLE

1½ tablespoons butter
1½ tablespoons flour
½ cup milk
3 eggs
½ cup grated cheese
Salt
Cayenne

Mix butter and flour in a saucepan. Add milk by degrees. Stir well till thick. Take off stove and let it cool a little. Beat in egg yolks one by one. Add grated cheese, salt and cayenne. Beat

egg whites to a very stiff froth. Fold whites into the mixture
very lightly. Butter a souffle mould and pour the mixture in.
Bake 35 to 40 minutes in a moderate oven. Serve immediately
it is taken from the oven.

SWEET SOUFFLES

STEAMED SOUFFLE

1½ tablespoons butter
1½ tablespoons flour
½ cup milk
2 tablespoons castor sugar
Lemon rind
3 egg yolks
4 egg whites
Raspberry sauce

Melt butter in a fairly large saucepan. Add flour and stir till
smooth. Add milk and stir constantly till cooked. Remove
from stove and allow to cool for a time. Add sugar and grated
lemon rind, then egg yolks one by one, beating all the time.
Beat egg whites to a stiff froth. Add to the mixture with a
metal spoon, folding in lightly. Pour into a lined and greased
souffle case, cover with buttered paper and steam 45 minutes.
When souffle is well risen and firm remove band of paper and
stand on a hot dish. Serve immediately with raspberry sauce.

LEMON, ORANGE, OR PASSIONFRUIT SOUFFLE

1 tablespoon butter
1 cup sugar
2 tablespoons flour
Grated rind and juice of 1 lemon
    or orange, or 4 passionfruit
1 cup milk
2 eggs

Cream butter and sugar. Add flour, rind and juice of lemon or orange (or 4 passionfruit), milk, and egg yolks. Fold in lightly the stiffly beaten egg whites. Pour into a pie dish and stand this in another dish containing cold water. Bake slowly 45 minutes to 1 hour. Serve souffle immediately it is taken from the oven, with thin custard or whipped cream.

COFFEE SOUFFLE

2 tablespoons butter
2 tablespoons flour
¼ cup milk
¼ cup strong black coffee
2 tablespoons castor sugar
3 egg yolks
¼ teaspoon rum essence
4 egg whites

Melt butter in saucepan, mix flour in until quite smooth, add the combined milk, coffee and sugar slowly, beating well away from heat after each addition to make quite smooth. Cook 1 minute, stirring well. Remove from heat, add egg yolks one at a time, beat each well. Fold in essence and egg whites which have been beaten to a firm froth. Pour into prepared dish and bake 40 minutes at 200°C. Serve immediately with whipped cream.

Chocolate Souffle

Make as for Coffee Souffle, but substitute for coffee 2 tablespoons cocoa made up with ¼ cup boiling water. Cool cocoa mixture and add ½ teaspoon vanilla before combining with milk and sugar.

PANCAKES AND WAFFLES

The Batter

A successful batter, whether for pancakes, fritters, waffles or Yorkshire pudding, depends upon its consistency and also upon being cooked at the right temperature*. Most batters are greatly improved if allowed to stand for two or three hours before being cooked. Cooking temperature is important. Fritters should be fried in deep hot fat at 190º - 195ºC and afterwards drained on absorbent paper. If possible pancakes should be cooked in a heavy iron pan lightly greased with butter or oil. A lightweight pan does not maintain even temperature. Do not allow fat to reach smoking point. It is a good idea to have the batter in a jug so that it can be poured on to the pan in small quantities. Have ready a broad spatula or palette knife. Tilt the pan so that the uncooked batter can get to the heat. Once bubbles show on the upper surface slide the knife under the pancake and flip over. Keep the pancakes hot in the oven or in a heat-resistant casserole on another hot plate. When filling and rolling, the side cooked first should be on the outside.

*Consistency can vary according to the size of the eggs and the grade of flour.

AUSTRIAN PANCAKES

2 eggs, separated
½ teaspoon castor sugar

1¼ cups milk (this quantity can vary according to the
    weather, the size of the eggs and the
    grade of flour)
1 cup sifted flour
⅛ teaspoon salt

Combine egg yolks, sugar and one-third of milk with the flour
and salt until smooth. Gradually beat in the remainder of milk
to make the batter the consistency of cream. Beat egg whites
to form stiff but not dry peaks and fold into batter. Stir
mixture lightly during the making of pancakes.

ITALIAN PANCAKES

2 eggs
Few drops orange flower water
1½ cups dry white wine or cider
1½ cups sifted flour
1 teaspoon salt
2 tablespoons oil
2 egg whites

Beat eggs with orange flower water and gradually add wine.
Have flour and salt sifted into a bowl. Very slowly add liquid
with the oil. Continue to beat until the whole is perfectly
smooth and the consistency of cream. Allow to stand 1-2
hours. Before cooking fold in the lightly but stiffly beaten egg
whites. Fry in the approved manner. Keep in a warm place
until ready to fill with sweet mixtures, such as : (i) banana,
honey and a little spice; (ii) date, grated rind and juice of an
orange, ½ teaspoon mixed spice; (iii) sweetened apricot pulp
and chopped toasted almonds; (iv) well-drained stewed apples
flavoured with lemon rind; (v) strawberries cut into large
pieces and sprinkled with castor sugar.

After being folded any of these pancakes may be flamed in
a copper skillet or chafing dish, at the table if possible. For the
sauce melt 4 tablespoons butter creamed with 4 tablespoons
sugar, stir until sugar dissolves. Add finely grated rind of 2
oranges and juice of one and 2 teaspoons cointreau or
curacao. When heated place pancakes in mixture four at a

time, turn until thoroughly heated. Have 1 tablespoon warm
brandy ready, pour on to pan, ignite and serve flaming.

HAM FILLED LAYERED PANCAKES

500 g finely chopped cooked ham
1 cup sour cream
2 egg yolks
Freshly ground black pepper

Combine ham with other ingredients. Place four pancakes in a
buttered baking dish. Cover with filling, repeat, finish with
ham layer, dot with butter, sprinkle with coarsely grated tasty
cheese. Serve hot garnished lavishly with chopped chives.

This ham filling may be spread over thin pancakes rolled up
and the ends folded in. Lightly beat two egg whites. Dip rolls
in egg, then flour, then egg again and lastly fine breadcrumbs.
Deep fry quickly until light brown. Drain well, serve hot in
quarters as appetizers or as an entree, garnished with dill
pickle, shallots and celery.

MUSHROOM FILLED LAYERED PANCAKES

250 g mushrooms
2 tablespoons butter
½ cup sour cream
4 rashers of bacon, finely chopped
½ teaspoon salt
Little pepper
1 lightly beaten egg

Trim, wash, dry, chop and lightly fry the mushrooms in
butter. Combine well with other ingredients except bacon.
Proceed as for layered pancakes. Top with bacon. Heat until
bacon is cooked and crisp. If rolling pancakes have bacon
rasher to wrap around each roll. Pack in ovenproof dish to
cook.

COTTAGE CHEESE FILLED PANCAKES

500 g cottage cheese
1 egg yolk
½ cup sour cream
125 g chopped raisins
Lemon juice
2 tablespoons castor sugar

Press cheese through sieve and beat until creamed. Mix with egg yolk and sour cream. (Alternatively, vitamize cheese, egg yolk and sour cream until smooth.) Add raisins. Spread mixture on each pancake, roll up, pack in dish, sprinkle with lemon juice and sugar. Bake 20 minutes in moderate oven.

COFFEE PANCAKES

1 cup flour
1 pinch salt
1 egg
½ cup strong black coffee
½ cup evaporated milk
Icing sugar
Whipped cream

Make batter with flour, salt, egg and coffee. Beat well and gradually add milk. Continue to beat until the consistency of cream and as smooth. Fry lightly, roll up, sprinkle with icing sugar, and spread with cream or if very hot garnish outside of rolls with cream, sprinkled generously with grated chocolate.

COFFEE PANCAKE SAUCE

1 tablespoon cocoa
3 tablespoons icing sugar
1 tablespoon cornflour
3 tablespoons evaporated milk
½ cup black coffee
½ cup evaporated milk (any brand)
½ teaspoon vanilla

Blend cocoa, icing sugar and cornflour in heavy saucepan, stir
in 3 tablespoons milk, cook slowly until thickened. Gradually
stir in the boiling coffee, cook 1 minute. Very slowly add
remaining milk but do not boil. Lastly stir in vanilla. Serve as
hot accompaniment with coffee pancakes or plain lemon
pancakes.

CREPE MIXTURE

4 cups sifted flour
2½ cups milk
2 eggs
1 teaspoon salt
1 teaspoon fine oil
1 teaspoon brandy
1 cup soda water

Gradually add milk to sifted flour, beating the whole time so
that batter remains smooth. Add eggs separately, then salt, oil
and brandy. Lastly add soda water and beat until smooth.
Make sure pan is heavy, lightly buttered and keep crepes very
thin. Store between layers of paper until needed. They may be
frozen and keep well.

CREPES SUZETTE

4 lumps loaf sugar
Juice of 1 large orange
5 tablespoons butter
½ lemon
2 tablespoons fine shred orange jam
½ cup grand marnier, cointreau or benedictine
½ cup brandy
Prepared pancakes or crepes, 2 per serve

Rub loaf sugar over grated surface of orange to absorb oil
then crush with 3 tablespoons butter. Pour into a chafing dish
2 tablespoons butter, orange juice, squeeze of lemon juice.

Stir over heat while adding jam and liqueur, lastly stir in the
butter and sugar mixture. Lay crepes in sauce, turn and fold
into four. Push in turn to side of pan. When all are done
sprinkle with ½ cup warm brandy, ignite and serve on vanilla
ice cream.

WAFFLES

1½ cups flour
¼ teaspoon salt
2 teaspoons baking powder
2 eggs, separated
1 cup milk
3 tablespoons melted butter.

Sift dry ingredients. Beat egg yolks well, add milk and melted
butter. Slowly add flour mixture beating until smooth. Fold in
stiffly beaten egg whites. Place in large jug and let stand. Heat
waffle iron, brush with oil, reheat. Pour about ½ cup batter
into centre of opened iron. Close, before batter spreads to
edges. After 3-5 minutes test. Batter should be light brown
and lift quite freely from iron. Open iron out flat to remove
waffle. Serve on warm plate. Accompaniments: *Savoury*:
creamed chicken, ham, mushroom, asparagus or corn. *Sweet:*
butter with jam, honey or maple syrup; ice cream with
chocolate or caramel sauce or syrup.

PASTRY

Many varieties of sweet and savoury dishes can be made with pastry. There are a number of kinds: (i) short crust (plain or rich); (ii) champagne or biscuit pastry; (iii) suet crust; (iv) rough puff pastry (plain or rich); (v) flaky pastry; (vi) puff pastry; (vii) choux pastry; and (viii) raised pie crust.

Rules for Making

To ensure success, the pastry should be made in a cool place, handled lightly, rolled evenly, using as little flour as possible during the rolling out process, and it should be baked in a hot oven. Sweet pastry may be glazed with white of egg or with sugar and water made into a syrup. Savoury pastry may be glazed with milk or with yolk of egg and milk.

RICH SHORT CRUST

2 cups flour
¼ teaspoon baking powder
Pinch salt
1 egg yolk
1 tablespoon water
Squeeze lemon juice
125 g butter

Sift flour, baking powder and salt. Beat egg, water and lemon juice together. Rub butter into flour very lightly till free from lumps. Add water gradually and make into a very dry dough. Turn on to floured board and smooth out into a round shape. Roll out lightly and evenly to size and shape required.

PUFF PASTRY

250 g flour, sifted and chilled
250 g butter, chilled and chopped
2 tablespoons iced water
1 tablespoon strained lemon juice, chilled

Place one-third of the flour with chopped butter into a bowl. Blend together with pastry blender or two forks. Form into a block about 10 cm square. Chill on waxed paper. Place remainder of flour into a bowl and with a wooden spoon or metal fork, mix in the liquid to make a soft but not sticky dough. Shape into a block 15 cm x 10 cm x 3 cm thick, chill. Place the first or fat dough on to an evenly floured board. Press out, then roll with steady even pressure until 30 cm in length. Try to keep edges smooth. Slide a spatula frequently underneath to make sure the dough does not stick. Keep the board dry, smooth and floured.

Place the chilled flour and water dough into the middle and bring the two ends of the rolled dough over into the centre, then fold in half. Give this rectangle of folded dough a quarter turn to the right. Seal the top and bottom by pressing with the rolling pin. Chill for 20 minutes.

Roll into a long strip, sprinkle lightly with flour. Fold top one-third down, bottom one-third up, press open edges and quarter turn to the right. Repeat this rolling, folding and turning 4 times. The last time roll to required shape and 7 to 10 mm thick. Cut sharply and cleanly.

Bake on a tray brushed with cold water, 10 minutes at 230°C then 10 minutes at 200⁰C.

Do not turn pastry over, roll one way until after the last folding then turn pastry round to roll to the required shape. Always trim off rolled folded edges.

QUICHE LORRAINE

250 g short crust pastry
125 g bacon
3 eggs
300 ml milk
150 ml cream
Little salt
Freshly ground black pepper
⅛ teaspoon nutmeg
plus one of the following:
(i)   125 g cheese — gruyere or emmental in slices, or
       parmesan, strong, matured, dry, grated
(ii)   ⅛ teaspoon fresh thyme and 1 teaspoon chopped
       parsley
(iii) 1 medium firm tomato peeled, seeded and chopped
(iv)   Asparagus tips, grated soft cheese, dash cayenne
(v)   Sweet corn niblets, grated strong cheese
(vi)   2 teaspoons chopped chives

Line 25 cm tart plate with fairly thin pastry. Make fluted
double thickness rim. De-rind and cut bacon into narrow
pieces. Fry until lightly crisped, allow to cool, cover pastry
case. Beat together eggs, milk, cream and seasonings. Pour
carefully over bacon. Bake in hot oven (232°C) for 10 minutes,
reduce heat to 177⁰C, bake 30 minutes or until the filling is set.
Slide thin, flat blade across middle to test for set. Serve hot
with side salad and cold as hors-d'oeuvres or entree.

The recipe can be varied (i) by using cream cheese instead of
the usual shortening; (ii) by adding half a packet of French
onion soup to the flour when rubbing in the shortening.

FILET NAPOLEON

1½ kg fillet steak in one piece
250 g puff pastry
½ cup chopped parsley
1 teaspoon lemon juice

Freshly ground black pepper
Salt
1 egg yolk

Trim the steak of fat. Roll out pastry to two and a half times size of steak. To one side of the middle make a base of chopped parsley mixed with lemon juice. Arrange steak on top, sprinkle well with freshly ground black pepper and salt. Brush around edge of pastry with egg yolk glaze. Fold pastry over and press edges to form a good seal. Edges may be turned under or trimmed with a sharp knife. Place on a flat tray, bake in a hot oven (232°C) middle shelf, 20 minutes. If the fillet is short and thick, bake 30 minutes. Serve immediately with mashed potato, baked tomatoes, greens and a vegetable in cream sauce.

AUSTRALIAN MEAT PIE

Pie Base:

2 cups plain flour
½ teaspoon salt
½ cup water
4 tablespoons beef dripping

Pie Top:

345 g puff pastry
Egg glaze

Filling:

½ kg coarsely minced beef
1 stock cube
1 teaspoon salt
Pepper
1¼ cups water
Good pinch nutmeg
3 tablespoons plain flour
Extra ½ cup water
Parisienne essence

Saute the meat in a saucepan until well browned. Do not add any oil. Drain off any surplus fat. Add crumbled stock cube, salt, pepper, and nutmeg. Add water, bring to boil, cook few minutes. Mix flour with extra water until smooth. Remove pan from heat, cool slightly, stir in flour thickening. Bring back to the boil, stirring continuously, until well thickened. Cook further few minutes. Add sufficient parisienne essence to give rich brown colouring.

For the base pastry sift flour and salt into basin. Place water and dripping in saucepan; heat gently to melt dripping. Pour hot liquid into well in centre of flour. Mix with knife to begin with and when cool enough, use hands. Knead on lightly floured board until free of cracks. Roll out, and line bases of pie dishes. Use small saucer to cut circles. Fill centres with prepared cooled filling.

For the pastry tops roll out puff pastry on lightly floured board, and cut with small saucer to make rounds for tops. Wet edges of base pastry, gently press tops into place. Pierce centre with pointed knife. Brush well with egg glaze. Place in hot oven approximately 10 minutes, until browned, then reduce heat to moderate and cook further 5 minutes.

VOL-AU-VENT

375 g puff pastry
1 egg yolk
1 teaspoon water

On a lightly floured board roll out pastry about 2 cm thick. Cut two 15 cm circles and place one on oven slide that has been brushed with cold water. Cut a 10 cm circle out of the second round. Put this on separate tray. Moisten the under surface of the cut-out rim and fit exactly over the base. Press together gently but firmly. Score the rim in diamond pattern with a sharp knife; make the same pattern on the lid. Glaze carefully with egg-water mixture. Do not allow any excess water to run down the side. Bake in a hot oven (232°C) 10 minutes. Reduce heat to 204°C and cook for 20 minutes. It should be 6-7 cm high and a good, even, shiny brown. The cut-out is the lid and needs shorter baking time (10 minutes) in a hot oven and 5 minutes in a moderate oven. Vol-au-vent may be filled with hot cream sauce and mixtures of sea foods, chicken, ham, mushrooms or asparagus. The vol-au-vent may be made large, medium or small.

PIZZA

6 teaspoons compressed yeast
1 cup water
1 tablespoon each butter and lard
500 g flour
1 teaspoon salt

Toppings:
Salt, pepper
¼ cup olive oil
3 cm strips mozzarella cheese
Anchovies
Skinned, seeded chopped tomatoes
¼-½ cup parmesan cheese
2 teaspoons dried oregano

Sprinkle with salt and pepper (fresh black), brush on a good covering of olive oil, arrange strips of cheese and anchovies, cover with chopped tomatoes. Sprinkle with parmesan, more salt and pepper and oil. Lastly sprinkle with dried oregano. Bake 10-15 minutes in a hot oven (232°C) or until pizza bubbles.

Topping variations:
(i)   Oil, tomato paste, sliced salami and capsicum
(ii) Oil, tomato paste, parmesan, prawns, anchovies
(iii) Oil, grated mozzarella, pineapple slices.
(iv) Soft butter, brown sugar paste, sliced banana, raisins, grated apple sprinkled with cinnamon and sugar.
(v)   Butter, sugar paste, dates chopped and mixed with grated rind and juice of orange, sprinkled with chocolate bits.

SMALL PIES AND TARTLETS

Quantity of homemade or commercial short crust pastry

Pastry Case:
1. Roll pastry carefully and evenly into a regular shape, about 5 mm thick.
2. Cut sharply with dry floured cutter.
3. Ease pastry into a dry container — a shallow patty tin or pie shape. Never stretch; it is much better to have a little fullness.
4. Large open tarts should have a double thickness of pastry over the rim of dish.
5. Cut or flute to decorate but do not press down.
6. For covered pies cut the same size and make a steam hole in centre.
7. Brush lower edge with cold water.
8. Have plenty of uncooked filling as it will shrink during cooking.
9. Glaze savoury pies with egg and water glaze.
10. Glaze sweet pies with egg white or water sprinkled with castor sugar.

Fillings — Covered Pies:
(i)	Minced steak mixed with chopped bacon, chopped onion, very small amount of flour, pepper, tomato and black sauce
(ii)	Sausage mince mixed with chopped peeled tomatoes, chopped parsley, salt, pepper.
(iii)	Creamed corn, grated cheese, chopped celery.
(iv)	Canned mushrooms, cooked rice, crisp bacon pieces
(v)	Any cooked fish bound with thick melted butter sauce flavoured with lemon juice.
(vi)	Minced cooked poultry or meats bound with left-over gravy or suitable sauce.
(vii)	Well-drained stewed spiced apple.
(viii)	Canned or homemade fruit mince.
(ix)	Stewed, drained quinces, chopped small.

(x)   Chopped dates mixed with drained crushed pineapple.

Fillings — Open Pies:

(i)   Very thick heavy jam.

(ii)   True lemon butter.

(iii) Grated apple and raisins chopped with a thick layer of cinnamon and sugar.

(iv)   Well flavoured custard made with 2 eggs and 1 cup evaporated milk.

(v)   Golden syrup or honey mixed to a very thick consistency with coconut and grated lemon rind.

(vi)   A little jam topped with sponge or butter cake mixture.

SWEET FRUIT FLANS AND TARTLETS

Quantity of good sweet pastry, biscuit or champagne
Plain or fluted flan ring
Shallow patty tins

Make sure pastry is of good rolling consistency, not likely to crumble. Roll the required amount only, this is easier to handle. Use a little cornflour instead of flour when rolling, and roll between layers of heavy waxed paper or plastic sheets. Slide the open hand underneath to lift and the paper will peel away easily. Ease pastry gently into container and carefully press into shape. Do not pull or stretch. Prick base of flan or tart case very well. Bake blind at 177°C for 10 minutes. Remove paper and filling. Glaze surface with egg white, cook another 10 minutes. Cover with white or brown paper if colouring too quickly. Pastry may be cooked on the outside of a greased plate or tin. Prick well. Stand inverted on a flat tray, leave until cooking time is completed. Small tart cases should be pricked and cooked in greased tins for 15 minutes. Cool quickly.

Fillings — large or small cases:

(i) Lemon, chocolate, rum, butterscotch, pineapple, creme de

menthe, coffee, mocha, topped with a good covering of
meringue cooked slowly to set or decorated with whipped
cream, coconut or almonds, plain or toasted.

(ii) Layer of rich cream custard filling, covered with preserved
or carefully stewed fruits, one kind or a well chosen
mixture. Thicken juice with gelatine or arrowroot, spoon
gently over fruit when cold. When quite cold decorate
with whipped cream, angelica, strawberries or cherries.

SWEET FRUIT SLICES

Quantity good sweet pastry, biscuit or champagne
Low-sided flat tin

Roll out pastry, prick all over. Lift into tin. Cover half with a
thick layer of non-juicy filling, e.g. minced raisins, currants,
lemon peel flavoured with mixed spice and sugar, or chopped
dates softened with orange juice and grated rind, little nutmeg.
Bring other half of pastry over top, firm gently, glaze with egg
white, sprinkle with sugar. Bake at 204°C for 20 minutes. Cut
while still warm. Lift on to cooler.

Variation:

Roll out pastry, line large Swiss roll tin, bring carefully up the
sides. Fill with well-drained, cooked, flavoured fruits. Cover
with top layer of pastry, press moistened edges together.
Make some small steam holes. Glaze and sprinkle with sugar
or cover with lemon flavoured icing. Cut when cold.

Note: Half quantity of wholemeal flour may be substituted.
Slices may be served hot with cream or custard for desert.

PEACH ALMOND FLAN

Pastry Base:
1½ cups plain flour
1 level teaspoon baking powder
1/3 cup sugar

125 g butter
1 egg yolk, lightly beaten

Almond Mixture:

½ cup almond or marzipan meal
½ teaspoon almond essence
½ level teaspoon cinnamon
425 g can sliced peaches, well drained

Crumble Topping:

½ cup flour
½ cup sugar
1/3 cup butter

Sift flour, baking powder and sugar into a bowl. Rub in butter. Add egg yolk and combine well. Place a 20 cm flan ring on a scone slide. If a flan ring is not available use a 23 cm pie plate. Lightly grease the whole flan area and press the pastry evenly over the base and up the sides of the flan. Combine almond meal, essence and cinnamon. Cover pastry with the almond mixture. Arrange drained peaches over the mixture and sprinkle with the crumble topping. To make the topping, combine the flour and sugar, and rub in the butter. Bake in a moderate oven (204°C) for about 25 to 30 minutes. Allow to cool slightly before removing from flan ring. Serve warm or cold with cream.

ALMOND TARTLETS

250 g good short crust
Some apricot jam

Filling:

2 tablespoons butter
2 tablespoons castor sugar
1 egg yolk
4 tablespoons ground almonds
Almond or coconut essence
1 egg white

Line small tins or boats with short crust. Place a little jam in each boat. Put some almond filling in each. This is made by blending butter, sugar, egg yolk, ground almonds, and almond essence together, lastly add egg white and mixing thoroughly. Bake slowly in a moderate oven till a pale brown.

BALMORAL TARTLETS

250 g short crust
¼ cup butter
¼ cup castor sugar
2 eggs
1 cup cake-crumbs or soft breadcrumbs
2 tablespoons candied peel
A few cherries
3 tablespoons cornflour
Icing sugar for decoration

Mix short crust, roll out, cut into rounds and line ungreased patty tins. Cream butter and sugar. Stir in yolks of eggs, cake-crumbs, candied peel, cherries and cornflour. Fold in stiffly beaten whites of eggs. Fill cases with mixture. Decorate with strips of pastry. Bake in a moderate oven 15 to 20 minutes. Sift icing sugar over warm cakes.

FRENCH TART

5 medium cooking apples
300 ml water
½ cup sugar
3 cloves or a piece of lemon rind
Cochineal
250 g puff pastry
Cream, crystallized cherries and angelica for decoration

Wash, peel, quarter and core apples. Bring water, sugar and

cloves to the boil. Add apples and allow to simmer without lid till tender (without breaking). Lift carefully on to a sieve to drain. Strain syrup, colour with cochineal, return to heat and cook till thick enough to coat apples. Make pastry and roll out about 1 cm thick. Cut with a knife, placing a plate upside down on pastry and cutting round it with a knife dipped in boiling water. With a smaller plate or cutter mark out the centre (cutting half way through pastry). Brush over with egg white and bake in a hot oven 8 to 10 minutes. Reduce heat and cook 15 to 20 minutes longer. When quite cold, remove centre and fill with prepared apples. Garnish with whipped sweetened cream and small pieces of cherries and angelica; arrange cream between fruit with a long rose pipe.

FRUIT PIE

185 g rich short crust
3 teaspoons gelatine
150 ml hot water
¼ cup or more sugar
150 ml orange juice
2 tablespoons lemon juice
150 ml cream
1 mashed banana
1 egg white
Pinch salt
1 or 2 passionfruit

Line a tart plate with rich short crust, prick well and bake. Dissolve gelatine in hot water, add sugar and the orange and lemon juice. Beat well till thick. Fold in the banana and half the whipped cream. Beat egg white and salt till stiff and fold into the mixture. Fill a pie shell with the mixture and serve with whipped cream and passionfruit on top.

PUMPKIN PIE

2 cups cooked pumpkin
2 teaspoons butter
1 egg, well beaten
½ cup sugar
Juice and rind of 1 lemon
¼ teaspoon nutmeg
1 tablespoon sultanas or raisins
250 g rich short crust
Icing sugar for decoration

Steam or boil pumpkin in very little water till tender, then strain. Beat with a fork till smooth. Add other ingredients and mix well. Make a rich short crust and roll out and line a tart plate with half. Place prepared mixture in and cover with the other half of pastry. Glaze with water and sugar. Bake in a hot oven 20 minutes. Sprinkle with icing sugar.

Note: If a vitamizer is available, the first six ingredients may be combined to make a smooth puree.

PRUNE WHIP TART

2 cups prunes
250 g rich short crust
½ cup sugar
1 cup chopped walnuts
2 egg whites
1 cup whipped cream
2 teaspoons castor sugar
½ teaspoon vanilla

Soak prunes for 12 hours or longer, and then simmer in the same water till tender. Make a rich short crust, roll out, and line a tart plate (prick the bottom of the tart well or place dry grain on it to prevent it rising in the centre). Bake in a hot oven 15 to 20 minutes. Remove prune stones, pulp or vitamize prunes, add sugar and nuts. Beat egg whites stiffly, fold them into warm mixture, and chill, then pour into baked pie shell.

Sweeten and whip the cream, flavour with vanilla. Pile thickly on top of tart.

Note: As a variation use 1 cup dried apricots soaked and simmered in 300 ml water.

VANILLA FRANCHONETTES

1½ tablespoons butter
2 tablespoons flour
1 cup milk
2 egg yolks
3 tablespoons sugar
3 tablespoons cream
½ teaspoon vanilla
1 teaspoon lemon juice
250 g rich short crust
Passionfruit
Preserved pineapple pieces
Preserved apricots
Glace ginger and cherries
Stewed apple
Prunes

Meringue:
2 egg whites
½ cup castor sugar
1 teaspoon lemon juice

Melt butter, add flour and beat till smooth. Cook for 2 minutes. Add milk and stir till boiling. Beat yolks of eggs and sugar, add to mixture and cook without boiling. Remove from heat, add cream, vanilla and lemon juice, beat well and allow to cool. Make pastry and roll out evenly. Cut out pastry and line some patty tins. To prevent rising unevenly, line cases with paper and fill with dry grain. Bake in a moderate oven 8 to 10 minutes. Remove grain and paper, return pastry to oven to dry for a few minutes. Place on a wire stand to cool. Place 1 teaspoon custard mixture in each case. Arrange fruit on custard. If liked, decorate with cream roses and toasted slivered almonds. Alternatively, make meringue from egg whites and sugar, flavoured with lemon juice. Decorate top of custard with meringue through a rose pipe. Place in a very slow oven to dry the meringue without browning (1 hour or longer).

Variation:
Make one large pastry case, fill with cream custard. Decorate with a good variety of fruit. Finish the top with flavoured whipped cream, instead of meringue.

PALMIERS

375 g puff pastry
Castor sugar
Warm pink icing

On a lightly floured board roll out pastry to make a rectangle about 35 cm x 20 cm. Sprinkle lightly with castor sugar after a very light glaze with water. Fold the long sides into the centre. Repeat glaze and sugar. Fold together lengthwise four thicknesses of pastry. With a sharp floured knife cut into pieces about 2 cm thick. Place cut side down on a tray, brush top with water, sprinkle with sugar. Allow plenty of room for sideways expansion. Refrigerate 10-15 minutes. Bake in a hot oven 10-15 minutes until light brown and crisp. If necessary turn with spatula. When cold pour a teaspoonful of warm pink icing on to the centre of each; or sprinkle well with sieved icing sugar.

CREAM HORNS

375 g puff pastry in two portions
Egg glaze
Sieved icing sugar
Whipped cream
Raspberry jam

Roll pastry fairly thin, cut into strips approximately 25 cm long and 1 cm wide. Moisten one edge of each pastry strip with water. Fix one end to the point of a metal cone or horn, and wind pastry round, overlapping the wet edge. Finish off the end neatly but leave the metal edge quite free to allow for removal of the cone. Place on a dry tray, brush lightly with egg glaze. Bake in a hot oven 15 minutes. Take tray from oven and carefully remove cones. Return pastry to oven, reduce heat to moderate and cook until pastry is dry and crisp but not too brown. When cold spread inside base with raspberry jam and fill with whipped cream. Sprinkle well with sieved icing sugar.

APPLE JALOUSIE

375 g puff pastry
Egg glaze

Filling:

2 cups dry stewed apple
½ cup soft brown sugar
½ cup sultanas
½ teaspoon cinnamon
¼ teaspoon nutmeg

Prepare filling by mixing all ingredients together. Cut pastry in two and roll each piece on a lightly floured board to rectangular shape about 30 x 15 cm, one slightly larger than the other. Spoon the filling down the centre of the smaller one, leaving 2 cm all round. Fold second piece of pastry in half lengthwise, cut strips across the fold 2 cm in width and about 2 cm from the far side. Open out flat. Glaze around edge of base and cover with top layer, press edges together, brush all over with egg glaze. Bake in a hot oven 15-20 minutes. When cooled sprinkle with sifted icing sugar or serve hot with whipped cream.

CHOCOLATE MARZIPANS

185 g puff pastry
Apricot jam
Milk for glazing
90 g dark chocolate
1½ tablespoons butter

Filling:
155 g marzipan meal
2/3 cup castor sugar
Grated rind of 1 lemon
1 small egg

Mix marzipan meal, sugar and lemon rind together. Add beaten egg, mix to a paste. Turn on to a floured board, knead well. Divide the mixture to make two rolls about 1½ cm in diameter. Roll the pastry out to a rectangular shape about 20 cm wide. Cut along middle lengthwise. Place a roll of filling on each pastry strip, brush all round with water, roll up and glaze top with milk. Cut into 5 cm lengths. Bake on a dry oven tray in a hot oven 12-15 minutes until golden brown. Brush with apricot jam while still hot. When cold melt chocolate with butter and pour a little on to top of each roll.

GATEAU ST HONORE (ST HONORE'S DESSERT CAKE)

185 g biscuit pastry
Choux pastry
Egg glazing
185 g sugar
½ cup water
St Honore cream
Whipped cream
Preserved fruits

Biscuit Pastry:
1½ cups flour
4 tablespoons butter

¼ cup castor sugar
1 egg yolk
1 teaspoon water
½ level teaspoon baking powder

Cream together the butter and sugar, add the egg yolk and water. Knead in the sifted flour and baking powder. Chill ½ hour in the refrigerator.

Choux Pastry:

125 g butter
300 ml or 1¼ cups water
155 g + 1 teaspoon plain flour
4 eggs

Place water and butter into a saucepan and heat over a low flame until the butter has melted. Increase the heat and bring to the boil, then immediately add the flour, stir, remove from heat. With a wooden spoon beat the mixture until smooth and leaves the sides of the saucepan. Cook 1 minute, stirring. Cool slightly, add eggs, one at a time, beating well.

St Honore Cream:

4 level tablespoons flour
¾ cup sugar
4 eggs
1 level tablespoon gelatine
2 cups warm milk
½ cup whipped cream
2 tablespoons brandy, kirsch or rum

Blend the flour and sugar together with the egg yolks until light and fluffy. Add the gelatine. Add the egg mixture to the warm milk and stir carefully over low heat until the mixture thickens. Allow to cool. Beat the egg whites until stiff, fold through cooled custard mixture and add ½ cup whipped cream. Flavour with spirits as desired.

Roll biscuit pastry into a circle 1 cm thick. Place on to a greased scone slide, prick with a fork. Pipe a choux pastry ring around the edge of the biscuit pastry with a 1 cm plain tube. Glaze with egg. Bake in a hot oven (204°C) for 10 minutes and then for 20 minutes at 177°C or until choux pastry is nicely browned and dry. Pipe the remaining choux pastry into small puffs on to a greased scone slide and bake at 232°C for 10 minutes, then 177°C for 20 minutes. Allow to cool. When cold fill with cream, using a forcing bag and a small plain pipe.

Boil the sugar and water to a pale honey colour, and carefully dip each puff into the toffee mixture, placing them immediately around the top edge of the pastry round. Drizzle remaining toffee over the small puffs. Fill centre with St Honore cream. Decorate with whipped cream and fruits as desired: dessert prunes soaked in orange juice, pineapple pieces, preserved apricots and pears.

FRUIT SALAD PUFFS — INDIVIDUAL DESSERTS

Double quantity choux pastry
Salad: pineapple, pawpaw, grapefruit segments, tart apple, canned mandarin segments, cut small and well drained
300 ml cream, whipped and sweetened
1½ tablespoons butter
90 g dark chocolate

Make puffs two or three times the usual size. Bake at 232°C for 15 minutes, reduce temperature to 177°C for 20 minutes or until puffs are well dried. When cold cut tops nearly off, spoon in fruit salad, cover with a thick layer of cream and replace tops. Melt butter and chocolate over hot water, spoon over each puff. Sprinkle with chopped almonds.

PASSIONFRUIT CHIFFON PIE

1 baked 23 cm pie shell (biscuit
   pastry or crumb crust)
2 teaspoons gelatine
2 level tablespoons cold water
¼ cup sugar

4 passionfruit
3 egg yolks
½ teaspoon grated lemon rind
3 egg whites
2 level tablespoons extra sugar

Biscuit Pastry:

1 small egg
¼ cup sugar
90 g butter or margarine
1¼ cups plain flour
½ level teaspoon baking powder
Pinch of salt

Beat egg and sugar until thick. Add softened butter or margarine and beat in thoroughly. Add sifted dry ingredients (1 tablespoon cornflour may be used in place of 1 tablespoon of the plain flour). Turn on to a floured surface and knead well. Roll out to fit a 23 cm pie plate, prick with a fork, and decorate the edge. Bake in a hot oven for about 15 minutes. Allow to cool thoroughly.

NEENISH TARTS

Shells:

1 cup ground almonds
½ cup icing sugar
2 tablespoons flour
1 egg white

Filling:

1 tablespoon butter
3 tablespoons icing sugar
1 tablespoon condensed milk
½ teaspoon vanilla
2 teaspoons honey or extra condensed milk

Icing:
1½ cups icing sugar
1 tablespoon boiling water
Peppermint flavour
Coffee or cocoa
Vanilla essence

For the shells, make almond meal, icing sugar, flour and egg white into a stiff paste, roll out and line well-greased small, deep patty tins. Trim the edges, prick well, and bake till firm.

For the filling, cream the butter and add gradually the other ingredients. Spread into the shells and chill.

For the icing, mix icing sugar and boiling water. Add peppermint flavour to half; cocoa and vanilla to the remainder. Cover each tart half white, half brown. Stand icing over hot water while working.

SWEET BISCUITS AND SLICES

These are often quite rich and very sweet, therefore it is a good plan to keep them small. Serve with black coffee or as a dessert.

CRUNCHY CHOCOLATE CASES

125 g dark chocolate
1 tablespoon white vegetable shortening
3 cups rice bubbles
Vanilla ice cream
Ice cream topping or lime marshmallow (optional)

Roughly chop chocolate, put in top of a double saucepan with white vegetable shortening, melt over simmering water. Do not overheat. Pour the melted chocolate mixture over rice bubbles, mix thoroughly. Lightly grease small bowls or small glass dishes, add enough chocolate mixture to press a thin layer over base and round sides of dish. Refrigerate until firm. To remove the chocolate case from bowl, stand the bowl in warm water for a few seconds and gently ease case out with a knife. Put a large scoop of vanilla ice cream in the centre of each chocolate case.

If desired, spoon any favourite ice cream topping, caramel, strawberry, etc, over the ice cream or fill with lime marshmallow.

Keep cases in refrigerator until ready to serve so that they remain quite crisp.

NUT LOGS

3 egg whites
3 tablespoons sugar
¾ cup ground hazelnuts
1½ cups ground almonds or marzipan meal
¼ cup plain flour
85 g dark chocolate

Beat egg whites until soft peaks form, gradually add sugar; beat until sugar is dissolved and mixture is of good meringue consistency. Fold in sifted flour, marzipan meal and hazelnuts. Put the mixture into a piping bag. Pipe 5 cm lengths on to greased oven slides sprinkled lightly with cornflour. Bake in a moderate oven 10 minutes. Melt chopped chocolate over hot water. When biscuits are cool, dip ends in melted chocolate.

CITRUS PEEL SLICES

Base:

½ cup plain flour
½ cup self-raising flour
½ cup icing sugar
½ cup butter or substitute

Topping:

1 tablespoon butter or substitute
1/3 cup sugar
1 teaspoon vanilla
1 tablespoon milk
1 cup mixed peel
½ cup slivered almonds

Sift flours and icing sugar into a bowl. Rub in butter. Press into a greased, greased-paper-lined 16 x 28 cm lamington tin. Bake in a moderate oven 15 minutes. Spread prepared topping over, cook a further 10 minutes. Cut into squares. For the topping melt butter in a saucepan, stir in sugar, vanilla and milk. Stir over low heat until sugar dissolves. Remove from heat, add mixed peel and almonds, stir until combined.

GINGER CRISPS

4½ tablespoons butter or substitute
½ cup castor sugar
1 egg
¾ cup self-raising flour
¾ cup plain flour
1 teaspoon ground ginger
½ cup preserved ginger, chopped and drained
1 cup crushed cornflakes

Cream butter and sugar until light and fluffy, add egg; beat well. Stir in sifted flours and ground ginger, add finely chopped ginger, mix until all ingredients are well combined. Roll teaspoonfuls of mixture in cornflakes. Put on greased oven slides, bake in a moderately hot oven 10 to 15 minutes.

ORANGE SHORTBREAD

1 cup soft butter or substitute
½ cup castor sugar
1 tablespoon finely grated orange rind
2 cups plain flour
½ cup ground rice

Cream butter and sugar until light and fluffy, add orange rind. Mix in sifted flour and ground rice to make pliable dough. Spread mixture into a greased 20 cm square slab tin. Bake in a slow to moderate oven 30 minutes or until light golden brown. Mark into squares while warm; cut into squares when cold.

SHORTBREAD

220 g butter
125 g icing sugar, well sifted
315 g plain flour, sifted

Cream the butter and icing sugar. Do not allow this to become too light and fluffy. Work in the sifted flour to form a pliable dough. Turn the mixture on to a lightly floured board. Shape into two rolls or logs. With the back edge of a dinner knife, cut 1½ cm slices. Cut surface should be rippled. Bake on a lightly greased tray 20 minutes at 180°C or until very lightly coloured. Cool on the tray before removing. Adjust size but not thickness to suit requirements. Excellent keeping quality.

CHERRY FINGERS

1 cup ground almonds
1 packet plain sweet biscuits, crushed finely
1 cup raisins, chopped
1 cup glace cherries, chopped
2 cups sugar
2 tablespoons condensed milk
1 tablespoon golden syrup
2 tablespoons butter
½ cup milk
¼ teaspoon almond essence

Combine ground almonds and crushed biscuits, mix well. Add raisins and cherries. Put aside. Place in saucepan sugar, condensed milk, syrup, butter, milk and almond essence. Bring slowly to boil, boil gently 10 minutes, then beat with wooden spoon until mixture just begins to thicken. Quickly add biscuit and fruit mixture. Mix thoroughly, pour into greased shallow slab-tin. When cool, refrigerate several hours. Cut into finger-lengths.

APRICOT MERINGUE SLICES

Base:

½ cup soft butter or substitute
½ cup sugar
½ teaspoon vanilla
1 egg
1 cup plain flour

½ cup self-raising flour

Topping:

250 g dried apricots
1 tablespoon sherry
½ cup boiling water
2 tablespoons sugar

Meringue:

2 egg whites
½ cup castor sugar
½ cup coconut
¼ cup flaked almonds (optional)

Cream the butter and sugar until light and fluffy. Add vanilla
and egg; beat well. Stir in sifted flours. Spread into a greased,
greased-paper-lined 16 x 28 cm lamington tin. Bake in a
moderate oven 20 minutes. To make the topping chop apricots
finely, add remaining ingredients. Stand 1 hour. Beat with a
wooden spoon until pulpy, or blend in an electric blender.
Spread topping evenly over base. For the meringue beat egg
whites until soft peaks form. Gradually add sugar. Beat until
sugar is dissolved and mixture is of thick meringue
consistency. Fold in coconut. Pile on to apricot topped base
and spread. If desired, sprinkle with ¼ cup flaked almonds.
Bake in a moderate oven a further 15 minutes.

PEANUT CRUNCH SLICES

2 tablespoons honey
½ cup butter or substitute
1 cup sugar
4 cups rice bubbles
1 cup coconut
½ cup salted peanuts

Put honey, butter, and sugar into a large saucepan, stir over
medium heat until mixture boils, boil gently 5 minutes.
Remove from heat. Add rice bubbles, coconut, and peanuts,
and mix thoroughly. Spread into a greased 16 x 28 cm

lamington tin, allow to stand 10 minutes, then cut into finger lengths. Remove from tin when biscuits are cold and crisp.

CHOCOLATE FRUIT SQUARES

1/3 cup drinking chocolate
1 cup coconut
¾ cup sultanas
½ cup crushed cornflakes
1/3 cup chopped walnuts
1/3 cup finely crushed plain sweet biscuits
2/3 cup condensed milk
1 tablespoon sherry or orange juice
114 g dark chocolate

Combine drinking chocolate, coconut, sultanas, cornflakes, walnuts, and crushed biscuits. Add condensed milk and sherry, mix well to a stiff spreading consistency. Spread mixture over the base of a lightly greased and paper-lined 16 x 28 cm lamington tin. Refrigerate 1 hour. Roughly chop chocolate, melt over hot water. Spread melted chocolate over fruit base, mark decoratively with fork. Allow chocolate to set, cut into squares for serving.

CHOCOLATE FUDGE FINGERS

½ cup butter or substitute, melted
½ cup brown sugar, firmly packed
1 egg
1 tablespoon cocoa
1 cup plain sweet biscuit crumbs
½ cup chopped walnuts
½ cup chopped raisins
1 tablespoon sherry or orange juice

Lemon Icing:

1 cup icing sugar
1 tablespoon butter
Lemon juice

Place melted butter in saucepan, add sugar, stir over heat 2 minutes. Remove from heat, allow to cool slightly. Add beaten egg, sifted cocoa, finely crushed biscuits, walnuts, chopped raisins and sherry; mix thoroughly. Press into greased and greased-paper-lined 20 cm square slab tin. Refrigerate 1 hour. Ice with lemon icing. When icing is firm, cut into fingers.

For the icing, sift icing sugar into a small saucepan, add butter and enough lemon juice (2-4 teaspoons) to mix to a stiff paste. Stir over hot water until icing is a smooth spreading consistency.

DATE AND SULTANA SLICES

2 pkts plain sweet biscuits (thin rectangular
  biscuits are best)
1 2/3 cups chopped dates
½ cup sultanas
2 teaspoons grated lemon rind
2 tablespoons lemon juice

Lemon Icing:

1½ cups icing sugar
1 teaspoon softened butter or substitute
2 teaspoons lemon juice
1 tablespoon hot water
Chopped walnuts

Line a 16 x 28 cm lamington tin with paper, bringing it up over the two long sides. Line base of tin with one layer of biscuits. Put dates, sultanas, lemon rind and juice into a small saucepan. Stir over low heat until mixture becomes soft and combines well. Spread date and sultana filling over biscuits. Place another layer of biscuits on top of filling; press gently. Ice with lemon icing, sprinkle with chopped walnuts. Cut into slices when icing is firm.

For the icing sift icing sugar into bowl, add butter and lemon juice; mix well. Add hot water and beat until icing is of smooth consistency.

ALMOND WAFERS

2/3 cup blanched almonds
½ cup sugar
½ cup butter or substitute
1 tablespoon plain flour
2 tablespoons milk
Whipped cream for serving

Grind almonds, then in a saucepan mix with all other
ingredients; stir over heat until butter melts. Drop teaspoons
of mixture about 10 cm apart on to greased and floured trays.
Bake in a moderate oven 8 to 10 minutes or until lightly
browned. Allow to cool slightly, but while still warm remove
from trays and place over rolling pin to shape; cool. Serve
with bowl of whipped sweetened cream so everyone can
spoon cream into the crisp lacy shells.
  Other accompaniments: pineapple cream cheese mixture;
any fruit chiffon; chilled egg custard — stir in 2 tablespoons
advocaat before chilling.

TOASTED ALMOND BREAD

1 cup butter or substitute
½ cup sugar
4 eggs
1 teaspoon vanilla
2 tablespoons grated lemon rind
2 tablespoons lemon juice
4 cups plain flour
2½ teaspoons baking powder
¼ teaspoon salt
1 cup blanched almonds
Melted butter
Cinnamon
Little sugar

Cream butter and sugar until light and fluffy. Add eggs, beat
well. Add vanilla, lemon rind, and lemon juice. Fold in sifted

flour, baking powder, salt, and blanched almonds. Divide mixture evenly between two small greased loaf-tins. Brush with melted butter, sprinkle with sugar and cinnamon. Bake in a moderate oven 30 to 35 minutes. Allow loaves to stand overnight. Next day cut into thin slices and toast very lightly. Crunchy and nutty when served alone; delicious as an accompaniment to fruit desserts and ice cream.

MARSHMALLOW BARS

½ cup chopped almonds
1 cup shredded coconut
4½ tablespoons butter
2 pkts marshmallows
4 cups cornflakes
114 g chocolate

Brown almonds and coconut under griller or in oven. Melt butter in saucepan, add marshmallows, cook over low heat until melted. Mix in almonds, coconut and flakes. Press into greased lamington tin or shallow tin; chill. Spread top with melted chocolate, cool, cut into bars for serving.

CHOCOLATE RAISIN DROPS

114 g dark chocolate
1 tablespoon butter
¼ cup chopped nuts
½ cup raisins
Corn cereal flakes

Chop chocolate roughly, place in top of double saucepan over warm water (or place in basin over warm water). Add butter, stir until smoothly melted. Add nuts and raisins and enough corn cereal flakes to bind mixture together. Drop in heaps on to greased paper, refrigerate until set.

CHOCOLATE RUM SLICES

Pastry:

1 cup self-raising flour
1 cup plain flour
½ cup butter or substitute
¼ cup sugar
1 egg
Few drops vanilla
Milk

Sift flours, rub in the butter, add sugar and mix thoroughly. Beat egg slightly, add vanilla, gradually work into the flour mixture, using a little milk, if necessary, to make a firm dough. Wrap in greaseproof paper, chill while preparing the filling and topping.

Filling:

1½ cups ground almonds
¾ cup icing sugar, sifted
2 tablespoons cocoa
1 egg white
2 tablespoons rum

Place the ground almonds in a bowl. Sift together icing sugar and cocoa, add to almonds, mix thoroughly. Lightly beat egg white, add to dry ingredients with rum. Mix thoroughly to make rather moist consistency.

Topping:

One egg white
2/3 cup icing sugar
2 teaspoons plain flour
Slivered almonds

Lightly beat the egg white, sift in icing sugar and flour. Beat until smooth and of pouring consistency.

To assemble, roll out pastry into a long rectangle on a lightly floured board. Lightly mark into three sections lengthwise, the middle section twice as wide as the two outside sections. Spread filling in the centre section; fold in outside sections to meet in centre. Grease oven slide and place roll, folded side down, on to tray. Pour topping over the roll, spreading evenly. Sprinkle with slivered almonds. Bake in moderate oven ½ to ¾ hour, or until golden brown. While still hot, cut into slices, leave to cool.

CHOCOLATE RUM BALLS

3 cups (approx.) cake crumbs
3 tablespoons cocoa
½ cup chopped raisins
3 tablespoons apricot jam
2 tablespoons rum
2 tablespoons water
2 tablespoons apricot jam, extra
Chocolate sprinkles

Mix together cake crumbs, cocoa, raisins, apricot jam and rum until a stiff paste is formed. Make into approximately 24 balls. Warm 2 tablespoons sieved jam with water; dip the balls in this jam mixture, then coat with chocolate sprinkles. Place in paper patty cases.

Note: For convenience, make 1 dark chocolate cake mix, for crumbs.

RUM TRUFFLES

1 cup stale cake-crumbs
¼ cup castor sugar
½ cup marzipan meal
1 tablespoon coconut
2 teaspoons cocoa
1 tablespoon rum
1 egg yolk
Melted chocolate
Chocolate sprinkles

Mix cake-crumbs, sugar, marzipan meal, coconut, cocoa, rum and egg yolk well together. Form into small balls, refrigerate until firm. Melt chocolate in top half of double saucepan and dip the balls. Drain, refrigerate until chocolate has set. Spoon a little extra melted chocolate over top of balls, coat with chocolate sprinkles; refrigerate again until topping has set.

CHOCOLATE CRUMBLES

½ cup butter
½ cup sugar
2 tablespoons milk
5 tablespoons powdered milk
1 tablespoon cocoa
Few drops vanilla
2 teaspoons sherry
1 cup coconut
½ cup sultanas, chopped
¼ cup currants
¼ cup raisins, chopped
2 cups cornflakes

Place butter, sugar and milk into a saucepan, stir until dissolved. Pour into a basin, sprinkle powdered milk on top; beat until well blended. Add cocoa, vanilla and sherry, mix well. Work in coconut, dried fruits and cornflakes. Place in small heaps on greaseproof paper, refrigerate until set.

WHITE CHRISTMAS

1 pkt white vegetable shortening
3 cups rice bubbles
1 cup coconut
¾ cup icing sugar
1 cup powdered milk
¼ cup chopped mixed peel
¼ cup chopped preserved ginger
¼ cup chopped glace apricots

¼ cup chopped glace pineapple
¼ cup sultanas
¼ cup chopped glace cherries

Melt chopped white vegetable shortening over gentle heat and
allow to cool. Combine rice bubbles, coconut, sifted icing
sugar, powdered milk, and chopped fruits; mix well. Add
cooled shortening and mix thoroughly. Press mixture into
lightly greased and paper-lined 16 x 28 cm lamington tin.
Refrigerate until firm, cut into bars for serving.

DARK CHRISTMAS

¾ pkt white vegetable shortening
2½ cups rice bubbles
1 cup powdered milk
1 cup icing sugar
2 tablespoons cocoa
1 cup mixed fruit
¼ cup chopped preserved ginger
¼ cup chopped glace cherries
Icing sugar to dust

Melt chopped white vegetable shortening over gentle heat and
allow to cool. Combine rice bubbles, powdered milk, sifted
icing sugar, sifted cocoa, and chopped fruits; mix well. Add
cooled shortening and mix thoroughly. Press mixture into
lightly greased and paper-lined 16 x 28 cm lamington tin.
Refrigerate until firm. Cut into bars, dust tops with icing
sugar.

CHOCOLATE PEPPERMINT SQUARES

Crumb Base:

1 cup crushed cornflakes
½ cup coconut
1/3 cup brown sugar, lightly packed
½ cup butter or substitute

Combine crushed cornflakes, coconut and brown sugar, add melted butter, mix well. Press over base of lightly greased and paper-lined 20 cm square slab tin. Refrigerate 1 hour.

Peppermint Filling:

1 lge pkt cream cheese
1/3 cup castor sugar
1 small can reduced cream
2 or 3 drops peppermint essence

Beat softened cream cheese until smooth. Gradually add sugar; beat well. Blend in reduced cream and peppermint essence. Spread over crumb base. Refrigerate until firm.

Chocolate Topping:

Melt 90 g chocolate bits over hot water. Add 2 tablespoons hot water and 1 to 2 drops vanilla essence, beat until smooth. Spread evenly over peppermint filling, refrigerate until firm. Cut into squares.

CONTINENTAL CHOCOLATE SLICES

1 pkt wheatmeal biscuits
½ cup butter or substitute
½ cup sugar
2 tablespoons cocoa
1 egg
1 teaspoon vanilla
¾ cup coconut
½ cup chopped walnuts

Cream filling:

1½ tablespoons butter or substitute
2 cups icing sugar
1½ tablespoons custard powder

Topping:

2 tablespoons hot water
125 g dark chocolate

Crush biscuits into fine crumbs. Combine butter, sugar and cocoa in a saucepan. Stir over low heat until well blended. Stir in beaten egg and vanilla. Cook, stirring, 1 minute. Remove from heat, stir in biscuit crumbs, coconut and walnuts, mix well. Press mixture into greased 16 x 28 cm lamington tin, refrigerate until set.

For the cream filling cream butter well. Sift together icing sugar and custard powder, add to butter alternately with hot water. Beat until light and fluffy. Spread over biscuit base, refrigerate.

As a topping melt chopped chocolate over hot water, spread evenly over firm, cold cream filling; refrigerate. Cut into small squares or fingers to serve.

YEAST COOKERY

Doughs

One of the important things about making yeast doughs is to acquire the "feel" of what you are doing. It is almost impossible to give exact measurements or weights for the flour needed in certain recipes because flours vary so greatly. Often you will find that the amount given is a little less than will be needed. The "feel" of the dough, how it sticks to the hands or the board, must tell you whether or not to add more. How long to knead is also judged by the "feel" of the dough; it has been worked enough when it is smooth and springy and no longer sticks to the board.

Yeast dough must be left covered in a warm place long enough for it to rise and become light. There are various ways to knead. Possibly the simplest is to turn the dough on to a floured board or large, warm tray, pull it towards you with the fingers of both hands, then push it down hard and away from you with the heels of your hands. Turn it a quarter way round and repeat until it feels smooth and springy and no longer sticks to the board. Sprinkle more flour as it is needed. The harder you work the better it is. Because wheat flour contains a high proportion of gluten it is possible through kneading to develop the texture wanted in a good dough. If flour from other grains is used it is usually combined with some wheat flour.

There are two kinds of yeast: (i) compressed yeast, which is a grey putty-like substance obtainable at selected bread shops, some food supermarkets and delicatessens. It keeps 3 to 4 days in the refrigerator; (ii) dry granulated yeast (Dribarm)

sold in packets or cans in grocery supermarkets. This yeast
will keep up to six months in a cool, dry cupboard.

FRENCH BREAD (BAGUETTE)

3 tablespoons compressed yeast, lightly crumbled,
    or ½ cup dry yeast
¼ cup warm water
½ cup milk
1 cup water
1 tablespoon sugar
1 tablespoon butter
2 teaspoons salt
5 cups flour

Dissolve the yeast in ¼ cup warm water. Scald the milk and
water, add sugar, butter and salt, let it cool and mix with the
yeast in a large bowl. Gradually stir in the sifted flour and
blend into a fairly soft dough. Turn on to the floured board and
knead well, adding more flour if necessary. When quite
springy place the dough into an oiled or greased bowl, brush
the top with oil or melted butter. Cover the bowl and stand it
in a warm place to allow the dough to rise to double its
original size — about 1¼ hours. When fully risen the imprint
of your fingers, after testing, will remain and the dough will
start to fall. Punch it down, pull the edges into the centre,
make a firm ball. Re-cover and let the dough rise again, about
30 minutes, to twice its size. Turn on to a floured board, cut
sharply into three or four sections. Shape each one into a long
cylinder about 4 cm in diameter. Place the loaves on a
greased tray, cover with towel and allow to rise in a warm
place until double their size (30 minutes). When half risen cut
six or seven diagonal slits 1 cm deep in the top of each loaf.
Brush with milk and bake in a hot oven (230°C) for 10 minutes
and then 200°C for a further 15 minutes until crust is brown
and crisp and the loaf sounds hollow when tapped. Cool,
uncovered, on a wire stand.

BRIOCHE

6 teaspoons crumbled compressed yeast
½ cup warm water
1 cup flour

Dissolve yeast in water, mix with the flour to make a ball of
dough. Cut a cross on the top and place the ball in a deep bowl
of warm water. When the ball rises to the top it is ready to
mix with the other ingredients:

3 cups flour
1 teaspoon salt
1 tablespoon sugar
250 g butter
4 eggs
¼ cup milk

Sift flour and salt into a bowl, add sugar, cut the butter, which
should be at room temperature, into the flour. Add the eggs
one at a time, mixing well after each. Stir in the milk to make
a fairly soft dough. When the ball of sponge has risen in the
water, take it out and work it into the egg dough by cutting
and folding it in. Work the dough into a large ball, sprinkle it
with flour, cover with a towel and leave at room temperature
for 2 to 3 hours. When dough has doubled in bulk, punch it
down, pull in the edges and re-shape. Sprinkle with flour,
cover and leave in a cool place for 6 or 7 hours or overnight.
Dough which is so rich in butter cannot be shaped when
warm. Punch down the dough again and pull off pieces to
half-fill well-greased fluted or plain round moulds. Cut a cross
on top and crown the brioche by pushing a small ball of dough
into the opening. Let the brioche rise in a warm place, about
30 minutes, until increased by about one-third. Brush carefully
with well-beaten egg and milk mixture. Bake in a hot oven
(232ºC) 15-20 minutes until well browned. Test with a fine
skewer. Remove from mould immediately.

CHELSEA BUNS

4 cups flour
1 teaspoon salt
125 g butter
¾ cup castor sugar
4 eggs
6 teaspoons crumbled compressed yeast
6 tablespoons lukewarm milk
1 tablespoon chopped lemon peel
1 cup currants
¾ teaspoon mixed spice

Sift flour and salt; rub in half butter. Add half castor sugar.
Cream yeast with 1 teaspoon of castor sugar. Beat eggs, mix
with milk and the liquefied yeast. Blend well. Make a well in
the centre of flour, add liquid to make a soft dough. Mix until
quite smooth. Cover and leave in a warm place about 1½
hours or until doubled in size. Have extra sifted flour ready.
Turn on to a well-floured board, spread lightly into shape and
roll out to square shape. Have remaining butter softened
enough to spread over dough, sprinkle with sugar. Fold in
three, top to bottom, then in half sideways. Roll out to square
shape again. Sprinkle with sugar, peel, currants and spice.
Roll up as for Swiss roll, cut into four slices, place flat on a
warm greased tray, almost touching. Leave in a warm place to
rise 15-20 minutes. Sprinkle with extra castor sugar. Bake at
232ºC until quite brown, about 15-20 minutes.

WREATH CAKE

Make as for Chelsea Buns but substitute chopped cherries and
walnuts for currants. Curve the roll to make a circle by
moistening and joining the ends. Slash the top at 5 cm
intervals and spread cuts outward. When cooked and cold
decorate with glace icing, extra cherries and peel.

CONTINENTAL YEAST SYRUP CAKE

3 teaspoons crumbled compressed yeast
3 tablespoons sugar
2 teaspoons cream
2 eggs
½ cup melted butter
150 ml milk
3 cups flour
¼ teaspoon salt
¼ cup finely chopped blanched almonds

Syrup:

90 g loaf sugar
6 teaspoons water
4 drops almond essence
2 drops lemon essence
½ teaspoon cinnamon
Chopped blanched almonds and thin strips of
    lemon peel, for decoration

Cream yeast with sugar, add cream, beaten eggs, butter and milk, mix well. Sift in the flour and salt which should be warm. Make a soft, but not sticky, dough. Knead in the bowl by bringing the outsides into the middle with a wooden or plastic spoon. Continue to turn the bowl and knead until mixture is quite smooth. Cover the insides of a large ring-mould or 20 cm round tin with a thick layer of butter. Sprinkle thickly with almonds. Three-quarters fill with dough and leave covered in a warm place to rise. When the mixture almost reaches the top, bake in a hot oven (205°C) for 30-40 minutes. Test with a fine skewer.

To make the syrup, boil loaf sugar and water. After sugar is dissolved to 120 or 125°C on a candy making thermometer, add essences mixed with cinnamon. When cake is cooked turn out and glaze the top with several applications of syrup. Allow each one to set before applying the next or leave cake upside down and very gradually spoon the syrup over it. In this way the syrup will soak down into the warm cake. Top with more chopped nuts and thin strips of lemon peel.

DANISH PASTRY

1/3 cup plain flour
12 tablespoons softened butter
1¼ cups milk
6 teaspoons crumbled compressed yeast
¼ cup sugar
1 egg
3½ cups plain flour

Sift 1/3 cup flour, cut in butter, using pastry blender or two knives. Put in refrigerator. Warm milk until lukewarm, crumble in yeast, leave a few minutes, then add sugar and lightly beaten egg. Sift in remaining flour gradually, mix in with wooden spoon until smooth and firm. Turn on to a well-floured board, roll out to about 35 cm square. Roll out butter-flour mixture on waxed paper to oblong about 15 cm by 30 cm. Put butter dough on half, fold other half over. Roll out into a long strip from top to bottom, fold in three, quarter turn. Do this three times, chilling if dough becomes at all soft and butter appears to soften. Chill half hour. Prepare fillings:

Filling 1:
¾ cup ground almonds
½ cup sugar
1 egg

Mix almonds, sugar, add lightly beaten egg and blend, working until smooth. Do not over-mix.

Filling 2:
1 tablespoon flour
1 tablespoon sugar
½ cup milk
1 egg yolk
Little yellow lemon rind, freshly peeled
1 teaspoon butter
Little vanilla
Warm icing

Mix flour, sugar; blend with milk, add beaten egg yolk, lemon peel. Cook, stirring over low heat until thickened; add butter, vanilla, remove lemon rind, cool.

Danish Envelopes
Roll dough out thinly, cut in 10 cm squares, spread with 1 tablespoon custard filling. Fold corners in to middle, pressing down edges.

Crescents
Roll dough out thinly, cut into triangles. Spread almond filling on base, roll up. Put on greased scone slide. Leave to rise. Brush with slightly beaten egg. Bake in hot oven until golden brown. When cold ice with a little warm icing.

CAKES

SMALL CAKES

CHERRY CAKES

90 g butter
1/3 cup sugar
2 eggs
2 tablespoons milk
Vanilla
1½ cups flour
1 teaspoon baking powder
Pinch salt
Crystallized cherries

Cream butter and sugar, gradually add well beaten eggs. Add milk and vanilla, then sifted flour, baking powder, salt and 12 chopped cherries, mixing lightly. Have some small paper containers ready and put 2 teaspoonfuls of mixture in each. Bake in a hot oven 10 to 15 minutes. Ice with pink butter icing.

Alternatively, leave mixture plain and cherries whole. After 5 minutes cooking place one whole cherry on top of each cake. Cook 10 minutes more. Cherry should be in middle of cake.

SAND CAKE

250 g butter
1 cup sugar
4 eggs
1 1/3 cups arrowroot or cornflour
½ teaspoon bicarbonate of soda
1 teaspoon cream of tartar

Beat butter and sugar to a cream, add well beaten egg yolks.
Add sifted dry ingredients, fold in stiffly beaten egg whites
until well combined. Pour into lined, greased Swiss roll tin.
Bake in a moderate oven 40 minutes.

   This cake has a very fine texture and is a suitable base for
fancy iced shapes, e.g. petits fours or lamingtons.

WALNUT CRISPIES

2 egg whites
1 cup castor sugar
1 cup chopped walnuts
4 cups cornflakes or crispies

Beat egg whites stiffly, gradually work in sugar until mixture
is the consistency of meringue. Add chopped walnuts,
cornflakes and mix. Place in small rough heaps on greased tins
and bake in a very slow oven 30 minutes until pale brown.
Allow to cool on tin.

RICE BUBBLE NUTTIES

1 cup rice bubbles
1 cup rolled oats
¾ cup flour
½ cup coconut
Pinch salt

½ cup sugar
½ cup melted butter
1 tablespoon honey
½ teaspoon bicarbonate of soda
2 tablespoons boiling water

Mix rice bubbles, rolled oats, flour, coconut, salt and sugar together. Add melted butter, honey and bicarbonate of soda dissolved in 2 tablespoons boiling water. Drop with a spoon on a greased tray, leaving space between each to spread. Bake in a slow oven and leave on tray till cold.

Note: Cornflake nutties may be made the same way, substituting cornflakes for the rice bubbles.

LITTLE APPLE CAKES

Quantity of flavoured stewed apple
3 tablespoons butter
¼ cup sugar
1 egg
1 cup self-raising flour
3 tablespoons cornflour
Pinch salt
Lemon icing
Chopped nuts

Strain stewed apples, retaining liquid for glazing. Cream butter and sugar (not too creamy). Add well beaten egg. Stir in sifted flours and salt and make into a dry consistency. Knead very lightly. Chill 30 minutes. Roll out thinly, cut rounds 5 cm. Glaze half these with apple liquid, place 1 teaspoon apple in middle, cover with plain round which has small hole cut in centre for escape of steam. Press edges, glaze with apple liquid, sprinkle with castor sugar. Bake on very lightly greased tray 10-15 minutes at 204°C until light brown. Cool, ice and sprinkle with chopped nuts. For special effect decorate with butter cream rose.

HONEY ROLLS

1½ tablespoons butter
1½ tablespoons honey
1 egg
1/3 cup milk
2 cups self-raising flour
Pinch salt

Cream butter and honey, add egg and beat. Add milk and lastly flour sifted with salt. Roll out 13 mm thick on floured board. Cut with 8 cm round cutter, brush with milk, fold over in halves, glaze tops. Bake in a moderate oven (218°C) on a greased baking dish 15 minutes. Serve warm. Very good with morning tea or coffee.

HONEY FRUIT DROPS

1 cup butter
½ cup honey
1 egg
1 cup chopped dates
1 cup seeded raisins
½ teaspoon cinnamon
2/3 cup chopped walnuts
2 cups flour
Pinch salt
½ teaspoon bicarbonate of soda

Cream butter and honey, add egg and beat. Add dates, raisins, nuts and flour which has been sifted with cinnamon, salt and soda. Place teaspoonfuls on a greased tray and bake in a moderate oven.

COFFEE KISSES

6 tablespoons soft butter
1/3 cup sugar
1 egg

1 tablespoon coffee essence (1 teaspoon instant coffee
  dissolved in 1 tablespoon boiling water)
1¼ cups self-raising flour

Filling:
1 tablespoon butter
2 tablespoons icing sugar
1 teaspoon coffee essence

Beat butter and sugar until just creamy. Add well beaten egg
and essence. Stir in flour; make a mixture to handle. Roll a
teaspoonful, place on a greased tin, press with a fork and bake
in a very moderate oven 15 minutes. Make coffee filling by
beating the butter, sugar and coffee essence to a cream. Join
kisses together with this filling and sprinkle with icing sugar.

DATE CHEWS

1 cup self-raising flour
3/4 cup chopped dates
¼ cup chopped walnuts
4 tablespoons butter
½ cup brown sugar
1 egg
Vanilla

Sift flour and mix in chopped dates and nuts. Melt butter in
saucepan, add sugar and stir till boiling. When cool, add well
beaten egg and vanilla. Add to flour mixture and stir well.
Spread evenly in a greased Swiss roll tin. Bake in a moderate
oven 20 minutes. Cut into fingers while hot and allow to cool
in tin.

LARGE CAKES

APRICOT FUDGE CAKE

½ cup chopped dried apricots
¾ cup boiling water
½ cup soft butter or margarine
¾ cup brown sugar
2 eggs
60 g chocolate
1 teaspoon vanilla
2 cups self-raising flour
¼ teaspoon bicarbonate of soda
¾ cup milk

Chocolate Icing:

2 tablespoons cocoa
¼ cup apricot juice
¼ cup soft butter
½ teaspoon vanilla
1 cup icing sugar

Soak apricots, tightly covered, at least 2 hours in ¾ cup boiling water. Drain and reserve the liquid. Cream butter and sugar. Add eggs one at a time, beating well after each addition. Melt chocolate in 1 tablespoon apricot juice, cool. Add melted chocolate, vanilla and apricots to mixture. Sift flour, bicarbonate of soda; add alternately with milk. Pour into greased 20 cm tin. Bake in moderate oven 1 hour. Leave in tin 10 minutes, then turn on to cooler. Leave until cold.

To make chocolate icing, blend cocoa, juice and butter and boil 2 minutes. Remove from heat. Add vanilla and icing sugar. Beat until spreading consistency. Cover top of cake. Increase butter and icing sugar by half if cake is to be iced around sides.

MAORI CAKE

1 cup dates
¾ cup cold water
1 teaspoon bicarbonate of soda
Squeeze of lemon juice
125 g butter
¼ cup sugar
2 eggs
1 cup coconut
2 cups plain flour

Soak dates in cold water 1 hour, beat well and add bicarbonate
of soda and lemon juice just before using. Cream butter and
sugar. Add well beaten eggs slowly and continue beating till
thick. Add date mixture, coconut and flour and stir lightly
together. Pour into a greased 20 cm square tin and bake in a
moderate oven 45 minutes.

CINNAMON SPONGE

4 eggs
1 cup sugar
1 cup flour
1 teaspoon cream of tartar
½ cup milk, heated
½ teaspoon bicarbonate of soda
2 teaspoons cinnamon
1 teaspoon cocoa
1 teaspoon butter
Pinch salt
Raspberry jam
Whipped cream
Coconut

Beat eggs and sugar 20 minutes. Add sifted flour and cream of
tartar and mix in lightly. Pour hot milk on to soda, cinnamon,
cocoa, butter and salt and stir into the mixture. Pour into

greased sandwich tins. Bake in a moderate oven 20 minutes. When cool fill with raspberry jam and sweetened whipped cream. Spread the top with raspberry jam, sprinkle with coconut.

CINNAMON APPLE CAKE

2 large apples
Rind and juice of medium lemon
2 tablespoons butter
2 tablespoons sugar
1 small egg
1 cup flour
2 teaspoons cinnamon
1 teaspoon baking powder
Icing sugar

Stew apples, flavour with rind and juice of lemon. Keep warm. Cream butter and sugar, add egg and beat well. Add sifted flour, cinnamon and baking powder. Turn on to floured board and divide in two. Slightly roll out half, fit it into a 18 cm round greased tin and spread with hot apple. Roll out other half and cover apple. Bake in a moderate oven 20 to 25 minutes. Cover with sifted icing sugar if serving warm, with lemon or chocolate icing if cold.

HONEY ROLL

3 eggs
¼ cup castor sugar
2 tablespoons honey
½ teaspoon bicarbonate of soda
2 teaspoons hot water
1 cup plain flour
1 teaspoon cinnamon
Extra castor sugar
Whipped cream
Icing sugar

Beat eggs 3 minutes, or until light in colour. Gradually add sugar, beat until dissolved. Add honey, beat until mixture resembles thick cream. Add bicarbonate of soda dissolved in hot water. Lightly fold in sifted flour and cinnamon. Put into greased, greased-paper-lined 23 x 35 cm Swiss roll tin. Bake in moderately hot oven 12 to 15 minutes. Turn out on to teatowel covered with greaseproof paper sprinkled with extra castor sugar. Peel off lining paper, quickly trim cake edges. Fold end of paper over cake. Lift up teatowel, gently roll it away from you toward other end of cake. Leave cake covered by teatowel until cold. Unroll cake, spread with whipped cream. Reroll carefully with hands. Cover well with sifted icing sugar.

FRUIT AND NUT CAKE

125 g butter
¾ cup sugar
1 egg
½ cup chopped walnuts
½ cup chopped raisins
2 cups plain flour
2 level teaspoons baking powder
2 level tablespoons cocoa
1 cup milk
1 level teaspoon bicarbonate of soda

Icing:
1 tablespoon butter
1 tablespoon condensed milk
½ teaspoon vanilla essence
1 tablespoon powdered chocolate
2 cups sifted icing sugar

Beat butter and sugar to a cream and add well beaten egg, chopped walnuts and raisins, sifted flour, baking powder and cocoa alternately with milk, in which the soda is dissolved. Place mixture in a greased loaf tin measuring 23 x 12 cm, and bake in a moderate oven 50 to 60 minutes. Stand 5 minutes before turning out of tin. When cold cover top and sides with chocolate icing, and decorate with walnut halves.

For the icing, cream butter, milk, essence and chocolate. Gradually mix in icing sugar until smooth spreading consistency.

ARMENIAN NUTMEG CAKE

2 cups brown sugar
2 cups self-raising flour
125 g margarine or butter
1 teaspoon bicarbonate of soda
200 ml milk
1 egg
1 teaspoon nutmeg, preferably freshly ground
½ cup walnut pieces

Combine brown sugar, flour and margarine. Rub till mixture resembles breadcrumbs. Press half mixture evenly over base of greased 20 cm cake tin. Dissolve soda in milk, add beaten egg and nutmeg, stir well in to balance of mixture, pour into tin and sprinkle walnut pieces on top. Bake in moderate oven for 1 hour and leave in tin 5 minutes before turning out.

BOILED FRUIT CAKE

4½ cups mixed fruit
1 cup dates
½ cup glace cherries
125 g butter or substitute
¾ cup brown sugar, firmly packed
1 teaspoon mixed spice
½ cup water
½ cup sweet sherry
2 eggs
2 tablespoons marmalade
1 cup self-raising flour
1 cup plain flour
¼ teaspoon salt

Line a deep 20 cm square or deep 25 cm round cake tin with two thicknesses of greaseproof paper, bringing paper 5 cm above edges of tin. Chop mixed fruit and dates, halve cherries; combine in saucepan with butter, sugar, spice and water. Stir over heat until butter is melted; bring to boil. Boil uncovered 3 minutes. Remove from heat, allow to become completely cold. Add sherry, beaten eggs and marmalade; mix well. Add sifted dry ingredients; mix well, spread evenly into prepared tin, bake in moderately slow oven approximately 2 hours. Cover with aluminium foil until cold, remove from tin, re-wrap in foil until required.

GLACE FRUIT CAKE

¾ cup red glace cherries
¾ cup green glace cherries
¾ cup glace pineapple
2/3 cup drained preserved ginger
½ cup glace apricots
1½ cups sultanas
¾ cup ground almonds
250 g butter or substitute
1 tablespoon grated orange rind
2 teaspoons grated lemon rind
1 cup castor sugar
4 eggs
1½ cups plain flour
¼ cup self-raising flour
¼ teaspoon salt

Line a deep 20 cm round cake tin with two thicknesses of greaseproof paper, bringing paper 5 cm above edges of tin. Halve cherries, chop pineapple, ginger and apricots; combine in a large basin with sultanas and ground almonds. Beat butter and rinds until creamy, add sugar; beat until light and fluffy. Add eggs one at a time, beating well after each addition. Add creamed mixture to fruit mixture, mix well. Stir in sifted flours and salt. Spread into prepared tin. Bake in slow oven

(150ºC) approximately 2 hours. Test through middle with a fine skewer, cake tester or straw. When cooked, cover, cool in tin.

PINEAPPLE FRUIT CAKE (BOILED)

1 cup sugar
425 g can crushed pineapple
3 cups mixed fruit
1 teaspoon bicarbonate of soda
1 teaspoon mixed spice
125 g soft butter or margarine
1 cup self-raising flour
1 cup plain flour
2 eggs

Place sugar, contents of can of pineapple, mixed fruit, bicarbonate of soda, spice and butter into a saucepan. Bring to boil. Boil for 3 minutes and remove from heat. Let cool completely. Sift flours together and mix into cold fruit mixture with well beaten eggs. Place mixture in greased and lined 20 cm tin. Bake in a moderate oven (149ºC) approximately 1½ hours. Reduce heat to 122ºC. Bake further 20-30 minutes or until a skewer inserted comes out clean and dry.

CHRISTMAS CAKE (WHITE)

1½ cups glace pineapple
1½ cups glace cherries
1 cup raisins, chopped
1½ cups blanched almonds
¾ cup lemon peel
Juice of 2 oranges
2 tablespoons sherry (optional)
250 g unsalted butter
1½ cups sugar
6 eggs
1 1/3 cups desiccated coconut

1 teaspoon rose-water
3 cups self-raising flour

Chop pineapple, cherries, raisins, blanched almonds and
lemon peel into small pieces. Mix and cover with 3
tablespoons of the orange juice, and the sherry. Allow to stand
overnight. Add the rose-water to the coconut, and allow to
stand 30 minutes. Cream butter with sugar. Add well beaten
yolks of eggs, then add coconut mixture. Beat in ½ cup
orange juice alternately with sifted flour. Fold in stiffly beaten
egg whites. Add fruits and nuts. Pour into a well-lined greased
tin and bake slowly 3 to 4 hours at 150°C. Allow to become
cold in tin.

DARK FRUIT CAKE

375 g butter
2¼ cups dark brown sugar
6 eggs
4 cups plain flour
1 teaspoon bicarbonate of soda
½ teaspoon salt
2¼ cups raisins, chopped
2½ cups currants
1½ cups peel, chopped
2/3 cup preserved ginger, chopped
2/3 cup prunes, chopped
1½ cups almonds, blanched and chopped
4 tablespoons treacle

Use 35 cm square or round tin, line with three layers of
paper. Cream butter and sugar, add eggs. Gradually add
flour to which bicarbonate of soda and salt have been added.
Add fruit, ginger, nuts and treacle. Bake in slow oven
(149°-177°C) about 4 hours.

Note: Use 6 large eggs or 6 medium eggs and 2 extra
yolks.

ORIENTAL FRUIT CAKE

2 cups self-raising flour
4 cups plain flour
1 teaspoon cinnamon
2 teaspoons mixed spice
1 teaspoon ginger
500 g butter
2¼ cups brown sugar
8 eggs
2¼ cups raisins
2¼ cups sultanas
1 2/3 cups currants
1 2/3 cups dates
¾ cup chopped dried figs or ginger
1½ cups chopped prunes
¾ cup blanched almonds
¾ cup mixed candied peel
½ cup crystallized cherries
1 tablespoon warmed treacle
1 cup rum or brandy
1 teaspoon bicarbonate of soda
1 tablespoon boiling water

Line one 35 cm or two 22 cm tins with three layers of paper,
two brown, one greaseproof. Clean and prepare fruit. Sift
both flours, cinnamon, spice, ginger and salt together.
Cream butter and brown sugar. Add eggs one by one,
beating well each time. Mix raisins, sultanas, currants,
dates, dried figs or ginger, almonds, candied peel and
cherries. Add alternate cupfuls of sifted flour and mixed
fruit to the butter, brown sugar and egg mixture. Mix well
together. Add warmed treacle, rum and bicarbonate of soda
dissolved in boiling water. Mix well together. Bake in a
moderate to slow (170°C down to 150°C) oven 3 to 4 hours.
As soon as cake is taken from oven, sprinkle surface with 2
tablespoons rum or brandy. Cover the top and allow to get
cold in tin, then wrap and store.

Note: Fruit may be prepared in advance and stored in a
large covered container. To do this, chop all fruits, peel and

nuts, combine with rum in container and stir occasionally.
For a wedding cake make 1½ or 2 times the quantity depending on the number of tiers.

DESSERT CAKES
AND PUDDINGS

CRUMB TART AND PIE SHELLS

For the crumbs use plain sweet biscuits; unless specifically stated do not use cream-filled or chocolate coated biscuits. Plain or cheese flavoured cracker type biscuits, milk arrowroot, coffee, rice, digestive and chocolate are some of the suitable ones.

CRUMB PASTRY

2 cups fine crumbs
½ cup sweetening — castor sugar, icing sugar, brown sugar
½ cup melted butter or substitute
Flavourings: 1 tablespoon cocoa, 1 teaspoon spice,
    nutmeg or cinnamon

If a vitamizer is available, prepare crumbs, a few broken biscuits at a time. If not, place several biscuits between sheets of thick plastic or in a bag. Roll to crush into crumbs. Combine dry ingredients, then using a fork slowly incorporate melted butter until well blended. Very thick cream or cream cheese may be used with cracker type crumbs if savoury filling is being used. Omit sugar, add prepared mustard, herbs or a large clove of garlic well crushed.

Make sure that the container, whether springform or plate, is covered with a heavy layer of greasing. Press mixture firmly into shape, avoiding bulky thickness at the joint of the sides and base. Shapes may be baked 10 minutes in the middle of a 177°C oven. Cool and refrigerate, or place immediately into refrigerator while filling is being prepared.

Savoury Fillings

Well flavoured heavy cream sauce, well flavoured stock set with gelatine, 2 teaspoons to 150 ml of liquid. Incorporate minced or diced, cooked or canned poultry, meat, fish and vegetables flavoured with herbs, spices, condiments, garlic, chives, parsley. Decorate with tomato, radish roses, celery curls or fancy shapes of cooked beet or carrots.

Sweet Fillings

There is a very wide range: cooked, canned or fresh fruits set in jelly or starch thickened syprup, cream cheese mixtures, cold souffles and chiffons.

MANGO CREAM FILLING

2 ripe mangoes
2 teaspoons lemon juice
¼ cup sugar
1 tablespoon cold water
2 teaspoons gelatine
300 ml cream
1 passionfruit

Peel mangoes, remove flesh from stone, mash fruit to a pulp with a fork (there should be 1 to 1¼ cups of pulp). Add lemon juice and sugar. Sprinkle the gelatine over the water, stand a few minutes, dissolve over hot water, add to mango mixture. Beat cream until firm peaks form, fold lightly into mango mixture. Spread into a crumb crust, refrigerate until firm. Decorate with extra whipped cream and passionfruit pulp.

STRAWBERRY MOUSSE FILLING

6 eggs, separated
2/3 cup sugar
¼ cup evaporated milk
1 tablespoon gelatine
¼ cup water
300 ml cream
2 punnets strawberries
2 tablespoons kirsch

Put egg yolks, sugar and evaporated milk in top of a double saucepan. Beat over simmering water until mixture doubles in bulk and becomes very thick and creamy. Remove from heat, pour into a bowl, allow to become cold. Sprinkle the gelatine over the water, stand over simmering water until gelatine dissolves. Allow gelatine mixture to become cold. Beat cream until soft peaks form. Wash and hull strawberries: keep a few for decoration and mash the remainder well. Beat 3 egg whites until stiff. Fold half the cream, the gelatine mixture, mashed strawberries and kirsch into egg yolk mixture. Blend in egg whites and pour into a prepared case. Refrigerate. Before serving decorate top with remaining cream and strawberries that have been brushed with egg white and rolled in castor sugar.

PINEAPPLE FILLING

3 x 125 g pkts cream cheese
½ cup brown sugar
2 eggs, separated
½ cup pineapple syrup
2 tablespoons gelatine
1 cup pineapple pieces, chopped finely
1 tablespoon lemon juice
1 cup whipped cream

Soften cream cheese, add brown sugar, beat until soft and well blended. Add egg yolks, beat well. Meanwhile bring pineapple juice to boil, add gelatine, stir to dissolve and cool. Stir into the cream cheese mixture the pineapple pieces, dissolved gelatine and lemon juice. Finally, fold through the whipped cream and stiffly beaten egg whites. Pour over the base which has been chilled in a springform pan. Refrigerate several hours. Garnish with pineapple pieces, cream and toasted almonds.

PASSIONFRUIT CHIFFON FILLING

1 tablespoon gelatine
¼ cup water
4 eggs
¼ cup sugar
½ cup passionfruit pulp
3 tablespoons castor sugar

Soften gelatine in water. Separate eggs. Beat egg yolks with ¼ cup sugar until thick. Cook, stirring, in the top of a double boiler over hot water until sugar has dissolved and mixture thickens. Add gelatine, stir until dissolved. Remove from heat, cool slightly, stir in passionfruit pulp. Refrigerate until thickened slightly but not set. Beat egg whites until stiff, gradually add castor sugar, and continue beating until stiff peaks form. Carefully fold passionfruit mixture into egg whites. Spread mixture into a 20-25 cm prepared pastry shell, refrigerate until set. Serve with whipped cream.

CIDER HAZELNUT CHIFFON

1 tablespoon gelatine
1/3 cup cold water
1/3 cup castor sugar
1 cup sweet apple cider
2 tablespoons lemon juice
½ cup apple puree
2 egg whites
1/3 cup extra sugar
Whipped cream
1 teaspoon grated lemon rind
2 tablespoons chopped hazelnuts

Soak gelatine in cold water, dissolve over boiling water. Place castor sugar, cider, lemon juice and apple puree into a basin, add dissolved gelatine; mix thoroughly. Allow gelatine mixture to partially set. Beat egg whites until stiff, gradually add extra sugar, beating until sugar has dissolved; add gelatine mixture, combine well. Pour into a prepared pastry case and refrigerate until firm. Decorate with whipped cream flavoured with grated lemon rind. Sprinkle generously with chopped hazelnuts.

COLD CHOCOLATE SOUFFLE

125 g dark chocolate
300 ml milk
3 eggs, separated
¼ cup castor sugar
1 tablespoon gelatine
2 tablespoons water
150 ml cream

Put half the milk in a saucepan with the chopped chocolate, stir over hot water until chocolate has melted. Add remaining milk, remove from heat. Beat egg yolks and sugar until thick and light. Gradually add chocolate mixture. Return to saucepan, stir until mixture thickens; do not boil. Sprinkle gelatine over water, leave to stand 5 minutes: dissolve over hot water. Whip egg whites until soft peaks form. Whip cream. Fold gelatine, cream and egg whites into chocolate mixture. Pour into a prepared case. Refrigerate until firm. Decorate with extra whipped cream and, if desired, grated chocolate.

HAWAIIAN CHOCOLATE PIE

1 1/3 cups sugar
½ cup flour
3 cups milk
3 tablespoons margarine

3 egg yolks
1 teaspoon vanilla
425 g can crushed pineapple
60 g cooking chocolate
½ cup chopped walnuts
Whipped cream

Combine sugar and flour in a saucepan, add milk gradually, mix well. Bring to boil, stirring constantly. Blend in margarine, egg yolks and vanilla. Divide in half. Stir drained pineapple into one portion, cover. Let it cool till lukewarm. Blend melted chocolate into second portion. Cover, cool till lukewarm. Sprinkle half the chopped nuts over the base of a pastry shell. Spoon over half chocolate mixture, cover with pineapple mixture, and then remaining chocolate mixture. Decorate with nuts and whipped cream. Cool thoroughly before serving.

CREME DE MENTHE MARSHMALLOW

1½ cups crushed chocolate cream-filled biscuits
3 tablespoons shortening, melted
48 white marshmallows (approximately 1½ packets)
1 teaspoon gelatine softened in 1 tablespoon water
¾ cup undiluted evaporated milk
½ teaspoon peppermint essence
Few drops of green food colouring
1 tablespoon creme de menthe
Extra 2/3 cup undiluted evaporated milk
1 tablespoon lemon juice

Mix biscuits and shortening together, press on the bottom and sides of a 25 cm pie plate, reserving one tablespoon to decorate top. Melt the marshmallows in the ¾ cup milk in the top of a double saucepan. Add peppermint and food colouring. Cool until thick and syrupy, add creme de menthe, stirring occasionally. Chill the 2/3 cup milk in the refrigerator tray until soft ice crystals form around the edges of the tray (10-15 minutes). Whip until stiff (1 minute). Add lemon juice;

whip very stiff (1 minute longer). Fold whipped milk into marshmallow mixture. Spoon into a pie shell and decorate with remaining biscuit mixture.

YOGHURT CHEESECAKE

6 teaspoons gelatine
½ cup hot water
3 x 125 g pkts cream cheese
1 cup yoghurt (plain)
1 tablespoon lemon juice
3 eggs
¾ cup sugar
¼ teaspoon salt
½ cup sugar (extra)
1 cup cream (whipped)
Crumb crust, well chilled
Nutmeg

Dissolve gelatine in hot water. Beat the cream cheese and yoghurt with lemon juice until smooth and creamy. Separate eggs. Combine yolks, salt and ¾ cup sugar in saucepan and gently cook over a low heat for a few minutes, stirring occasionally. When thick, remove from heat. To this add gelatine solution, mixing in well. Cool slightly. Add to yoghurt cheese mixture. Beat egg whites until stiff, but not dry, gradually beating in ½ cup sugar. Blend into cheese mixture with whipped cream. Pour carefully into the pie case, refrigerate for at least 8 hours before serving. Sprinkle top with nutmeg.

As a variation, use fruit yoghurt.

BASIC BAKED CHEESECAKE

3 x 250 g pkts cream cheese
1 teaspoon vanilla
4 eggs
1 cup sugar

2 teaspoons lemon juice
20 cm crumb crust
Whipped cream
Cinnamon or nutmeg

Press cream cheese through a strainer, blend with vanilla.
Beat eggs until thick, beat in sugar gradually. Continue beating
while adding cheese mixture in small portions, mixing each
time until smooth. Mix in lemon juice. Spread into the crumb
crust, bake in a moderate oven 25 to 30 minutes. Cool, then
refrigerate. Just before serving, top with whipped cream,
sprinkle with cinnamon or nutmeg.

This mixture may be baked in a sweet biscuit pastry shell.

APRICOT NECTAR CHEESECAKE

Crumb Crust:

1 cup plain sweet coconut biscuit crumbs
½ cup butter or substitute

Filling:

425 ml can apricot nectar
1 tablespoon gelatine
½ cup castor sugar
3 x 125 g pkts cream cheese
1 tablespoon lemon juice
300 ml cream

Topping:

1 tablespoon sugar
3 teaspoons arrowroot
Apricot nectar
2 teaspoons rum (optional)
Whipped cream for decoration

For the crumb crust combine crumbs with melted butter, mix well. Press mixture firmly on to the base of a 20 cm springform pan, refrigerate 1 hour. To make the filling measure 1 cup apricot nectar from the can (reserve remainder for the topping). Pour the 1 cup nectar into a small saucepan, sprinkle gelatine over. Stir over low heat until gelatine is dissolved, allow to cool and thicken slightly. Beat softened cream cheese and sugar until mixture is smooth and creamy, beat in lemon juice, then apricot mixture; fold in whipped cream. Pour on to crumb crust, refrigerate until firm. For the topping put sugar and arrowroot in a saucepan, gradually stir in the reserved apricot nectar. Bring mixture to the boil, stirring constantly. Remove from heat, add rum. Continue stirring a few minutes to cool mixture slightly. Spread the topping over the cheesecake, refrigerate 1 hour. Decorate top with additional whipped cream.

LEMON CHIFFON PIE

Crumb Crust:

2 cups crushed plain biscuits
½ cup melted shortening
¼ cup sugar + 2 teaspoons honey
½ teaspoon each cinnamon and nutmeg

Filling:

1 cup lemon juice
1 cup sugar
1½ tablespoons custard powder
2 egg yolks
1 tablespoon gelatine softened in ¼ cup water
300 ml cream
2 egg whites
1 firmly packed tablespoon grated lemon rind

Make up crumb crust, press into sides and base of a 23 cm pie plate. Chill. Place sugar and lemon juice in a saucepan and bring to the boil. Blend custard powder with ¼ cup cold water. Stir in hot lemon syrup, return to the pan and cook, stirring until boiling. Cook for 2 minutes after it comes to the boil. Beat in the egg yolks. Add softened gelatine and stir to dissolve; allow to partially set. Whip cream to stiff peaks, mix half into the lemon custard. Fold in whipped egg whites and lemon rind. Pile into pie shell, chill until set. Serve with whipped cream or ice cream.

PINEAPPLE CRUNCH

Crunch Mixture:

1 cup very finely crushed cornflakes
¼ cup brown sugar
½ teaspoon allspice
1/3 cup melted butter

Pineapple Filling:

1 tablespoon gelatine
¼ cup cold water
3 eggs, separated
1 cup crushed pineapple
½ cup passionfruit pulp
2 tablespoons lemon juice
¾ cup sugar
1 cup cottage cheese
Whipped cream and cherries

Combine the crushed cereal, sugar, spice and melted butter. Reserve 3 tablespoons crunch for topping. Press remainder firmly into a buttered rectangular dish. Chill.

To make filling, soften gelatine in cold water. Combine pineapple, lemon juice, rind, ¼ cup sugar and passionfruit pulp. Heat until sugar is dissolved. Pour on to the well beaten yolks. Reheat but do not boil. Stir constantly. Remove from heat. Add the gelatine, stir until dissolved. Add sieved cottage cheese, beat until smooth. Chill until partially set. Whip egg whites until stiff, add remaining sugar. Fold in gelatine mixture, pour on to crunch crust. Sprinkle with the reserved crumbs. Press firmly on to the mixture. Refrigerate for 6 hours. Loosen edges, turn on to a board, cut into squares. Serve with cream, decorated with cherries.

If a vitamizer is available, blend the cheese with just sufficient fruit mixture to make a pouring consistency.

ORANGE AMBROSIA

Crumb Crust:

2 cups crushed coconut dessert biscuits
1/3 cup melted shortening + 1 tablespoon golden syrup

Filling:

1 pkt orange jelly crystals
½ cup sugar
1½ cups desiccated coconut
2 tablespoons grated orange rind
½ cup orange juice
1 2/3 cups undiluted evaporated milk, icy cold
¼ cup lemon juice
Whipped cream

Combine crushed biscuits with melted shortening and golden syrup. Press into the sides and base of a 20-25 cm pie plate. Chill. Dissolve the orange jelly and sugar with 1 cup hot water. Add coconut, orange rind and juice. Chill till partially set. Whip milk to soft peaks, add lemon juice and whip till stiff. Fold in jelly mixture. Allow to almost set if necessary, then pile into the biscuit crust. Refrigerate till set. Decorate with whipped cream.

CRUNCHY AMBER TORTE

Cake Mixture:

125 g butter or margarine
¾ cup brown sugar, closely packed
1 teaspoon vanilla essence
1 whole egg
1 extra egg yolk
1½ cups self-raising flour
¼ cup milk

Meringue:

2 egg whites
½ cup sugar

Topping:

1 level tablespoon sugar
1 level teaspoon cinnamon
1 level tablespoon coconut (or ¼ cup finely
   sliced almonds)

Butterscotch Cream Filling:

4 level tablespoons brown sugar
2 level tablespoons cornflour
Pinch salt
1 egg yolk
1 tablespoon butter
1 cup milk
Vanilla essence to taste
Apricot jam

Cream butter and sugar thoroughly and add vanilla. Add the whole egg and the extra yolk and beat well. Sift flour and fold in alternately with milk. Place in two well-greased and floured

20 cm sandwich tins. These are covered with the following meringue mixture before baking: beat egg whites stiffly, add ½ cup sugar gradually and beat again until stiff. Spread this over the uncooked cake mixture in the sandwich tins and sprinkle with a topping of sugar, cinnamon and coconut (or almonds) mixed. Bake in a moderate oven for 30 to 35 minutes. Great care is needed when turning the cakes out. Let them stand for 5 minutes then turn on to sugared paper. To make the butterscotch cream filling combine sugar, cornflour and a pinch of salt, add egg yolk and beat thoroughly, then add butter and milk and stir over heat until thick and smooth. When cold, stir in vanilla essence.

Split each cake, being careful not to break meringue, and fill with butterscotch cream. Spread apricot jam over one meringue top, and cover with other cake.

CHOCOLATE HAZELNUT TORTE

Meringue:

4 egg whites
¾ cup castor sugar
½ cup ground hazelnuts
6 teaspoons melted butter
¼ cup plain flour

Rum Cream:

300 ml cream
2 teaspoons rum
½ teaspoon vanilla
1 tablespoon sugar
1 teaspoon instant coffee

Chocolate Cream:

300 ml cream
¼ cup sugar

½ teaspoon vanilla
2 tablespoons cocoa

With a pencil, mark five 10 x 20 cm rectangles on three scone trays. Grease and dust with flour. Beat egg whites till stiff, gradually beat in the sugar. Beat till dissolved; this is important. The mixture should be of good meringue consistency. Carefully fold in the nuts, butter and sifted flour. Divide evenly between the trays, spreading to fit the rectangles. Bake in a moderately slow oven 30 minutes. Remove carefully from the trays immediately; use an egg slice for this so the wafers will not break. Allow to cool on wire racks on greased paper.

For the rum cream whip all ingredients together till thick. Sandwich the meringue layers together with rum cream. Refrigerate.

For the chocolate cream mix together all ingredients, cover, refrigerate 1 hour. Then whip together till thick. Cover top and sides of torte decoratively. Decorate, if desired, with whole hazelnuts. Refrigerate cake several hours.

PEACH LAYER CAKE

1 small can sliced peaches
½ cup soft butter or substitute
1 cup castor sugar
2 eggs
1 teaspoon vanilla
2 cups self-raising flour
½ cup milk
1 tablespoon brown sugar
1 teaspoon cinnamon

Drain peaches well; reserve a few slices for decoration. Chop remaining peaches. Combine softened butter, sugar, eggs, vanilla and sifted flour and milk in a bowl, beat 3 minutes. Spread half cake mixture into greased deep 20 cm round springform cake tin. Top with chopped peaches, sprinkle with sugar and cinnamon. Spread evenly with remaining cake mixture. Arrange reserved peaches decoratively on top. Bake in moderate oven approximately 50 to 60 minutes. Allow cake to stand in tin 5 minutes before turning out. Dust with sifted icing sugar.

CHOCOLATE ROLL

4 eggs
1 cup castor sugar
125 g dark cooking chocolate
6 teaspoons water
1 tablespoon cocoa

Filling:

¾ cup cream
Vanilla
5 teaspoons icing sugar
Little extra cocoa

Grease and line with greased paper a 25 x 35 cm Swiss roll tin. Separate eggs. Beat yolks and sugar until very pale and fluffy. Melt chopped chocolate with water stirring with a wooden spoon until chocolate has melted. Cool. Mix gently through the egg yolk mixture. Beat egg whites until soft peaks form. Do not overbeat. Fold the chocolate mixture into the egg white mixture very carefully until evenly distributed. Carefully spoon the mixture into prepared tin and spread evenly. Bake in moderate oven (190°C) 15 minutes. Remove from oven, cover cake with two layers of paper towelling wrung out in cold water and one layer of dry paper towelling. Chill 20 minutes. Remove paper towels carefully. Loosen cake along the long sides, using a sharp knife. Dust top with sifted cocoa. Turn out. Remove lining paper. Whip cold cream until thick. Beat in vanilla with icing sugar and cocoa sifted together. Spread cake with cream mixture, roll up, and dust with extra cocoa.

MARSHMALLOW CHOCOLATE SPONGE

90 g chocolate, melted
2 cups brown sugar
1 cup milk
1 egg yolk
1 teaspoon vanilla
¼ cup butter
2 eggs
2 cups self-raising flour
¼ teaspoon salt
1 teaspoon bicarbonate of soda
1 tablespoon boiling water

Filling and Frosting:

2 cups sugar
½ cup water
⅛ teaspoon cream of tartar
Whites of 2 eggs
½ teaspoon vanilla
½ cup quartered marshmallows
Chocolate chips
Glace orange peel

Blend melted chocolate, half brown sugar and half milk. When hot, add egg yolk beaten with 1 tablespoon cold milk. Cook 1 minute longer, allow to cool, and add vanilla. Cream butter with remaining half of brown sugar, add yolks of 2 eggs, sift flour and salt and add it and milk alternately. Add soda dissolved in boiling water, then cooled chocolate mixture, lastly fold in stiffly beaten whites 2 eggs. Bake in two 20 cm sandwich tins in a moderate oven 20-30 minutes. For icing, boil sugar, water and cream of tartar (make sure that sugar is dissolved before boiling) till the mixture threads when dropped into cold water. Add mixture slowly to stiffly beaten egg whites and flavour with vanilla; beat till thick and fold in marshmallows. Fill sponge with some of mixture and spread remainder all over cake. Decorate with chocolate chips and glace orange peel.

LAYERED STRAWBERRY ICE CREAM DESSERT CAKE

2 x 20 cm sponge cakes
1 litre strawberry ice cream
500 g frozen strawberries, chopped or 1 large can
2 tablespoons cornflour
2 tablespoons lemon juice
2 tablespoons cold water
Fresh ripe strawberries, washed and well drained
Whipped cream

Split each cake in two layers, put all together with fairly generous layers of ice cream, cover and freeze. Place chopped or mashed strawberries in a saucepan. Blend cornflour with lemon juice and cold water. Stir until it becomes a heated puree. Bring to boil, stirring, cook 3 minutes. Cool, stir occasionally. Have cake on serving plate, cover with thickened sauce. Decorate with fresh strawberries and whipped cream.

DOBOS TORTE

Cake:

4 eggs
1 teaspoon vanilla
½ cup granulated sugar
¼ teaspoon salt
½ cup sifted self-raising flour

Caramel Frosting:

1 cup granulated sugar
½ cup water
½ teaspoon cream of tartar

Chocolate Creme de Cacao Butter Cream:

4 egg yolks
1½ cups granulated sugar
¾ cup water
Cream of tartar
230 g dark sweet chocolate
1 cup soft unsalted butter
4 tablespoons water
2 tablespoons creme de cacao

For the cake, beat eggs, vanilla, sugar, and salt until very stiff and fluffy, either over a bowl of hot water or in an electric mixer. Carefully fold in sifted flour. Grease seven scone trays with vegetable shortening and dust lightly with flour. Mark a 23 cm circle on each. Place 2 tablespoons of batter in the centre of each circle and spread evenly with a spatula until it just covers the circle. Bake 7 or 8 minutes in a moderate oven or until lightly browned all over. Loosen each circle at once and use the same 23 cm marker to trim off edges evenly. Allow to become quite cold. Take one of the best layers and place on a scone tray which has been well oiled with vegetable oil. Cover with the caramel frosting.

To make caramel frosting put sugar, cream of tartar and water into a heavy pan. Stir over a slow fire until it dissolves. Allow to cook to a dark, golden brown. Remove and place over a bowl of ice at once to cool a little. When thick, but not set, pour over the top of the cake layer to completely cover it. Trim off any bits that run over the side, using an oiled knife. Use the same oiled knife to mark criss-crosses on the top of the cake to make eight even servings. (This should be done quickly because the caramel sets very rapidly.) Set aside to cool.

To make chocolate creme de cacao butter cream beat egg yolks until light and fluffy. Put sugar, water and cream of tartar into a pan. Cook to a light thread (104°C). Pour over yolks, beating all the time. Continue beating until very thick and cold. Cream butter and add it, bit by bit. Cut up the sweet chocolate and put into a pan. Add the water and stir over low heat until it melts. Cool. Add this with the creme de cacao to the butter cream.

To serve, sandwich six layers generously with the butter cream, ending with the layer covered with caramel frosting. Spread more butter cream smoothly around the sides of the cake and stick coarsely grated chocolate round the edge. Put the rest of the butter cream into a pastry bag with a star tube and pipe small rosettes around the edge of the cake. Cool in the refrigerator for at least one hour before serving.

ICE CREAM CAKE

2 1/3 cups milk
1 cup condensed milk
1 plain junket tablet
2 teaspoons water
1 teaspoon vanilla
1½ tablespoons gelatine
4 tablespoons water
1/3 cup cleaned raisins
1/3 cup cleaned sultanas
1/3 cup drained ginger
1/3 cup red and green glace cherries
½ cup slivered almonds
3 tablespoons marsala
1 teaspoon grated lemon rind
300 ml cream, whipped
Whipped cream and some red and green
    glace cherries for decoration

Combine the milks in a saucepan, stir over low heat until lukewarm. Remove from heat. Dissolve crushed junket tablet in 2 teaspoons water. Stir into milk with vanilla. Dissolve gelatine, which was softened in 4 tablespoons cold water. When cool stir into milk mixture. Refrigerate in ice cream trays until set. Spoon mixture into large electric mixer bowl which has been well chilled; beat on high speed for 10 minutes. Should be doubled in quantity and have a marshmallow consistency. Fold in the fruits which had been previously cut up and mixed with the marsala and 1 teaspoon of grated lemon rind. Mix in 1 cup whipped cream. Pour mixture into deep 20 cm tin which has been greased, lined with greaseproof paper and greased again. Cover top with double thickness of greased paper or film. Leave in freezer at least 12 hours. Unmould on to serving dish. Decorate with whipped cream and some red and green cherries. Leave in refrigerator 30-40 minutes to make cutting and serving easier.

DATE AND APPLE ROLL

2 large apples
1 2/3 cups dates
250 g rich short crust
Little more than ¼ cup brown sugar
Nutmeg or cinnamon
2 teaspoons butter
¾ cup boiling water
Cream or custard

Peel, core and dice apples. Remove stones from dates. Make a short crust and roll out to a thin sheet about 6 mm thick. Cover with apples and dates, leaving about 2 cm margin all round. Sprinkle with brown sugar and cinnamon or nutmeg. Roll up, close ends and place in piedish. Dissolve brown sugar with butter in the boiling water and pour this round the roll. Bake in a hot oven with a decreasing heat for 30 minutes. Serve with cream or custard.

APPLE SHORTCAKE

Filling:

6 apples
6 cloves
2 tablespoons butter
Rind of ½ lemon
Juice of 1 lemon
2 tablespoons honey or sugar

Biscuit Pastry:

90 g butter
¼ cup castor sugar
1 egg yolk
1 cup flour (plain)
¼ cup self-raising flour
⅛ teaspoon salt
1 tablespoon lemon juice
1 tablespoon water

Garnish:

300 ml cream, whipped
Sugar to flavour
Essence
Cochineal

Stew apples with cloves, 2 tablespoons butter, lemon rind, juice and honey. Mix butter and sugar until combined, add egg until absorbed. Do not beat. Have flour and salt sifted. Add half to the mixture, then lemon juice and 1 tablespoon water. Add remainder of the flour. Turn on to a floured board, knead slightly and roll into two round shapes between greaseproof paper. Place pastry into a prepared tray, prick well and bake 15-20 minutes at 175°C.

When cold spread apple on one layer with cream, cover with the other layer. Decorate top layer with cream and large seeded prunes filled with apple. For individual serves make rounds 8 cm across.

Variations: Any fresh fruit in season or a combination of fruits; well drained preserved fruits; pears stewed with ginger and lemon.

STRAWBERRY SHORTCAKE

125 g butter
¼ cup sugar
1 egg

¾ cup flour
4 tablespoons cornflour
1 teaspoon baking powder

Filling and Topping:

2 tablespoons melted butter
150 ml cream, whipped
1 punnet strawberries

Beat butter and sugar to a cream. Add well beaten egg. Lastly add flour, cornflour and baking powder sifted together. Place in two greased 18 cm sandwich tins and bake 15 minutes at 190°C. Turn out carefully and allow to cool. Brush melted butter over tops, join with half the cream and half the strawberries. Place other portion of cake on top and spread remainder of cream over it. Decorate with whole strawberries.

Peaches, bananas, or pineapple may be substituted for the strawberries.

GRAND CHOCOLATE LAYER

1 cup soft unsalted butter
½ cup sugar
6 eggs, separated
½ cup plain flour
1 cup milk
Few drops vanilla
Drinking chocolate
300 ml cream

Grand Marnier Sauce:

1½ tablespoons grand marnier (or other liqueur)
1 tablespoon icing sugar
1 cup cream, whipped
1½ teaspoons grated orange rind

Put aside 2 tablespoons of the butter for buttering pan. Beat the rest of the butter until creamy, gradually add the 6 egg yolks and the sugar, beat well. Add sifted flour and mix thoroughly. Add milk, beat until mixture is a fairly thick consistency. Stiffly beat egg whites and fold into mixture. Add vanilla. Heat pan and grease well by dipping a crumpled piece of paper into the reserved butter. Place 1 tablespoon of mixture in pan; when the pancake is lightly cooked on one side, slide it off with the help of spatula or egg slice on to an ovenproof dish with sides at least 5 cm high. Cook pancakes on one side only. Sprinkle lightly with drinking chocolate between each pancake as they are piled one on top of the other. Let stand until serving time. Then pour cream over pancakes, cook in moderate oven approximately 30 minutes. Serve hot, cut into wedges, with Grand Marnier Sauce. To make Grand Marnier Sauce simply combine all ingredients and blend well.

UPSIDE-DOWN SPONGE PUDDING

Dried apricots
Prunes
2 level tablespoons butter or margarine
4 level tablespoons brown sugar
Blanched almonds

Batter

¼ cup butter or margarine
½ cup sugar
1 egg
1½ cups self-raising flour
Pinch salt
½ cup milk
½ teaspoon vanilla essence

Soak apricots (and prunes if necessary) in warm water until soft. Cream 2 level tablespoons butter and 4 level tablespoons brown sugar and spread on the bottom and 1 cm up the sides of a deep 23 cm sandwich tin; or grease the tin and line with one layer of buttered paper and spread mixture on this. Arrange a design in the middle with the fruit and almonds, using half an almond in place of each prune stone. Place apricots and prunes alternately round the edge. For the batter, cream butter and sugar, add egg and beat well. Sift flour and salt and add alternately with milk and vanilla. Cover fruit with this batter and bake in a moderate oven 20 to 30 minutes. Turn on to a hot serving dish and serve with custard sauce.

Pineapple, cooked apple, peaches or cherries may be substituted for apricots and prunes.

UPSIDE-DOWN PEAR GINGERBREAD

284 g plain flour
1 level teaspoon bicarbonate of soda
1 level tablespoon ginger
½ level teaspoon spice or cinnamon
125 g butter or margarine
½ cup brown sugar
1 beaten egg
150 ml milk
4 tablespoons treacle or golden syrup
2 level tablespoons extra butter or margarine
1/3 cup extra brown sugar
8 halves small, cooked or preserved pears
Crystallized ginger
Lemon peel

Sift flour, bicarbonate of soda, ginger and spice. Rub in shortening with the tips of the fingers. Add ½ cup brown sugar. Mix beaten egg, milk, and golden syrup and pour into flour, mixing in lightly and quickly. Grease a lamington tin (approximately 20 cm x 30 cm) or two 18 cm sandwich tins. Cream the extra butter and brown sugar and spread it over the bottom and sides of the tin. Arrange pear halves hollow side down with crystallized ginger, lemon peel in hollow and pour in batter mixture. Bake in a moderately hot oven about 25 to 30 minutes. Turn out and serve hot with custard or lemon sauce.

PLUM PUDDING

This recipe will make two medium sized plum puddings, each making 6 servings. Good keeping quality.

1½ cups sultanas
4 cups seeded raisins
1 cup currants
2/3 cup mixed peel
2 cups plain flour
⅛ teaspoon salt
1 level teaspoon mixed spice
1 level teaspoon ground nutmeg
1¼ cups soft butter
4 cups soft white breadcrumbs
1 cup white sugar
6 eggs
6 tablespoons brandy, sherry or orange juice
300 ml milk

Prepare two medium-sized basins of about 15 cm diameter. Grease well. Cut two thicknesses of greased paper to fit the top of each basin. Flour the pudding cloths. Have string ready to tie the pudding cloths down. Chop the sultanas, raisins and peel into uniform pieces. Sift the flour, salt, spice and nutmeg together and rub in the butter. Then add the fruit, breadcrumbs and sugar. Beat the eggs and add the brandy, sherry or orange juice, and milk. Gradually add this liquid to the dry ingredients, making a soft mixture. Put the mixture into the greased pudding basins. Cover each basin with the double thickness of greased paper and tie the pudding cloth over the top. Place each pudding basin in a saucepan of boiling water. The water should reach halfway up the sides of the basins. Cover tightly with the saucepan lid and boil steadily for 6 hours. As the water boils away, replace it with more *boiling* water. The day each pudding is to be served, boil it for a further 2 hours. Serve with cream, custard or Hard Sauce.

Hard Sauce:

½ cup butter
1 cup sifted icing sugar
1-2 tablespoons brandy

Cream butter and icing sugar till light and fluffy. Gradually beat in brandy. Pipe in 4 cm rosettes on to a tray lined with greaseproof paper. Chill well. Place rosettes on to hot pudding when serving.

FROZEN CHRISTMAS PUDDING

2 teaspoons gelatine
¼ cup cold water
¾ cup sugar
1 cup water
3 eggs
2 tablespoons brandy or orange juice
1 cup sultanas
1 cup seeded raisins
¼ cup currants
½ cup chopped cherries
¼ cup chopped mixed peel
½ cup chopped almonds (optional)
1 cup soft white breadcrumbs
1 cup cream
1 cup seeded raisins
Whipped cream and cherries
   for decoration

Soak gelatine in the ¼ cup cold water and then dissolve over boiling water. Place sugar and the other cup of water in saucepan and stir until the sugar has dissolved, forming a syrup. Bring to boil and boil for 5 minutes. Separate whites from yolks of eggs and beat yolks until creamy. Add the syrup and continue beating. Return mixture to heat and cook until it coats back of spoon. Remove from heat and stir in dissolved gelatine. Allow to become almost cold. Whip egg whites until stiff and fold in, together with the brandy or orange juice. Stir in the sultanas, raisins, currants, chopped fruits, nuts and breadcrumbs. Whip cream until stiff and fold in mixture. Line enamel basin with aluminium foil, then pour in the pudding mixture. The foil will make the pudding easy to remove when set. Place pudding in the refrigerator (it does not need to go in the freezer section) and chill for at least 12 hours. Unmould it into a serving dish and trim with whirls of whipped cream and some cut cherries.

This pudding is excellent for hot Christmas days.

RICH CHRISTMAS PUDDING

2 cups seeded raisins
1½ cups sultanas
1 cup currants
¼ cup candied lemon peel
1 level teaspoon grated orange rind
½ cup brandy or rum
1¼ cups plain flour
1 level teaspoon salt
1 level teaspoon cinnamon
1 level teaspoon ground cloves
1 level teaspoon ground nutmeg
2 cups finely minced beef suet
¾ cup breadcrumbs
1 cup brown sugar
60 g grated unsweetened chocolate
½ cup chopped almonds
½ cup finely chopped crystallized ginger
1 grated apple
5 eggs
½ level teaspoon bicarbonate of soda
¼ cup milk

Prepare fruits, peel and rind and place in a large screw-top jar; pour brandy or rum over, screw lid tight and allow to steep for a week. Sift flour, salt and spices thoroughly into a large bowl. Add minced suet, breadcrumbs, brown sugar, chocolate, almonds, ginger and apple. Stir well. Add prepared fruit and any remaining liquid from the jar. Mix well. Add beaten eggs and mix well. Dissolve bicarbonate of soda in milk and mix in slowly and thoroughly. Two-thirds fill a greased bowl, cover with buttered greaseproof paper, tie securely and steam for 5 to 6 hours. This may be cooked in two smaller bowls for 3½ to 4 hours, or in individual moulds for 45 minutes to 1 hour. Re-steam on the day the pudding is to be eaten — 2 hours for a large one, and 1 hour for a small one.

To flame pudding have ½ cup warmed brandy ready. Turn pudding on to heated serving plate, pour brandy around, ignite. Serve with Hard Sauce (p. 119).

If a boiled pudding is desired, have 45 cm square of well boiled unbleached sheeting prepared. Dip centre into boiling water, place over large bowl, sprinkle well with plain flour. Spoon pudding into prepared cloth, gather up all material leaving room for expansion. Tie very tightly. Have sufficient boiling water to cover pudding in large boiler. Immerse pudding. Boil 5-6 hours. Remove immediately from boiling water and hang to dry. On day of serving place in rapidly boiling water and cook 1 hour. Remove from water, drain a few minutes, remove string, turn on to serving plate, and flame and serve.

FROSTINGS, ICINGS AND FILLINGS

FROSTING

3 egg whites
1 cup castor sugar
Juice of 1 lemon

Beat egg whites stiffly. Add sugar, 1 tablespoon at a time, and beat well. Add lemon juice and beat for 5 minutes after all the sugar is added. Spread portion of mixture over cake with a knife. Place remainder into a bag and ornament the top, using a plain forcing pipe. Place in a slow oven to set and dry.

SEVEN MINUTE FROSTING

2 egg whites
1½ cups sugar
Pinch salt
1/3 cup water
2 teaspoons liquid glucose
1 teaspoon vanilla

Beat all ingredients except vanilla together in a bowl. Place over boiling water and beat until mixture thickens — about 7 minutes. Remove from water, add vanilla. Beat until spreading consistency. This mixture will frost the top and sides of a 24 cm layered cake.

Marshmallow Add 16 chopped marshmallows before spreading.

Chocolate: Add one 90 g block of dark semi-sweet chocolate, melted, before spreading.

VIENNA ICING

4 tablespoons icing sugar
2 tablespoons butter
2 teaspoons sherry
Chocolate or vanilla flavouring

Sift icing sugar. Cream the butter, add icing sugar gradually and beat until white and fluffy. Add sherry gradually. Add chocolate or vanilla flavouring.

CARAMEL ICING

1 cup brown sugar
2 tablespoons milk
1 tablespoon butter

Mix well together in a heavy saucepan and boil 6 minutes. Cool. Beat well until thick, pour on to centre of cake, allow to spread evenly to edges. Decorate with nuts while still soft.

FRUIT SYRUP GLAZE FOR FLAN

2½ teaspoons gelatine
½ cup fruit juice
¼ cup sugar

Dissolve gelatine in a little of the fruit juice. Boil the remaining juice and sugar, pour on to gelatine and stir till dissolved. Do not boil.

Note: Melted red currant jelly forms the best glaze for fruit tart.

CHOCOLATE WHIPPED CREAM FROSTING

¾ cup sifted icing sugar
2 tablespoons cocoa
1 teaspoon vanilla
300 ml cream
1 teaspoon rum or sherry (optional)

Sift sugar and cocoa together, mix in a bowl with vanilla and cream. Do not beat. Leave in refrigerator 2 to 3 hours. When ready to use beat vigorously until thick enough to fill and cover cake.

RICH CHOCOLATE FILLING AND TOPPING

125 g semi-sweet dark chocolate
½ cup butter
½ cup castor sugar
2 egg yolks
1 teaspoon vanilla
Cherries, nuts or chocolate shapes for decoration

Melt chocolate over hot water, cool to room temperature. Cream butter until very light, gradually add sugar and beat until quite fluffy and sugar completely dissolved. Add egg yolks one at a time; beat until smooth and creamy. Beat in vanilla and cooled melted chocolate. Spread over cake. Pipe decoration on smooth surface, finish with whole cherries, nuts or chocolate shapes.

FONDANT ICING

2¼ cups pure icing sugar
2 tablespoons liquid glucose
1 small unbeaten egg white
2 teaspoons glycerine
Few drops lemon juice
Few drops white vanilla essence or
    other flavouring

Roll and sift icing sugar into a basin. Melt glucose over hot water. Make a well in centre of icing sugar, add egg white, glucose, glycerine, lemon juice and flavouring. Begin the mixing with a wooden spoon; when mixture stiffens use one hand to work fondant into a firm consistency. Turn on to a surface dusted with icing sugar and knead well. If colouring the fondant, add a little at this stage and knead until colour is evenly distributed. Brush top of cake with a little unbeaten egg white. Roll fondant out evenly to size of cake and to about 13 mm thickness. Fold over a rolling pin and unroll on to cake. Work fondant on to cake with the hands, trim if necessary or pinch a frill around edge if desired. Decorate with pipe work, sugar flowers, motifs, etc.

This quantity is sufficient to cover the top only of a 20 cm square or round cake.

Note: This fondant is also used for moulding flowers and fruits. When moulded and allowed to dry it can be painted with vegetable colourings to imitate the natural colourings of flowers and fruit.

CHOCOLATE COATING FOR LAMINGTONS

3 cups sugar
1 cup water
1/3 cup cocoa
1 teaspoon vanilla

Put sugar, water and cocoa in a saucepan, bring slowly to boil, stirring occasionally. When boiling remove from heat, wash down saucepan sides with wet pastry brush. Return to heat but do not stir again. Boil gently for 12 minutes. Remove from heat. Add vanilla. Stir 1 minute. Cool slightly. Hold cake on large fork. Dip quickly into the chocolate mixture and toss in coconut.

LEMON CHEESE 1

125 g butter
4 eggs
2 cups sugar
3 large lemons

Use a double saucepan or a jug standing in a saucepan of water. Melt butter in saucepan. Add vitamized or well beaten eggs, sugar and grated rind and juice of lemons. Stir mixture over gently boiling water for 1 hour, or till it is as thick as honey. Pour into clean jars. When cold, seal and label.

LEMON CHEESE 2

½ tin condensed milk
¼ cup lemon juice
Rind of 1 lemon
1 egg

Beat all ingredients together. Allow to stand 30 minutes before use.

APRICOT NUT FILLING

125 g dried apricots, washed and soaked overnight
1 tablespoon orange juice
1 teaspoon lemon juice
2 tablespoons sugar
½ cup chopped walnuts

Drain apricots, cook with fruit juice and sugar until quite soft. Put through a sieve or blender to make a pulp. Stir in nuts.
  1 cup whipped cream and 1 tablespoon kirsch may be added to the mixture for special cakes.

HONEY CREAM

2 tablespoons butter (soft)
1 tablespoon honey
2 teaspoons warm water
1 teaspoon lemon juice

Beat butter and honey to a cream. Gradually beat in water and lemon juice.

WASHED BUTTER CREAM

4 tablespoons butter
4 tablespoons sugar
Cold water
1 teaspoon vanilla

Cream butter until very pale. Gradually beat in the sugar until well mixed. Cover with cold water, stir once, pour water off. Beat well. Repeat process of washing and beating until mixture has texture of whipped cream. Add vanilla. Do not refrigerate as butter will set hard.

This quantity fills two sponges.

Grated rind of orange or lemon, passionfruit pulp, finely chopped nuts, chopped preserved ginger and other flavourings may be substituted for the vanilla.

CONFECTIONERS' CUSTARD

2 tablespoons butter
3 tablespoons flour
1½ cups milk
2 egg yolks
2 tablespoons castor sugar
2 tablespoons cream
½ teaspoon vanilla

Melt butter, add flour, stir until smooth. Remove from heat, gradually add milk. Beat well. Return to heat, stir until boiling and very thick. Cook 2 minutes. Remove from heat. Add beaten egg yolks. Cook and stir without boiling 2 minutes. Remove from heat. Beat in sugar, cream and vanilla.

Use to fill choux pastry cases and sponges or as a base for fruit in rich flans.

CHOCOLATE DECORATIONS

Melt 200 g dark chocolate. Draw small rounds or leaf shapes on heavy waxed paper or foil. Fill outlines with a layer of chocolate. Chill well. Peel away paper backing. Will keep in freezer.

SWEETS

SWEET-MAKING

Utensils Required

The utensils necessary for making sweets are: a sugar boiling thermometer; a spatula or wooden spoon; a medium-sized enamel saucepan, free of chips or cracks; a dipping fork; and a sheet of brightly-polished tin, a marble slab or heavy waxed paper.

Use and Care of the Thermometer

A sugar boiling thermometer registers up to 230°C. A thermometer ensures success and saves the time and labour usually spent in continually testing the syrup. The thermometer should be handled carefully and washed, dried and put away in a box after use. A cold thermometer should not be placed in boiling syrup; keep a jug of hot water ready to dip the thermometer in before and after use.

Degrees for sugar boiling are as follows:

Soft ball, 113° - 115°C
Hard ball, 122° - 128°C
Small crack, 143°C (syrup clear)
Hard crack, 149° - 157°C (syrup golden brown)

Cold Water Testing

If no thermometer is available the following test will help to determine when the syrup is ready. Put some cold water into a cup and drop a little syrup into it. If the syrup dissolves it is not ready and the water should be replenished and further tests made till the result is a soft ball, a hard ball, or a definite crack is heard.

Rules for Success

- Use good quality ingredients.
- Avoid stirring syrup after it comes to the boil.
- Keep the sides of the saucepan free from grains while boiling, by brushing with a wet brush or placing the lid on for a minute or two.
- Allow the bubbles to subside before pouring the syrup into a basin or slab previously rinsed with cold water.
- Allow the mixture to become quite cool before commencing to beat it.

Chocolate Dipping

Chocolate dipping must be done in a dry, cool place, and only the best quality chocolate should be used. Care should be taken that no steam or cold air is brought into contact with the chocolates during the dipping process. If centres are sweet, use unsweetened chocolate with a small proportion of sweetened added to it for dipping; for nut or semi-sweet centres have sweet chocolate plus smaller amount of unsweetened chocolate. Do not overheat the chocolate when dissolving it. Milk chocolate is an excellent coating.

Fondant

Fondant forms the foundation of the following creams, and it may be coloured and flavoured according to taste:

Ribbon creams: Colour and flavour small pieces of fondant, roll out and then place one on top of another. Press and cut into shapes.

Walnut creams: Colour, flavour and shape fondant in small rounds, and press a walnut on either side.

Almond creams: Prepare in the same manner as walnut creams.

Prune creams: Remove the stone, then fill prune with coloured and flavoured fondant.

Date, raisin and cherry creams: These may be prepared in the same manner as prune creams.

CANDIED ORANGE, LEMON OR GRAPEFRUIT PEEL

Peel of 6 oranges, lemons or grapefruit
Water
1 level tablespoon salt
2 cups crystal sugar
Fine dry castor sugar

Remove peel and cut into strips 3 mm wide. Cover with cold water and add salt. Boil until tender (about 20 minutes). Strain. Bring crystal sugar and 1 cup water to the boil, add strips of peel, then cook slowly until syrup is absorbed. Roll strips in castor sugar, spread out on trays, and dry in a cool oven (about 53°C) for 30 to 45 minutes, longer if necessary; or dry in the sun. *Do not* overdry. Roll strips in sugar again after drying.

These candied peels may be served as a confection.

AUSTRALIA ROCK

2 cups sugar
¾ cup liquid glucose
½ cup water
2 egg whites
1 cup blanched almonds

Stir sugar, glucose and water over low heat until sugar dissolves. Boil to 128°C, or until a little of the mixture dropped in cold water forms a hard ball when rolled between finger and thumb. Cool slightly and beat until thickening. Combine well with stiffly beaten egg whites and almonds.

Press into buttered bar tin. Cut into shapes. Wrap in waxed paper.

CARAMELS

125 g butter
250 g brown sugar
2 tablespoons golden syrup
1 tin condensed milk

Melt butter, then mix in other ingredients in a heavy saucepan. Stir over low heat while boiling until 120°C is reached or until a deep caramel colour, and mixture leaves sides of saucepan. Pour into well-greased tray. Mark into sections before completely cold. Cut and wrap in waxed paper.

FUDGE

1 cup brown sugar
2 tablespoons milk
1 tablespoon butter
½ teaspoon cream of tartar or 1 tablespoon glucose

Place all ingredients in a heavy saucepan, stir over heat until sugar is dissolved and mixture boils. Boil to 115°C. Allow to cool. Beat until a stiff pouring consistency. Spread onto a greased tray. When almost set mark into squares. Cut sharply.
   Chocolate Fudge: Add ½ cup cocoa to the sugar.
   Fruit and Nut Fudge: Add 2 tablespoons chopped nuts and fruit or 1 tablespoon of each before beating.

DIVINITY FUDGE

2 cups sugar
½ cup water
1 tablespoon glucose
1 cup chopped walnuts or almonds
4 egg whites

Stir sugar, water and glucose over heat in a heavy saucepan until quite clear. Chop nuts and grease tray. Beat egg whites stiffly while syrup boils to 128°C — about 10 minutes. Test. If it cracks in cold water, remove from heat. Pour slowly on to egg white, beating all the time. Add nuts. Pour on to tray and mark into shapes. When cold, cut and wrap in waxed paper.

BUTTERSCOTCH

2 cups sugar
1 cup vinegar
½ cup butter

Stir all ingredients over heat in a heavy saucepan until sugar dissolves and mixture boils. Boil until 149°C or until a little dropped into cold water separates into hard brittle threads, making a clear cracking sound. Pour on to tray and mark into shapes. When cold, cut and wrap in waxed paper.

HONEYCOMB TOFFEE

4 tablespoons golden syrup
4 tablespoons sugar
2 teaspoons bicarbonate of soda

Place syrup and sugar in a large heavy saucepan over low heat and stir to dissolve the sugar. Boil (not rapidly) for 10 minutes. Remove from heat and immediately stir in bicarbonate of soda, from which all lumps have been removed. While mixture is still bubbling, pour on to well-greased tray. Mark while warm and break when cold.

GLACE FRUIT AND NUTS

2 cups sugar
1 cup water
¼ teaspoon cream of tartar

Fruit, e.g., orange or mandarin segments, large grapes, cherries, strawberries, brazil nuts, almonds, halved walnuts

Place sugar and water in heavy saucepan, cook and stir to dissolve sugar. Add cream of tartar. Boil without stirring until temperature of 143°C is reached or to the small crack stage. Remove from heat and stand saucepan in dish of boiling water to prevent hardening. Dip each piece of fruit or nut one at a time into the hot syrup. Make sure that it is completely covered. Then lay on buttered trays. Leave in a cool place to harden. Put into fancy paper cases.

These are delicious served with coffee.

FRUIT ROLL

250 g fondant
8 dessert dates
2 slices glace pineapple
2 tablespoons chopped raisins
2 tablespoons chopped cherries
2 tablespoons finely chopped walnuts
1 teaspoon brandy
Coloured sugar
Colouring and lemon flavour

Make up or buy white fondant. Chop or mince fruit and nuts, add 1 teaspoon brandy and 1 tablespoon of the fondant. Mix well. Divide mixture and mould into rolls about 20 cm long and 2 cm in diameter. Chill. Colour and flavour the fondant. Roll out thinly on a dry board. Brush with egg white. Cut strips 20 cm x 8 cm, place fruit in position, roll over like a sausage roll. Firm the outer coating on to the filling. Brush all over with egg white and roll firmly on to coloured sugar. Cut into 2 cm pieces. Place cut side up in waxed sweet containers.

Coloured Sugar: Place 2 tablespoons sugar into a small glass container, add 1 or 2 drops of food colouring, mix well with a spoon until all the sugar is coloured as desired.

JAMS AND PICKLES

MELON AND LEMON JAM

3 kg melon
3 kg sugar
600 ml water
6 large lemons

Peel, seed and dice or mince melon. Weigh it and place in a
large bowl, sprinkle with half the sugar. Stand overnight.
Grate lemon rind and squeeze lemons. Boil left-over lemon
rinds in water for 20 minutes in covered saucepan or pressure
cooker. Strain, add to the melon and boil until tender. Add
lemon juice and grated rind with remainder of sugar. Boil until
a little sets on a cold saucer. Bottle in hot, sterile jars. Cover
and label.

GRAPE AND APPLE JAM

1 kg cooking apples (green skin)
3 kg dark grapes
1 cup iced water
4 kg sugar

Peel and core apples, cut into thin slices. Wash grapes and
crush lightly in large saucepan with apple, cook covered until
apple is clear. Add 1 cup iced water. Remove as many seeds
as will come to surface, using large spoon or skimmer. Add

heated sugar, stir briskly to dissolve. Boil uncovered until a little sets on a cold saucer. Remove from heat. Stir well for 3 minutes and remove more seeds. Pour into hot sterile jars. Cover and label.

RASPBERRY JAM

3 kg freshly picked, ripe raspberries
3 kg sugar

Place raspberries and sugar into large saucepan. Using a wooden spoon stir well for 5 minutes. Place over heat and bring to boil. Cook 10 minutes. Remove from heat. Pour into medium-sized, hot, sterile jars. Cover and label.

FIG JAM

3 kg figs, freshly picked, ripe, firm and dry
1 teaspoon salt
3 kg sugar
4 tablespoons lemon juice
Rinds and seeds of 2 lemons, tied in muslin

Check figs. Cut off the thick stem end. Cut up figs, place in preserving pan, add salt and one-third of the sugar, with lemon juice and rinds and seeds in muslin. Bring to boil, cook 30 minutes. Remove lemon rinds and seeds. Add remainder of sugar. Boil quickly, uncovered, until a little sets on a cold saucer. Bottle quickly in hot, sterile jars. Cover and label.

QUINCE JAM (PRESSURE-COOKED)

4 large, firm quinces
½ small lemon
4 cups cold water
Sugar
½ cup chopped preserved ginger (optional)

Wash, peel and dice or mince quinces. Measure diced quinces in cups. Place peel, cores and half a small lemon in the pressure cooker with 4 cups of cold water. Bring up to cooking pressure on large hot plate with high heat. Switch to "off" as soon as cooking pressure is reached. Cook 3 minutes. Cool under cold water.

Strain, discard peel and cores. Put liquid and diced quinces into cooker. Cover, bring up to pressure on high. Turn off. Cool quickly. Remove lid, add warmed sugar. Allow 1 cup to each cup of the diced quinces. Add ginger. Stir well, boil rapidly. Boil until a little sets on a cold saucer. Bottle in hot, sterile jars. Seal and label.

PEACH CONSERVE

3 kg ripe peaches
2 kg sugar
5 cups water

Peel and stone peaches and cut into large pieces. Make a syrup by boiling sugar and water 10 minutes. Add prepared fruit and cook until the mixture sets. Pour into hot, sterile jars. Seal and label.

TOMATO AND PINEAPPLE JAM

3 kg tomatoes
¼ cup salt
1 large pineapple
2 kg sugar
1 teaspoon tartaric acid or juice of 3 lemons

Remove skin from tomatoes by immersing them in boiling water for 2 minutes and then into cold water. Cut into large pieces, sprinkle with salt and allow to stand overnight.

Pour liquid off tomatoes, peel and chop. Chop pineapple finely, and add. Boil mixture gently until pineapple is quite tender. Add heated sugar and boil quickly 30 minutes. Add tartaric acid or lemon juice and boil for 5 minutes. A little of the mixture should now set on a cold saucer. Bottle in hot, sterile jars. Seal and label.

ROSELLA JAM

500 g rosellas
Water
Juice and grated rind of 1 lemon
Sugar

Separate bulbs and red leaves. Take bulbs, cover them with water, add lemon juice and rind and boil for 1 hour. Strain through a muslin bag. To the juice add the rosella leaves and boil for 20 minutes. Measure and add equal quantities of warm sugar. Boil rapidly, stirring now and then, for 20 minutes, or until a little sets on a cold saucer. Bottle in hot, sterile jars. Cover and label.

FRUIT MINCE

500 g tart apples
500 g beef suet
500 g raisins
500 g sultanas or currants
½ cup red and green glace cherries
125 g glace apricots
½ cup citron peel
½ cup lemon peel
½ cup orange peel
125 g almonds
1½ cups sugar
⅛ teaspoon salt
¼ teaspoon ground cloves
¼ teaspoon grated nutmeg
¼ teaspoon ground ginger
1 teaspoon cinnamon
¼ teaspoon ground mace
2 lemons
½ cup rum
½ cup brandy

Peel, core and chop apples. Mince suet finely. Chop or mince fruits and citron, lemon and orange peel. Blanch and chop almonds. Mix all fruit, almonds and suet together. Add sugar, salt, spices, grated rind and juice of lemons, rum and brandy. Mix thoroughly. Pot and seal as for jam.

PICKLED ONIONS

Small onions
Malt vinegar
1 tablespoon allspice
1 teaspoon salt
1 tablespoon peppercorns

} to every 2 cups vinegar

Peel onions, wash, and pack into jars. Pour vinegar over onions until jar is filled. Add allspice and salt. Put equal number of peppercorns in each jar. Cover tightly, allow to stand for 3 weeks, inverting jars twice during this period.

CUCUMBER RELISH

2 green cucumbers
2 medium onions
2 large green apples
300 ml malt vinegar
¾ cup sugar
2 teaspoons salt
¼ teaspoon cayenne pepper

Peel cucumber (if desired), mince and drain. Peel onions and mince. Peel apple and mince. Cook apple with vinegar, sugar, salt and pepper until soft. Cool. Combine the drained cucumber, onion and cooled apple and vinegar. Bottle, dividing any remaining liquid equally between jars. Seal well. Allow to stand for at least one week before eating.

PICKLED RED CABBAGE

1 red cabbage
Salt
Vinegar

Wash cabbage leaves and remove thick stalk. Dry and shred very finely. Sprinkle with salt and allow to stand overnight. Drain very well, pack into straight-sided jars, fill with vinegar and shake to release air bubbles. Seal well. Allow to stand for 3 days.

Note: This does not keep for long periods, so make up only one cabbage at a time.

SPICED VINEGAR

1 litre vinegar
Small stick cinnamon
½ teaspoon allspice
½ teaspoon mace
8 peppercorns
1 tablespoon sugar

Tie spices loosely in muslin and put with vinegar into saucepan. Cover, heat slowly to boiling point. Simmer 5-6 minutes. Remove from heat. Cool while still covered. Remove spices.

BEVERAGES

LEMON SYRUP

1/3 cup citric acid
2 teaspoons lemon essence
1 kg sugar
5 cups water

Mix citric acid and sugar together. Pour on boiling water. Allow to cool, add lemon essence then bottle.

MOCK OYSTER COCKTAIL

1 egg
Dark pepper
Salt
Tomato sauce
Worcestershire sauce
Vinegar
Lemon juice
Red pepper

Put whole egg into a shaker with a dash of each of the other ingredients. Shake well. Pour into a medium sized goblet and serve.

PEP COCKTAIL

1 egg yolk
1 teaspoon honey

Juice of 1 orange
Juice of 1 lemon

Mix well together.

FIFTY FIFTY

2 kg sugar
2 litres water
1 tablespoon tartaric acid
1 tablespoon citric acid
1 packet Epsom Salts
6 oranges
4 lemons

Boil water and sugar 5 minutes and allow to cool. Place dry ingredients in a mixing bowl, add grated rind and juices of oranges and lemons and cooled syrup. Stir well. Bottle and cork.

GRAPEFRUIT SHERBET

4 cups water
1 cup sugar
2 cups grapefruit juice
1 cup orange juice

Make syrup by boiling water and sugar together 10 minutes. Allow to cool. Add strained fruit juices and freeze. Stir before ice becomes solid, then spoon into individual containers.

TOMATO SOUP DRINK

1 440 g can condensed tomato soup
¾ cup milk (evaporated)
¼ cup cream
1 egg
½ teaspoon ground nutmeg
Dash of tabasco sauce

Combine all ingredients. Use blender or shaker, mix until very smooth; add more milk if too thick. Serve in chilled glasses sprinkled with nutmeg, with fresh crisp shallot as stirrer and potato crisps for accompaniment.

SUMMER PUNCH

1/3 cup castor sugar
2 or 3 tablespoons water
A few mint leaves
1½ lemons
370 ml bottle ginger ale
Crushed ice

Put castor sugar and water into a saucepan and heat till sugar is dissolved. Leave to cool. Pick over mint leaves, wash thoroughly and drain. Put mint into a jug with juice of lemons and syrup. Add ginger ale and ice just before serving.

EGG ORANGEADE

1 egg
250 ml orange juice
Squeeze lemon juice
Sugar to taste
Ice (optional)
Soda water

Beat egg very thoroughly. Add orange juice, lemon juice, sugar and some ice if desired. Pour into a tumbler. Fill up with soda water. Serve very cold.

CLARET CUP

1 bottle claret
2 tablespoons sugar
Juice of 1 lemon
Rind of ¼ lemon
1 slice cucumber
1 liqueur glass of curacao or brandy

1 cup crushed ice
2 x 370 ml bottles soda water

Pour wine over sugar and allow to stand about 1 hour. Just before serving add all other ingredients, soda water last.

HOCK CUP

1 bottle hock
1 liqueur glass brandy
½ cup diced canned pineapple
3 x 370 ml bottles soda water
1 cup crushed ice
1 slice cucumber

Pour hock and brandy over diced pineapple. Allow to stand 6 hours. Add all other ingredients just before serving.

HOT CHOCOLATE

½ cup unsweetened chocolate
1 tablespoon sugar
2 tablespoons hot water
2 cups scalded milk
Vanilla
Whipped cream

Break chocolate into pieces. Add sugar and hot water. Heat until melted and smooth. Add scalded milk. Cook in double boiler 5 minutes. Add vanilla and top with whipped cream.

CIDER CUP

1 lemon
1 tablespoon castor sugar
10 slices cucumber
2 tablespoons sherry
1 bottle cider
1 370 ml bottle soda water
Chipped ice

Put juice of lemon and castor sugar into jug with sliced cucumber. Add sherry and cider and stir together. Allow liquid to stand for 1 hour in a cool place or on ice. Strain liquid, add soda water and some chipped ice.

TOMATO COCKTAIL

1 glass tomato juice
2 teaspoons lemon juice
1 teaspoon Worcestershire sauce
Pinch salt

Mix all ingredients together. Place on ice and leave till very cold. Serve in cocktail glasses, decorated with lemon twist and mint.

RECIPES FROM OTHER LANDS

Albania

SWEET SESAME BISCUITS (Ismir Simit)

2 eggs
1/3 cup sugar
2 tablespoons milk
1/3 cup melted butter
1½ cups sifted flour
¾ teaspoon baking powder
¼ cup sesame seeds or
   ¼ cup ground blanched almonds

Preheat oven to 175ºC. Beat 1 egg in a bowl. Add the sugar and beat until light. Add the milk and melted butter and mix well. Sift flour and baking powder together. Gradually add to the egg mixture, kneading until a dough is formed. If the dough is too soft, add a little more flour. Divide into about 18 small balls. Roll each ball between the hands into a 25 cm strip. Fold each strip in thirds. Pinch the ends together. Place biscuits on a buttered baking sheet. Beat the remaining egg and brush some on each biscuit. Sprinkle with the sesame seeds or almonds. Bake for 20 minutes or until delicately browned.

Bahamas

PEAS AND RICE, BAHAMAS STYLE

2 cups canned dried peas
3 tablespoons salad oil
1 onion, chopped
3 tomatoes, chopped
3 cups boiling water
2 teaspoons salt
¾ teaspoon pepper
1 cup rice, washed and drained

Drain peas and force through a strainer. Heat the oil in a saucepan and add the onion. Saute for 10 minutes, stirring frequently. Add the tomatoes and cook over low heat for 5 minutes. Add water, pea puree, salt and pepper. Bring to a boil. Add rice and mix together lightly. Cover and cook for 25 minutes, or until rice is tender. Watch the liquid carefully, adding small additional quantities of boiling water if necessary to prevent burning.

Bermuda

BAKED BERMUDA ONIONS

4 large sweet Bermuda or white onions
3 slices buttered toast
1 cup grated cheese
3 eggs
1 cup milk
½ teaspoon salt
3 tablespoons butter

Peel onions and place in a saucepan. Cover with water and bring to a boil. Cook for 5 minutes. Drain well and cool for 10 minutes. Cut onions into 1 cm slices. Cut toast in half diagonally, so as to form triangles. Place buttered side of toast face down in a large, deep pie plate or casserole. Arrange onion slices over the toast. Sprinkle grated cheese on top. In a separate bowl beat the eggs well and add milk and salt. Again beat well, then pour mixture over onions. Dot with butter. Bake in a moderate oven for 30 minutes, or until the egg mixture is firm.

Bolivia

PEPPER PORK (Aji de Carne)

½ cup olive oil
5 onions, chopped
3 cloves garlic, minced
3 tablespoons rice
1½ kg pork or beef, cut into 2 cm cubes
4 tomatoes, chopped
¼ teaspoon saffron
2 teaspoons salt
½ teaspoon pepper
¼ teaspoon dried ground chilies
1 clove
¼ teaspoon cinnamon
2 cups stock or 1 can consomme and ½ can water
6 potatoes, peeled and quartered
2 green bananas, peeled and quartered
½ cup ground peanuts
½ cup heavy cream
1 tablespoon molasses

Heat olive oil in a large saucepan. Add onions and garlic and saute for 5 minutes, stirring frequently. Add rice and meat and cook over high heat until meat is brown. Add tomatoes, saffron, salt, pepper, chilies, clove, cinnamon and stock. Cover and cook over low heat for 30 minutes. Add potatoes and bananas and cook 15 minutes longer. Add peanuts, cream and molasses. Cook for 15 minutes, or until the meat and potatoes are tender. Correct seasoning. Serve hot.

Brazil

BRAZIL NUT CAKE (Torta de Castanha-do-para)

10 eggs, separated
1¾ cups castor sugar
3 cups ground Brazil nuts
⅛ teaspoon salt
2 tablespoons brandy
2 tablespoons breadcrumbs
2 teaspoons instant coffee in
   2 tablespoons boiling water
1½ cups heavy cream
3 tablespoons icing sugar
Brazil nuts, sliced or chopped, for decoration (optional)

Beat egg yolks in a bowl. Gradually add castor sugar, beating until thick. Add nuts, salt, brandy and breadcrumbs, mixing well. Preheat oven to 175°C. Beat the egg whites until stiff but not dry and fold into the nut mixture. Butter a 25 cm springform pan and dust lightly with breadcrumbs. Pour the batter into it. Bake in a 175°C oven for 45 minutes or until a cake tester comes out clean. Leave cake in the oven with the heat off and door open for 5 minutes after baking is finished. Cool for 2 hours. Mix coffee and water, chill. Whip cream and add coffee and icing sugar, mixing lightly. Remove cake from pan and split. Spread some cream between the cake halves and place the rest on top. Chill. Some sliced or chopped Brazil nuts may be sprinkled on top if desired.

Burma

GINGER BEEF (Ahme Hnat Hin)

5 onions, chopped finely
4 cloves garlic, minced
2 teaspoons turmeric
2 fresh chilies, chopped or
   ½ teaspoon dried ground chilies

2 cm piece fresh ginger, chopped or
  2 teaspoons powdered ginger
2 teaspoons salt
1½ kg beef cut into 4 cm cubes
½ cup sesame oil or peanut oil
8 tomatoes, chopped
2 cups stock or 1 can consomme and ½ cup water

Combine onions, garlic, turmeric, chilies, ginger and salt. Chop or pound together until very fine. Place beef in a bowl and add the spice mixture. Coat meat as thoroughly as possible. Leave in bowl for 3 hours, turning frequently. Heat oil in a deep saucepan until it fumes. Add beef and spices and brown well. Add tomatoes and cook over medium heat for 10 minutes. Add stock. Cover and cook over low heat for 1 hour or until meat is tender. Serve with parsley rice.

Canada

PORK PIE (Tourtiere)

Pastry:
3 cups sifted flour
1 teaspoon salt
¾ cup shortening (butter or lard)
1 egg, beaten
4 tablespoons cold milk

Filling:
1½ kg pork or 750 g pork and
  750 g veal
3 slices bacon
2 onions
1 clove garlic, minced
½ cup boiling water
1½ teaspoons salt
½ teaspoon pepper
Pinch sage
3 tablespoons chopped parsley
1 tablespoon gelatine   } if pies are to be
1 cup meat stock   served cold

Sift flour and salt together. Cut in shortening with a pastry blender or two knives until the consistency of coarse breadcrumbs. Combine beaten egg and milk and add to flour mixture. Toss lightly with a fork until a ball of dough is formed. Wrap in wax paper and chill for at least 1 hour. If possible, use both pork and veal, as the combination of meats gives the dish a better flavour. Grind meat, bacon and onions. Add garlic and mix. Place in a heavy ungreased saucepan, and cook over medium heat for 5 minutes, stirring constantly. Add water, salt, pepper, sage and parsley. Cover and cook for 20 minutes. This mixture should not be allowed to become too dry, and small quantities of boiling water should be added if required. Cool for 15 minutes.

Remove dough from the refrigerator and divide into four pieces, two of which should be slightly larger than the others. Preheat oven to 232°C. Roll out the four pieces of dough on a lightly floured surface. Line two 20 cm pie plates with the larger pieces of dough. Fill with meat mixture. Cover each pie with the smaller pieces of dough. Make a few slits across the top of each pie. Glaze with egg-milk mixture. Bake in a 230°C oven for 10 minutes. Reduce heat to 175°C and bake for 25 minutes, or until well browned. If pies are to be served cold have ready 1 tablespoon gelatine dissolved in 1 cup meat stock. As pies cool pour liquid through steam hole, a teaspoonful at a time.

Central America

COSTA RICAN TAMALE (Tamale Ticos)

1 kg pork, cubed
2 cups water
2 tablespoons butter
4 onions, chopped
5 cloves garlic, minced
1 cup rice

1½ cups boiling water
2 cups canned tomatoes
2 green peppers, diced
4 teaspoons salt
2 teaspoons pepper
3 boiled potatoes, peeled
4 rashers fried bacon
2 cups corn kernels, drained
1 cup canned chick-peas, drained
1 cup canned small green peas, drained
¼ cup seedless raisins
3 pimentos, sliced thin

Combine pork and water in a saucepan. Cook over medium heat for 1 hour. Melt 1 tablespoon of the butter in a saucepan. Add 2 of the onions and half of the garlic and saute for 10 minutes, stirring frequently. Add rice and cook over low heat for 5 minutes, stirring constantly. Add boiling water, tomatoes, green peppers, 2 teaspoons of the salt, 1 teaspoon of the pepper and the remaining butter. Cover and cook over low heat for 45 minutes. Drain pork and reserve the stock. Grind pork, potatoes, bacon, and corn. Add remaining onions, garlic, salt, and pepper. Add reserved stock and mix well. Place in a saucepan and cook over low heat for 10 minutes, stirring almost constantly. Add chick-peas, green peas and raisins to the rice mixture and mix carefully. In a large buttered casserole or baking dish arrange successive layers of the pork mixture, followed by the rice mixture, until they are all used up. Arrange pimentos on top. Cover the casserole. If the cover is not tight-fitting, cover with a piece of aluminum foil and then put the casserole cover on top. If a baking dish is used, tie a piece of aluminum foil over the top to make a tight seal. Place in a pan of hot water and bake in a 175°C oven for 45 minutes. Serve hot.

Note: In Costa Rica tamales are made individually in plantain or banana leaves. If desired, wrap small quantities of the two mixtures in aluminum foil. Boil in salted water for about 30 minutes.

China

LOBSTER BALLS (Loong Har Kow)

250 g can lobster meat
1 tablespoon pork dripping
1 teaspoon cornflour
¼ teaspoon pepper
Pinch salt
¼ teaspoon monosodium glutamate
1 teaspoon sherry
1 egg
4 slices white bread (crusts removed)
Oil for frying
Garnish:
2-3 slices tomato
1 slice pineapple
1 glace cherry
Parsley

Mash lobster with dripping to a paste. Add cornflour, pepper, salt, monosodium glutamate and sherry and bind all together with the beaten egg. Shape into 12 balls. Crumble bread into a shallow bowl. Roll the lobster balls in the bread and deep fry for about 5 minutes. Drain and serve garnished with tomato, pineapple butterflies, glace cherry and parsley.

Note: Lobster balls are very good as an hors-d'oeuvre or at cocktail parties.

FRAGRANT DUCK (Nghong Auck)

1½ cups dark brown sugar
3 teaspoons cinnamon
2 cloves
1 cup water
1 tablespoon salt
1 large duck, washed and dried
2 teaspoons soy sauce
2 teaspoons powdered ginger

Optional sauce:
½ cup vinegar
3 cloves garlic, minced

Place sugar in a saucepan and cook over low heat until it melts. Add half the cinnamon, the cloves and water. Cook until syrupy. Combine salt and remaining cinnamon and rub into duck thoroughly, inside and out. Place duck on a roasting pan. Combine syrup with soy sauce and ginger and mix well. Pour over duck. Roast in a 220°C oven until golden in colour, basting frequently. Reduce the heat to 175°C and roast until tender, about 2½ hours altogether, including browning time. Add additional water if pan becomes dry, and baste frequently. Cut the duck into small pieces and serve.

The Chinese serve the duck with a sauce made by mixing ½ cup of vinegar and 3 cloves of minced garlic. The pieces of duck meat are dipped into this sauce.

STUFFED POCKETS OF DOUGH (Won Ton)

Dough:

2 cups sifted flour
1½ teaspoons salt
2 eggs
1/3 cup water

Filling:

1½ cups cooked beef, pork or chicken, chopped
2 teaspoons soy sauce
¼ teaspoon pepper
2 shallots, chopped finely
6 cups salted boiling water

Soup:

6 cups chicken stock or 2 cans chicken consomme and 2½
    cans water
1 cup cooked beef, pork or chicken, sliced
½ bunch green spinach, shredded

Sift flour and salt together twice. Beat eggs and combine them with water. Add to flour and mix until well blended. Place on a lightly floured board and knead until smooth. Set aside while preparing filling. Mix chopped meat, soy sauce, pepper and shallots until well blended. Roll out dough as thinly as possible. Cut into 6 cm squares. Place a heaped teaspoonful of meat mixture in the centre of each square and fold over diagonally. Press the edges together, using a little water. Bring the salted water to boiling point and drop the won ton into it. Boil for 12 minutes. Drain. Heat the stock and add the sliced meat and the spinach. Cook for only 2 minutes. Place three won ton in each soup plate and pour the soup over.

Note: A combination of beef, pork and chicken may be used, if desired.

CHICKEN WITH GREEN PEPPER (Gong Bo Gai Deng)

2 cups raw chicken meat, diced
White of 1 small egg
1 teaspoon cornflour
Pinch salt
Pinch pepper
Little monosodium glutamate
Peanut oil for frying
3 tablespoons unsalted roasted peanuts
2 tablespoons bamboo shoots, diced
3 tablespoons water chestnuts
1 green pepper, diced
1 clove garlic, crushed
1 spring onion, chopped
1 piece fresh ginger
2 chilies
1½ tablespoons soy sauce
1 teaspoon sherry
½ teaspoon sugar

Mix chicken meat with egg white, cornflour, salt, pepper and a pinch of the monosodium glutamate. Put to one side. Heat oil in a pan and fry the peanuts over medium heat, without burning. Remove to a plate. Add the bamboo shoots, water chestnuts and green pepper to the oil left in the pan and cook for 1 minute. Remove to a plate. Wipe out the pan, heat another 4 tablespoons peanut oil, add the crushed garlic, chopped onion, ginger, chilies and chicken meat mixture and fry all together until the chicken is cooked. Add bamboo shoots, water chestnuts and green pepper and mix well. Add soy sauce, sherry, sugar and a pinch of monosodium glutamate. Cook for 1 minute, then stir in fried peanuts and serve hot with boiled rice.

Ecuador

SWEET FRITTERS (Bunuelos)

2 tablespoons butter
½ cup sugar
2 tablespoons grated lemon rind
1 cup water
8 tablespoons sifted flour
3 eggs
Fat for deep frying

Sauce:

1 cup dark brown sugar
3 tablespoons flour
1 cup water
2 tablespoons heavy cream
1 tablespoon butter
½ teaspoon vanilla

Combine butter, sugar, lemon rind and water in a saucepan. Bring to a boil, stirring occasionally. Add flour all at once, beating hard. Cook until the dough leaves the sides of the pan. Remove from heat. Add eggs one at a time, beating hard after each addition, and until the dough is smooth and shiny. Heat the fat to 190°C in a very deep saucepan. Drop the batter by the teaspoon into the fat. Fry until light brown, approximately

5 minutes. Cook only 3 or 4 at a time as fritters puff up. Drain.

To make the sauce, combine sugar and flour in a saucepan. Add water, stirring to a smooth paste. Cook over medium heat until mixture boils and becomes thick, stirring all the time. Add cream, butter and vanilla, mixing well. Pour over the fritters and serve either hot or cold.

Fiji

MOCK TURTLE SOUP (Baigan Soup)

2 large eggplants
5 cups milk
3 cups stock or 1 can consomme and 1 can water
2 tablespoons flour
1 tablespoon anchovy paste
2 tablespoons butter
½ teaspoon salt
¼ teaspoon pepper
3 tablespoons chopped parsley

Peel eggplants and cut into 2 cm cubes. Place in a saucepan with milk and stock and bring to a boil. Cook over low heat for 45 minutes, or until eggplant is very soft. Mix flour and water to a smooth paste and add it to eggplant mixture, stirring constantly. Cook for 5 minutes, stirring frequently. Remove eggplant from the saucepan, force it through a sieve, then return it to the saucepan. Add the anchovy paste, butter, salt and pepper. Correct seasoning. Heat again but do not allow to boil. Serve with chopped parsley.

France

POULET AU PORTO

1.4 kg or No. 14 chicken
3 tablespoons butter or substitute

2 tablespoons flour
1 2/3 cups white port wine
300 ml cream
Salt, pepper
220 g can champignons

Cut chicken into serving-sized pieces. Heat butter in pan, add chicken pieces, cook gently until light golden brown; remove from pan. Add flour to pan, stir until flour is light golden brown, remove pan from heat. Add port wine, stir until combined, return to heat, stir until sauce boils and thickens. Reduce heat, simmer gently, uncovered, 10 minutes. Return chicken to pan, simmer gently, covered, 45 minutes or until chicken is tender; remove chicken. Gradually add cream, stirring constantly. Season with salt and pepper. Return chicken to sauce with drained champignons. Simmer gently, uncovered, 5 minutes.

Note: If white port is not available, chablis may be substituted.

CREVETTES PAULETTE

1 tablespoon butter or substitute
500 g green prawns
½ cup tomato juice
2 teaspoons tomato paste
2 tablespoons dry white wine
Pinch saffron
Salt, pepper
Chopped parsley

Heat butter in frying pan, add shelled prawns, fry gently 2 minutes. Add tomato juice and paste, blended, wine, saffron, salt and pepper. Simmer, uncovered, 5 minutes. Serve very hot sprinkled with finely chopped parsley.

GREEN SALAD (Salade Verte)

1 cup olive oil
¼ cup wine or tarragon vinegar
1 teaspoon salt
¼ teaspoon black pepper
1 clove garlic, crushed
1 head romaine lettuce (long leaf)
2 endive (curly leaf)
1 head escarole (broad flat leaf)

Combine olive oil, vinegar, salt, pepper, and garlic in a bowl. Beat vigorously with a rotary beater, or place liquid in a bottle and shake vigorously. Chill. Wash, drain, and chill lettuce, endive and escarole. Tear, do not cut, lettuce into 5 cm pieces. Cut endive into 1 cm pieces. Tear escarole into small pieces. Combine greens in a salad bowl. Add the dressing just before serving and toss lightly.

Note: Any combination of green vegetables may be used with this simple, classic dressing.

APPLE CHARLOTTE (Pommes de Charlotte)

4 large cooking apples, peeled and thinly sliced
½ cup water
4 tablespoons sugar
¼ teaspoon cinnamon
1 tablespoon sherry (optional)
Thinly sliced stale bread (leave crusts on)
2 tablespoons butter or margarine (approx.)
Extra 2 teaspoons sugar
Extra ¼ teaspoon cinnamon

Cook apples with water over low heat until very soft, keeping lid on saucepan. Add sugar, cinnamon and sherry and stir over low heat until apples are quite clear. Taste and stir in more sugar if necessary. Remove from stove and beat apples with a wooden spoon until very soft and pulpy. Set aside. Cut bread into strips 3 cm wide and estimate how many you will require to line and cover the dish to be used. This dessert may be cooked in a round pyrex pie plate or an oblong piedish and the amount of bread must be adjusted to the size of the dish. (It is estimated that the apples will fill a round pie plate, 20 cm in diameter.) The strips should overlap or fit closely and there should be enough to cover the apples when they have been added. Melt the butter and dip each piece of bread into it, then press all over the bottom and sides of the dish, melting more butter if required. Fill the bread case with the prepared apple and cover with more strips of bread dipped in melted butter. Sprinkle with the extra cinnamon and sugar. Cook in a moderate oven until bread is crisp and golden brown. This should take about 30 minutes for a shallow dish or 40 minutes for a deeper dish. Serve warm with cream or custard.

Note: It is correct to serve this dessert turned out onto a warmed plate and sprinkled with more cinnamon and sugar, but this step may be omitted.

CREME BRULEE A L'ORANGE

1½ cans evaporated milk
1 tablespoon sugar
2 teaspoons cornflour
4 eggs
2 teaspoons grated orange rind
Brown sugar

Blend milk, sugar and cornflour. Cook over direct heat until *just* boiling, stirring all the time. Remove from heat and stir 1 minute to prevent skin forming. Beat eggs until white and yolk are very well blended. Add 1 tablespoon hot milk mixture and stir through. Stir egg mixture gradually into milk mixture which is still in the saucepan. Stand over simmering (not boiling) water and cook until the custard coats a silver spoon, stirring all the time. Remove from heat at once. Very gently fold in the grated orange rind. Pour into ovenware dish and chill thoroughly (preferably overnight). About 1 hour before serving, sprinkle brown sugar through a fine strainer over the entire surface of the custard 10 mm thick so that no custard is visible. Place under a preheated griller until sugar melts and caramelizes. (This takes a very short time so it must be watched carefully to prevent burning.) Return at once to the refrigerator and chill again before serving.

Note: The original recipe is made with 600 ml cream and 8 egg yolks so this is a very simple version. It is served alone in France but, if desired, it could be spooned over chopped orange segments.

CRYSTALLIZED FLOWERS

¼ cup rose-water
3 teaspoons powdered gum arabic } obtainable from chemists
1 teaspoon sugar
Castor sugar
Flowers

Place rose-water, gum arabic and sugar in a small basin. Stand this in a saucepan containing hot water and heat the water very gently until the gum arabic dissolves, stirring occasionally. Remove from the stove but leave the basin in the hot water to prevent the gum arabic setting again. Using a clean, new, fine paintbrush, coat petals and calyx of flowers thinly with the solution, taking care that every part of the flower is covered. It is best to hold the flower with a pair of tweezers while doing this as fingers are sometimes clumsy. Dip the flower into castor sugar, making sure all parts are covered on both sides. Shake off loose sugar, but be sure no portion of the flower is left bare. Place on greaseproof paper on a cake cooler and leave to dry, away from steam, for three or four days. Store in an airtight container in the refrigerator.

Note: Many flowers are poisonous so it is advisable to use crystallized flowers for decoration only. Violets are safe to eat, but do not touch anything else. Flowers keep almost indefinitely by this process and look very attractive on party foods. The sugar and the gum arabic seal the pores of the flowers and prevent decay and the rose-water gives a delicate odour. (Rose-water has a very pleasant flavour and may be used in icings.)

Germany

LEMON SOUFFLE (Zitronenauflauf)

3 tablespoons butter
1 cup flour
Pinch salt
2 cups milk
4 eggs, separated
½ cup castor sugar
Grated rind 1 lemon
½ cup lemon juice
2-3 large green apples, peeled and cored
1 tablespoon extra sugar

Melt butter over low heat in saucepan, blend in flour and salt; gradually stir in milk. Cook over low heat until smooth and thick. Beat egg yolks and sugar well, stir into flour mixture. Stir in grated rind and lemon juice. Fold in stiffly beaten egg whites. Cut apples into paper thin slices. Arrange slices on base and sides of large well-greased souffle dish; sprinkle with extra sugar. Carefully pour batter over apples. Bake in moderate oven 45 minutes. Serve with wine sauce.

Sauce:

1 cup sugar
1¼ cups white wine
1 orange
½ lemon
1 tablespoon arrowroot

Place in saucepan, sugar, 1 cup of the wine, grated rind and juice of orange and lemon, bring to the boil while stirring. Blend arrowroot and remaining ¼ cup wine, combine with boiling syrup. Stir until boiling and quite clear.

PEACH CAKE (Pfirsich Kuchen)

1 cup self-raising flour
2 tablespoons butter or margarine
1 tablespoon sugar
Pinch salt
6 or 8 canned peach halves
¼ cup sugar
¼ teaspoon cinnamon
1 egg
½ cup milk
Reserved peach syrup
Pink colouring

Rub butter into flour, sugar and salt to make fine crumbs. Press this dry mixture into a greased round ovenware dish 20 cm diameter. Fill with drained peach halves, round side up. Sprinkle with sugar and cinnamon. Cook on centre shelf in a moderate oven 15 minutes. Remove. Beat egg and milk until well blended. Spoon gently over peach halves in pastry case. Return to oven and cook 30 minutes. Heat reserved syrup and colour pink. Serve pudding hot or warm with syrup as a sauce.

Note: Sliced peaches may be used for this dish if halves are unobtainable.

BAVARIAN STRUDEL

Filling:
½ cup blanched almonds
1½ cups canned pie apple
½ cup sugar
¼ cup sultanas
1 tablespoon cinnamon
750 g puff pastry
Egg glazing
Icing sugar

Toast almonds and chop roughly. Mix almonds with apples, sugar, sultanas and cinnamon to make filling. Roll out pastry to 35 cm square. Place filling across one end, wet pastry edges, roll up loosely. Seal ends firmly. Place on oven slide. Glaze with egg and make a few diagonal slashes across top. Bake in hot oven approximately 20 minutes until golden. Sprinkle with sifted icing sugar. Cut into diagonal pieces to serve.

VIENNESE PASTRIES

1 cup butter
¼ cup castor sugar
½ teaspoon vanilla
2 cups plain flour
Pinch salt
Melted chocolate

Syrup:

1 cup sugar
2 tablespoons lemon juice
1 teaspoon grated lemon rind
¼ cup finely chopped mixed peel

Cream together butter and sugar until light, fluffy and creamy. This is most important. Add vanilla, carefully fold in sieved flour and salt. Put into piping bag with large star pipe. Pipe into plain or fancy finger lengths on lightly greased oven slide. Bake in moderately hot oven approximately 15 to 20 minutes. Pastries can be left plain or dipped into melted chocolate at one end and syrup at the other.

To make syrup, place sugar, juice and rind into saucepan. Stir over low heat until sugar is dissolved. Boil until it becomes honey coloured or hard ball forms in cold water. Add mixed peel. Keep syrup warm while dipping.

MEATBALLS IN CAPER SAUCE (Klopse)

4 tablespoons butter
3 onions, chopped
6 slices white bread
1 cup light cream
750 g beef, ground
250 g veal, ground
250 g pork, ground
4 anchovy fillets
3 eggs
2 teaspoons salt
1 teaspoon pepper
½ cup iced water
3 cups boiling water
¼ teaspoon marjoram
3 sprigs parsley
3 stalks celery
2 tablespoons flour
2 tablespoons lemon juice
¼ cup capers, drained

Melt 2 tablespoons of the butter in a pan and add the onions. Saute for 10 minutes stirring occasionally. Soak bread in cream for 10 minutes. Press the excess liquid from it. Grind the bread with the sauteed onions, ground beef, veal, pork and anchovies in a food chopper. Add the eggs, 1 teaspoon of the salt, ½ teaspoon of the pepper, and the iced water. Mix together and shape into 5 cm balls. Combine in a deep saucepan the boiling water, remaining salt and pepper, marjoram, parsley and celery. Drop the meatballs into it and boil for 20 minutes. Melt the remaining butter in a saucepan. Add the flour and mix to smooth paste. Strain the liquid in which the meatballs were cooked, and add, stirring constantly until boiling point is reached. Cook over low heat for 5 minutes. Add lemon juice and capers and stir well. Place meatballs on a platter and pour the sauce over them.

ALMOND CRISPBREAD

1 cup whole shelled almonds
2 egg whites
½ cup sugar
¾ cup plain flour, sifted

Note: There is no raising agent

Wash and dry the almonds but do not remove the brown skins. Prepare a 25 cm x 8 cm bar pan (no larger) by lining with greased paper. Beat egg whites on high speed until soft peaks form, then beat in ½ cup sugar gradually until all sugar is dissolved and meringue holds stiff peaks. Gently fold in sifted flour, then almonds. Spread in prepared pan. Cook on centre shelf in a slow oven (150°C) for 30 minutes (mixture will not brown). Turn out, remove paper and cool. Wrap in a teatowel and store in a cupboard (not the refrigerator) for one week. Cut in very thin slices with a long-bladed, very sharp knife. Cook on ungreased slides in a slow oven (150°C) 40 to 45 minutes or until brown and very crisp.

Greece

EGG AND LEMON SOUP (Avgolemono Soup)

2½ l rich chicken stock
Salt, pepper
¾ cup long grain rice
3 egg yolks
¼ cup lemon juice
½ cup water

Bring chicken stock to boil in large saucepan, season with salt and pepper. Add rice, simmer uncovered 15 minutes or until rice is tender. Remove pan from heat. Put egg yolks into bowl, gradually beat in lemon juice and water, then gradually beat in 1 cup of the hot stock. Return egg mixture to chicken stock, beat well. Return pan to heat, stir over moderate heat until soup is hot; do not allow to boil or mixture will curdle.

Note: The rice can also be cooked separately. Put 1 or 2 tablespoons of cooked rice into each soup bowl and spoon hot soup over.

MEATBALLS IN THE OVEN (Soutzoukakia Sto Fourno)

2 thick slices bread
750 g minced steak
2 cloves garlic, crushed
1 teaspoon finely chopped parsley
1 egg
Salt and pepper
2 tablespoons butter or substitute
2 tablespoons dry white wine
425 g can tomato puree

Put bread into a bowl, cover with water, stand 5 minutes. Drain off water and squeeze excess water from bread. Combine meat, bread, crushed garlic, parsley, egg, salt and pepper; mix well. Form tablespoonfuls of mixture into oval shapes. Heat butter in large frying pan, add meatballs, fry gently for 3 minutes on each side. Remove from pan, put in ovenproof dish. Drain off fat from pan. Add wine and tomato puree to pan, stir until sauce boils. Add salt and pepper. Pour sauce over meatballs. Bake uncovered in moderate oven 25 to 30 minutes.

MOUSSAKA

4 aubergines (eggplant), sliced, unpeeled
7 tablespoons olive oil
10 small onions, finely diced
Butter
500 g minced beef or lamb
Salt and pepper
1 bay leaf
1½ cups meat stock

Tomato sauce (makes 3½ cups):

1 kg large, ripe tomatoes, peeled and chopped
4 lumps sugar
1 clove garlic, chopped
1 medium onion, chopped
2 tablespoons minced beef
½ teaspoon chopped basil or fennel
Salt and pepper

Topping:

1 egg
6 tablespoons cream or milk
Salt and pepper
Parsley

Sprinkle aubergine slices with salt and allow to stand for 15 minutes. Drain. Fry in 6 tablespoons olive oil for 3-4 minutes until soft. Fry onions in butter. Take medium roasting pan and pour in 1 tablespoon oil. Arrange a layer of fried aubergines, then a layer of mince, sprinkle with salt and pepper and the one bay leaf, then a layer of fried onions. Fill the dish with these layers. Pour over meat stock and 3½ cups of tomato sauce, made by putting all ingredients into a pan and simmering for 30 minutes, then sieving. Cover the dish and cook in a slow to moderate oven 45 minutes or until the liquid has been reduced considerably. For topping, beat egg, milk or cream with salt and pepper and pour over meat layers. Cook approximately 30 minutes in a very slow oven to form a custard on top of the dish. Garnish with parsley.

FILO PASTRY

3 cups plain flour
½ teaspoon baking powder
½ teaspoon salt
¾ cup iced water (approx.)

Sift dry ingredients into bowl, mix to stiff dough with the water. Knead on lightly floured board until smooth. Place in warm bowl, cover with damp cloth. Leave in warm place 30 minutes. Divide dough into eight pieces. Remove one piece at a time for working, and roll out on floured board as thinly as possible. Work quickly while rolling. Place on lightly floured surface when rolled, cover with damp cloth. Repeat with remaining pastry. Keep sheets separate, do not stack on top of each other.

Note: Filo is easier to handle if kept moist. Lay filo sheet on table, brush or sprinkle with water. The pastry dries rapidly, so work with only one or two sheets at a time (keep remainder covered with towel). Have filling prepared, ready for use. Filo can also be purchased, ready for use, from Greek and other Continental shops.

BAKLAVA

8 sheets homemade filo pastry
2 cups finely chopped blanched almonds

Syrup:

2 cups sugar
2 cups water
Small piece cinnamon stick or 10 cardamom seeds
250 g unsalted butter, melted
Thin strip of lemon or orange rind
1 cup honey

Cut filo into 20 cm squares. Line base of greased 20 cm cake tin with one sheet of filo; brush with melted butter. Sprinkle with 2 tablespoons chopped almonds. Reserving two sheets of pastry for the top layer, repeat this process until filling and pastry are used. First and last sheets should be whole and strong; any broken sheets or trimmings can be placed in between. Brush top with melted butter. Score top sheets with a pointed knife in square or diamond shapes. Bake in moderate oven 50 minutes, then increase oven temperature to moderately hot for 10 minutes, or until pastry is golden brown. Allow to cool in tin.

Place sugar, water, fruit rind and cinnamon or cardamom seeds in saucepan, bring to boil and boil 15 minutes. Remove fruit rind after 5 minutes. Add honey, boil further 5 minutes. Remove cinnamon or seeds. Pour hot syrup over the baklava in tin, let stand until cool. Cut pieces through to absorb syrup. Allow baklava to stand in tin until most of syrup is absorbed, then turn out carefully. Cut into pieces, following the square or diamond cuts at top.

Note: Bought filo pastry is much thinner (like tissue-paper) than the homemade variety. You would need sixteen sheets of bought filo for the baklava. Use two sheets of bought filo to separate each filling layer, and three layers of bought filo to top the baklava.

BISCUITS (Finika)

1 cup olive oil
Juice of 2 oranges (½ cup)
½ level teaspoon grated orange rind
½ cup sugar
2 level teaspoons cinnamon
¼ level teaspoon ground cloves
3½ cups self-raising flour
Honey
Toasted sesame seeds

In a bowl combine oil, orange juice, orange rind, sugar and spices and mix to a soft dough with the flour. Roll into small balls, place on greased trays, flatten with a fork and bake in a moderate oven (190°C) for about 15 minutes. Loosen from trays, brush with honey and sprinkle with toasted sesame seeds.

Hawaii

MARINATED STEAKS ON SKEWERS (Tariyaki)

1 cup soy sauce
1/3 cup sake or sherry
1 teaspoon powdered ginger
4 tablespoons dark brown sugar
3 tablespoons grated onion
1 clove garlic
18 pieces (3 cm x 3 cm) sirloin steak, 2 cm thick
12 cubes canned pineapple
12 mushroom caps, sauteed
1 tablespoon cornflour
2 tablespoons water

Combine soy sauce, sake or sherry, ginger, brown sugar, onion, and garlic in a bowl. Mix well. Marinate steak in the sauce for 2 hours. Drain steak, strain the marinade and reserve. Cook steak in a very hot oven or grill for 2 minutes on each side. Alternate steak, pineapple and mushrooms on six skewers, starting and ending with steak. Set aside and keep hot. Mix cornflour and water to a smooth paste in a saucepan. Add marinade gradually. Cook over low heat, stirring constantly, until smooth and thick. Serve hot. Arrange skewers of hot meat on a dish of boiled brown rice garnished with small grilled tomatoes.

Holland

DUTCH APPLE CAKE

Pastry:
2 cups plain flour
6 tablespoons castor sugar
1 egg
5 tablespoons butter or substitute
Pinch salt

Filling:
1 tablespoon soft breadcrumbs
6 large cooking apples
¼ cup sugar
Few strips lemon rind
3 tablespoons water
3 tablespoons sultanas

Topping:
2 teaspoons cinnamon
2 tablespoons sugar

Sift dry ingredients into a bowl, rub in butter or substitute until resembling breadcrumbs. Add sufficient beaten egg to make a stiff dough; chill.

Peel and slice apples, place in saucepan with water, sugar and lemon rind. Cover and cook over low heat until apples are soft but not broken up; cool.

Roll out two-thirds of the chilled pastry, line base and side of 25 cm square tin, trim off excess and pinch a frill on top edge. Sprinkle base of pastry with breadcrumbs. Place cooled, cooked apples on top of breadcrumbs, sprinkle sultanas over top. Roll out remaining one-third of the pastry thinly in rectangular shape and using fluted pastry cutter cut into 1 cm wide strips. Place these crosswise over filling, brush with milk or remaining egg and sprinkle with mixture of sugar and cinnamon. Bake in moderate oven approximately 45 minutes. Serve hot or cold.

Hungary

DUMPLINGS (Nokedli)

3 cups sifted self-raising flour
1 teaspoon salt
2 eggs
¾ cup water
1 tablespoon melted butter
2 litres boiling lightly salted water
¼ cup melted butter

Sift flour and salt into bowl. Beat eggs in a separate bowl, add the ¾ cup water with the butter and mix into the flour to make a soft smooth mixture. Have the boiling salted water in a deep saucepan. Drop the batter from an oiled spoon into the water. The dumplings will float on the surface as they are done. Remove them immediately. Drain well, keep hot and pour the melted butter over the top. These dumplings may be served with other meat dishes in place of potatoes.

HUNGARIAN GOULASH (Gulyas)

6 tablespoons butter
5 onions, chopped
2 tablespoons paprika
2 teaspoons salt
½ teaspoon pepper
1½ kg beef (cross rib, chuck or blade bone)
1 can tomato puree
1 clove garlic, minced (optional)
½ cup sour cream

Melt 4 tablespoons of the butter in a heavy saucepan. Add onions and saute for 15 minutes, stirring frequently. Remove onions and set aside. Combine paprika, salt and pepper. Cut meat into 5 cm cubes and roll in mixture. Melt remaining butter in saucepan. Add meat and brown well on all sides. Return onions to saucepan. Add tomato puree and garlic and stir. Cover and cook over low heat for 3 hours, stirring occasionally. Add sour cream and stir. Heat but do not allow the mixture to boil. Serve hot with boiled nokedli (dumplings).

India

VEGETABLE RELISH (Sambal)

3 tablespoons butter
2 onions, chopped

2 cloves garlic, minced
¾ teaspoon dried ground chilies
½ teaspoon powdered ginger
1 teaspoon turmeric
¼ teaspoon ground cumin seed
2 cucumbers, thinly sliced
2 tomatoes, thinly sliced

Melt butter in a saucepan. Add onions, garlic, chilies, ginger, turmeric and cumin seed. Saute over low heat for 10 minutes, stirring frequently. Divide mixture in half and place in two bowls. Add cucumber to one bowl and tomatoes to the other. Mix gently. Allow to stand for 1 hour before serving. Serve at room temperature.

Note: Sambals are served with curries.

CHICKEN KORMA (Morgee Korma)

2 No. 17 chickens, jointed
1 cup buttermilk or yoghurt
4 cloves garlic, minced
4 tablespoons butter
2 onions, chopped fine
½ teaspoon powdered ginger
2 cloves
1½ teaspoons salt

Indian Korma Mixture:

2 teaspoons ground coriander
2 teaspoons ground almonds
¾ teaspoon ground turmeric
¾ teaspoon ground cumin seed
⅛ teaspoon dried ground chilies

Clean chicken pieces carefully and place in large bowl. Mix buttermilk or yoghurt with half the garlic and pour over chicken. Marinate at room temperature for 2 hours, basting frequently. Melt butter in a casserole or heavy saucepan. Add onions, remaining garlic, ginger, cloves and salt. Saute over low heat for 5 minutes, stirring frequently. Mix Indian korma ingredients in a bowl. Add to onion mixture and stir well. Cook for 5 minutes, stirring frequently. Add chicken and its marinade. Cover and cook over low heat for 1½ to 2 hours, or until chicken is tender, stirring occasionally. Serve with boiled rice.

Indonesia

JAVANESE CHICKEN LIVERS (Sambal Hati Hati)

1 cup fresh or dried grated coconut
1 cup milk
4 tablespoons butter
1 onion, chopped
3 cloves garlic, minced
2 chilies, sliced thin, or ½ teaspoon dried ground chilies
750 g chicken livers, coarsely chopped
¼ cup ground almonds
2 tablespoons grated lemon rind
2 tablespoons orange juice
1 tablespoon lemon juice ⎫
1 tablespoon plum jam ⎬ or 1 tablespoon tamarind
1 teaspoon sugar
1 teaspoon salt

Combine coconut and milk in a saucepan. Bring to the boil, remove from heat, and allow to soak for 15 minutes. Press all the liquid from the coconut and discard the pulp. Melt butter in a saucepan. Add onion, garlic and chilies. Saute for 5 minutes, stirring frequently. Add chicken livers and saute for 10 minutes, stirring occasionally. Add coconut milk, almonds, lemon rind, orange juice, lemon juice, plum jam, sugar and salt. Cook over low heat for 10 minutes, stirring occasionally. Serve hot with boiled rice.

Ireland

CHOCOLATE SANDWICH CAKE

½ cup butter
2/3 cup castor sugar
1/3 cup cooked mashed potato
57 g plain chocolate, melted, or 4 level tablespoons cocoa
2 eggs
1½ cups self-raising flour
½ teaspoon salt
4 tablespoons milk

Cream butter and sugar with mashed potato, then add melted chocolate or cocoa. Add beaten eggs alternately with flour and salt. Finally pour in milk, mixing well, to make a soft dropping consistency. Grease two 20 cm sandwish tins well and divide the mixture equally between them. Cook in a moderate oven (205°C) for 25-30 minutes. The top will be firm and springy to the touch when it is cooked. Let the cakes cool for a few minutes, then turn out on to a wire rack. The two sides are sandwiched together with whipped cream or chocolate icing.

Note: The mashed potato in this cake makes it hold the moisture and so prevents it becoming dry.

ROAST GOOSE

1 large goose (5 kg)
Goose giblets cooked in salt water

Stuffing:

750 g boiled potatoes or 4 cups soft white breadcrumbs and 500 g potato
1 medium onion, chopped
½ cup diced salt bacon
Salt and pepper
Liver of the goose
1 tablespoon chopped parsley
1 tablespoon chopped sage

Mix all ingredients well together, check seasoning, add more if necessary. Fill goose which has been washed and dried. Place in baking dish with 1 cup giblet stock. Cover the bird with foil and cook at 210°C for half an hour then reduce to 175°C. Cooking time 20 minutes for each 500 g. Baste and add more stock if dish is drying. Remove foil 15 minutes before removing from the oven. Serve with onion sauce, baked potatoes and pumpkin, green beans and boiled celery in cream sauce.

Onion Sauce:
2 onions, chopped
2 tablespoons chopped turnip
½ cup water
½ cup milk
Salt
Pepper
Nutmeg

Boil onions and turnip until soft, push through a sieve, flavour with salt, pepper and nutmeg. Blend to a smooth consistency with either butter or cream.

IRISH TREACLE BREAD

2 cups plain flour
4 teaspoons baking powder
½ teaspoon salt
½ teaspoon ground ginger
½ teaspoon mixed spice
2 tablespoons butter
6 tablespoons milk
2 tablespoons black treacle
3 tablespoons moist brown sugar
1 egg

Sift together flour, baking powder, salt and spices. Melt butter in milk, cool slightly and add treacle, brown sugar and beaten egg. Stir the liquid into the dry ingredients and mix well. Turn into a greased 20 x 8 x 10 cm loaf tin and cook at 179°C for about 1 hour. Turn on to a wire rack to cool. Serve sliced with butter.

Italy

SHRIMPS IN WINE SAUCE (Scampi nella Salsa di Vino)

1 kg green shrimps (or prawns), shelled and cleaned
½ cup flour
½ cup olive oil
½ cup dry white wine
2 teaspoons tomato paste
4 tablespoons warm water
1 teaspoon salt
½ teaspoon pepper
Dash cayenne pepper
1 tablespoon chopped parsley
2 shallots, chopped
2 teaspoons lemon juice

Wash and drain shrimps. Roll them in the flour. Heat the olive oil in a skillet. Add shrimps and brown on both sides. Drain oil but reserve it. Add wine to the shrimps and cook over low heat until wine is absorbed. Combine reserved olive oil, tomato paste, water, salt, pepper and cayenne pepper in a saucepan. Cook over low heat for 5 minutes. Pour this sauce over the shrimps, add parsley and shallots and cook for 5 minutes. Remove from the pan, add lemon juice and serve.

POTATO BALLS (Gnocchi)

8 large potatoes
2 egg yolks, beaten
2 tablespoons salt
1 cup sifted flour
Boiling water
1/3 cup grated parmesan cheese
¼ cup melted butter

Boil and mash potatoes. Add egg yolks and 2 teaspoons of salt, beating well. Add flour gradually, adding just enough so that a dough is formed: it may not be necessary to use all of the flour. Knead the dough until very smooth. Break off pieces and roll into balls about 3 cm diameter. Add the remaining salt to a large saucepan of boiling water. Drop the gnocchi into it, about ten at a time. When they come to the surface remove them immediately, drain and keep warm. Continue until all of the gnocchi have been cooked. Place the gnocchi in a serving dish and sprinkle with parmesan cheese and melted butter. If desired, serve with a little hot tomato sauce.

RAVIOLI

4 cups plain flour
Pinch salt
2 eggs
1 tablespoon olive oil
¾ cup water (approx.)
Egg glaze
Salted water

Filling:

250g roast beef or fried steak
1 roasted breast of chicken
90 g salami
2 rashers bacon
2 slices ham
½ cup chopped cheddar cheese
5 cloves garlic
½ cup parsley
½ teaspoon allspice
½ teaspoon salt
4 eggs
½ cup cooked spinach (optional)

Sauce:

2 tablespoons butter
1 tablespoon olive oil
4 cloves garlic
1 kg tomatoes
½ teaspoon allspice

½ teaspoon rosemary
½ teaspoon basil
Salt and pepper

Sift flour and salt into a bowl. Beat eggs lightly, add with olive oil to bowl. Stir gently, gradually adding water to make soft but firm dough. Do not make dough too wet or it will be difficult to handle. Knead lightly on floured board. Refrigerate 15 minutes.

To make filling remove bacon rind. Put all ingredients except eggs through mincer. Beat eggs well and add to mixture. Mix well. Put aside.

For sauce, put butter and oil into saucepan. Heat through, add chopped garlic, allow to turn golden. Add tomatoes, which have been skinned, seeded and chopped. Strain juice from seeds and add. Place tomatoes with herbs and seasoning into pan. Simmer gently, covered, 1 hour stirring occasionally.

Roll out half the dough paper-thin, mark in 10 cm strips. Place 1 teaspoonful of filling at 5 cm intervals along strips of pastry. Brush round the mounds of filling with egg glaze and lift a second sheet of pastry over filling. Seal edges. Press with back of teaspoon between mounds of filling, and then cut to separate ravioli. Place ravioli in large saucepan of boiling water to which has been added 1 tablespoon of salt. Cook approximately 15 minutes. Remove and drain. Serve covered with sauce and liberally sprinkled with grated parmesan cheese.

Jamaica

STUFFED LOBSTER

Lobsters, split (half per serve)
½ cup butter
2 onions, chopped
125 g mushrooms, chopped
1 tablespoon flour
½ cup stock or ½ teaspoon anchovy paste
  dissolved in ½ cup water
1 teaspoon salt
¼ teaspoon pepper
Dash of cayenne pepper
½ cup breadcrumbs
½ cup grated cheese

Remove meat from the lobsters and cut in small pieces. Reserve the shells. Set aside. Melt 3 tablespoons of the butter in a saucepan. Add onions and mushrooms and saute for 15 minutes. Add flour, stirring constantly. Add stock, continuing to stir until the mixture boils. Add lobster meat, salt, pepper and cayenne pepper. Cook for 15 minutes. Correct seasoning and mix gently. Place the lobster mixture in the shells. Sprinkle with the breadcrumbs and cheese. Dot with the remaining butter. Place on a baking sheet. Bake in a 175°C oven for 15 minutes, or until lightly browned on top. Serve with lime or lemon wedges.

Japan

BEEF AND SOY SAUCE (Sukiyaki)

4 tablespoons sesame oil or salad oil
1 kg sirloin steak, cut into strips, 1 cm x 5 cm
½ cup stock or ½ bouillon cube dissolved in ½ cup boiling
  water

¾ cup soy sauce
¼ cup sugar
1 tablespoon sherry
3 onions, sliced thin
1 cup sliced celery
1 cup sliced, canned bamboo shoots
250 g mushrooms, sliced thin
1 cup shredded spinach
4 shallots, chopped, using at least 5 cm of green top
500 g vermicelli, boiled and drained

Heat oil in large frying pan. Add meat and brown on all sides. Combine stock, soy sauce, sugar and sherry in a bowl. Add half of this mixture to the meat, reserving the balance. Push the meat to one side of the frying pan. Add onions and celery and cook over low heat for 3 minutes. Add remaining stock mixture, bamboo shoots, mushrooms and spinach. Cook over low heat for 3 minutes. Add shallots and cook for 1 minute. Place vermicelli on one side of a platter and sukiyaki on the other side and serve immediately.

Note: In Japan this dish is made at the table. This custom may be duplicated by preparing the sukiyaki in a chafing dish. It is very important to follow the specified cooking times, as the vegetables should be very crisp when they are served.

JAPANESE HONEY CAKE (Kasutera)

5 eggs
¾ cup sugar
¼ cup honey
½ cup sifted flour
2 tablespoons confectioners' sugar

Beat eggs, sugar and honey in a bowl until very thick. Add flour, beating well. Preheat oven to 175°C. Pour the batter into a greased oblong pan, about 23 cm x 30 cm. Bake in a 175°C oven for 15 minutes. Stir the cake mixture with a spoon. Continue baking a further 30 minutes. Allow the cake to cool in the pan. Dust with confectioners' sugar, cut into strips and serve.

Note: The baking instructions are unusual; in Japan the cake is stirred every 15 minutes. A modification has been made for convenience and appearance. This cake is not part of the ancient authentic cuisine, as it has been known in Japanese cooking for only four hundred years.

Korea

CASSEROLE FISH WITH VEGETABLES (Sang Suhn Jim)

6 fillets of white-meat fish
250 g beef, ground
2 tablespoons sugar
5 tablespoons soy sauce
3 shallots, chopped
2 cloves garlic, minced
3 tablespoons peanut or salad oil
½ cup sliced mushrooms
2 onions, sliced
1 carrot, peeled and sliced
2 stalks celery, sliced
¼ teaspoon dried ground chili
½ teaspoon powdered ginger
2 teaspoons salt
1 teaspoon pepper
2 cups water
1 fried egg

Wash fish and cut into 5 cm pieces. Drain well. Combine beef, sugar, 2 tablespoons of the soy sauce, shallots and garlic in a bowl. Mix well. Heat the oil in a casserole or heavy saucepan. Spread half the meat mixture on the bottom. Add half the fish. Combine mushrooms, onions, carrot, celery, chilies, ginger, salt and pepper. Spread half the mixture over the fish in the casserole. Repeat the layers in the same order. Add the water and remaining soy sauce. Cover and cook over low heat for 1 hour. Shred the fried egg and sprinkle on top before serving.

Mexico

PICKLED SHRIMPS

¾ cup olive oil
4 onions
3 cloves garlic, chopped
1 kg shrimps (or prawns), peeled and cleaned
½ cup vinegar
1½ teaspoons salt
¼ teaspoon dry mustard
½ teaspoon pepper
¼ teaspoon dried ground chilies or 2 pickled chilies, cut into
    strips

Heat ¼ cup of the oil in a saucepan. Chop 2 of the onions coarsely, add to oil with garlic and saute for 10 minutes, stirring frequently. Add shrimps and saute for 7 minutes, stirring occasionally. Remove from heat and let cool for 15 minutes. Slice remaining onions thinly, combine with remaining olive oil, vinegar, salt, mustard, pepper, and chilies in a bowl. Add the shrimps and baste. Marinate for 24 hours, basting several times. Serve cold as an appetizer.

STUFFED CHICKEN PANCAKES (Enchiladas de Pollo)

1 cup salad oil
6 tomatoes, peeled and chopped
1 onion, chopped
2 green peppers, chopped
1 teaspoon salt
½ teaspoon pepper
1 cup chopped cooked chicken
1 tablespoon chopped seedless raisins
3 tablespoons chopped green olives
12 tortillas, fresh or canned, or 12 pancakes
2 eggs, beaten
Onions, finely sliced, lettuce, radishes, avocado, sliced for
   garnish (optional)

Heat 3 tablespoons of the oil in a saucepan. Add tomatoes, onion, peppers, salt and pepper. Cook over low heat for 20 minutes, stirring occasionally. Combine chicken, raisins and olives in a bowl and mix well. Dip tortillas or pancakes in the beaten eggs. Place a tablespoon of the chicken mixture in the centre of each. Roll up and fasten with a toothpick. Place the balance of the salad oil in a saucepan and heat to 190°C. Fry the tortillas for 3 minutes. Drain. Place them on a plate and cover with the tomato mixture. This dish may be garnished with finely sliced onions, shredded lettuce, radishes and avocado slices.

Middle East

LAMB AND EGG SOUP (Dugun Chorbasi)

1½ kg lamb necks
1 onion
1 carrot, peeled
2 teaspoons salt
Dash of cayenne pepper

2¾ litres water
4 tablespoons butter
4 tablespoons flour
3 egg yolks
3 tablespoons lemon juice
1/3 cup melted butter
½ teaspoon paprika

Cut the meat away from the bones. Combine lamb, bones, onion, carrot, salt, cayenne pepper and water in a saucepan. Bring to boil; cover and cook over low heat for 3 hours. Strain the soup, reserving meat. Chop meat and return to soup. Melt butter in a separate saucepan. Add flour and mix to a smooth paste. Gradually add to the soup, stirring constantly until boiling point is reached. Cook over low heat for 15 minutes. Beat egg yolks and lemon juice in a bowl. Gradually add to the soup, stirring constantly. Do not allow soup to boil after the eggs are added. Add 1 teaspoon of butter to each portion and sprinkle with paprika.

Note: This is the traditional "wedding soup" of Turkey.

LIMA BEAN AND MEAT CASSEROLE (Chulent)

1 cup dried lima beans
3 tablespoons rendered chicken fat or salad oil
3 onions, chopped
4 potatoes, peeled and quartered
½ cup barley
1½ kg fresh pork spareribs
1 tablespoon salt
1 teaspoon pepper
1 teaspoon paprika
1 tablespoon flour

Wash lima beans thoroughly. Soak them in warm water to cover for 1 hour. Drain. Heat chicken fat in a heavy saucepan. Add the onions and saute for 10 minutes, stirring frequently. Add beans, potatoes and barley and stir. Place meat in the centre of the pot. Combine salt, pepper, paprika and flour and sprinkle on top. Add hot water up to 15 mm above the top of the ingredients. Cover and cook over very low heat for 5 hours. Check frequently to see that casserole does not burn, adding a little water if necessary.

TONGUE WITH OLIVES (Limba cu Masline)

1 ox tongue, fresh or pickled
3 tablespoons butter
2 onions, chopped
1 clove garlic, minced
2 tablespoons flour
½ cup tomato paste
½ cup white wine
2 tablespoons vinegar
½ teaspoon pepper
1 bay leaf
½ teaspoon powdered ginger
1 cup black olives

Place tongue in a deep saucepan with water to cover and boil for 3 hours or until tender. Drain, reserving 1½ cups of the stock. Remove the skin carefully and slice the tongue into 1 cm slices. Set aside. Melt the butter in a saucepan and add onions and garlic. Saute for 5 minutes, stirring frequently. Add flour and mix until smooth. Combine reserved stock, tomato paste, wine and vinegar. Add to the onion mixture gradually, stirring constantly until the boiling point is reached. Add pepper, bay leaf, ginger, olives and the slices of tongue. Cook over low heat for 15 minutes. Correct seasoning, add salt if necessary. Serve hot with tiny boiled potatoes.

OKRA STEW (Bamiyeh)

4 tablespoons butter
2 No. 15 chickens, jointed
2 cloves garlic, minced

½ teaspoon coriander
1 kg okra, stems removed
2 cups tomato juice
2 cups water
1 teaspoon salt
½ teaspoon pepper

Melt butter in a saucepan, reserving 2 tablespoons. Add chicken pieces and brown well on all sides. Add garlic and coriander and mix well. Cover and cook over low heat for 30 minutes. In a separate saucepan melt the remaining butter, add the okra, and fry for 5 minutes. Add to the chicken with the tomato juice, water, salt and pepper and stir. Cover and simmer over low heat for 45 minutes. Stir carefully so as not to break the okra. Correct seasoning. Serve hot, being careful to lift the okra out of the saucepan gently.

ISRAELI "HOT DOGS" (Falafel)

2 cups chick-peas
3 cloves garlic, minced
1½ teaspoons salt
¼ teaspoon dried ground chilies
1 egg, beaten
2 tablespoons water
½ cup flour
Fat for deep frying

Wash the chick-peas in several changes of water. Drain. Soak overnight in water to cover. Drain. Grind twice in a food mincer. Add the garlic, salt, chilies, egg and water and mix well. Use 1 tablespoon of the mixture to form a small croquette and continue until all of the mixture is used up. Dip them lightly in the flour. Heat the fat to 188°C in a deep saucepan. Fry the croquettes until brown on both sides, about 1 minute. Drain well and serve hot.

STUFFED FISH (Gefulte Fisch)

2½ kg jewfish, filleted
6 onions
4 teaspoons salt
2 teaspoons pepper
1 teaspoon sugar
¼ cup cracker or matzo meal

2 eggs, beaten
½ cup cold water
Head, skin and bones of the fish
6 cups boiling water
2 carrots, sliced

Grind the fish and 2 of the onions in a food mincer. Place in a wooden bowl, add 2 teaspoons of the salt, 1 teaspoon of the pepper, the sugar, cracker meal, eggs and cold water. Chop until fine in texture and well blended.

Place the fish head, skin and bones in a deep saucepan. Slice the remaining onions and add with the boiling water, remaining salt and pepper, and the carrots. Bring to an active boil. Shape the fish mixture into balls about 1 tablespoon between wet hands. Drop into the saucepan. Cover and cook over low heat 1½ hours. Stir gently occasionally. Correct seasoning. Remove the fish balls from the saucepan carefully. Strain the fish stock into a separate bowl. Serve very cold. If a well set gravy is desired, add 1 teaspoon of softened gelatine to the hot fish stock before chilling.

TURKISH FRUIT SALAD (Mevye Salata)

2 teaspoons powdered ginger
½ cup brandy
2 oranges, peeled and thinly sliced
1 cup fresh or canned pineapple, cubed
1 cup strawberries, halved

Dissolve the ginger in the brandy. Combine oranges, pineapple and strawberries in a bowl. Pour brandy over the fruits, basting them for a few moments. Cover the bowl and chill 3 hours. Arrange the salad on lettuce leaves and serve.

Note: Any combination of three fruits may be used with the ginger-brandy dressing for an unusual fruit salad.

Pakistan

LAMB AND FRUIT (Huzoor Pasand Fulao)

1 cup rice
½ cup butter
1½ kg boneless lamb, cut into 2 cm cubes
3 onions, thinly sliced
4 cups sour milk, buttermilk or yoghurt
2 cloves garlic, minced
1 teaspoon coriander
2 cm piece fresh ginger, chopped, or 2 teaspoons powdered ginger
½ teaspoon pepper
2 cloves
3 cardamom seeds
1 tablespoon salt
1 teaspoon saffron
2 tablespoons boiling water
½ cup sliced mixed nuts (almonds, pistachios, etc.)
2 oranges, peeled, segmented, and pitted
½ cup seedless grapes (remove seeds if grapes are not seedless)

Wash rice thoroughly in several changes of water. Soak in cold water for 15 minutes. Drain well. Melt butter in a saucepan. Add lamb and onions, brown well on all sides. Add milk or yoghurt, garlic, coriander, ginger, pepper, cloves, cardamom seeds and salt and stir well. Place rice over it. Dissolve saffron in boiling water and add to the saucepan, stirring well. Arrange sliced nuts, oranges and grapes on top. Cover and cook over medium heat 10 minutes. Reduce heat to low and cook 25 minutes, or until the lamb and rice are tender.

NUT CANDY (Halva)

1 cup butter
2 cups farina or semolina
2 cups confectioners' sugar
½ cup ground almonds
½ cup ground pistachio nuts
½ teaspoon ground cardamom seeds
4 tablespoons light cream

Melt the butter in a saucepan. Add the farina or semolina, stirring constantly with a wooden spoon until lightly browned. Remove from the heat. Add the sugar, almonds, pistachio nuts, and cardamom and mix well. Add the cream and cook over low heat, stirring constantly, until the mixture forms a ball and leaves the sides of the saucepan. Butter an oblong baking dish. Pour the mixture into it and spread evenly. Cut into desired shapes and allow to cool. When cool, cut out the shapes completely. This dessert will keep very well in the refrigerator for more than a week.

Paraguay

CHEESE BREAD (Chepa)

2/3 cup shortening
2 eggs
1½ cups grated American or Cheddar cheese
2¼ cups corn meal
¾ teaspoon salt
1/3 cup milk

Cream shortening. Add eggs, beating well. Add cheese and mix until smooth. Combine corn meal and salt. Add to the cheese mixture, alternately with the milk, mixing steadily. Knead together with the hands until well blended. Preheat oven to 190°C. Place the dough in a buttered 23 cm loaf pan. Cover the top with a piece of aluminium foil. Bake in a 190°C oven for 35 minutes or until firm. Cool and slice with sharp knife.

Peru

PERUVIAN CRULLERS (Picarones)

1 cake or package of yeast
½ cup lukewarm water
½ cup fresh or canned sweet potatoes, pureed
¼ teaspoon salt
1¾ cups sifted flour
¾ teaspoon mace
2 eggs, beaten
3 tablespoons brandy
Fat for deep frying
Icing sugar to dust

Combine yeast and water in a cup and allow to soften for 5 minutes. Mix until smooth. Place sweet potatoes in a bowl. Add yeast mixture, salt, flour and mace and mix well. Add eggs and brandy, beating well until smooth and creamy. Cover the bowl with a cloth and put in a warm place for 2 hours, or until double in bulk. Heat the fat to 190°C in a deep saucepan. Drop the batter into it by the teaspoonful. Fry for 5 minutes, or until browned on both sides. Sprinkle with icing sugar and serve with syrup or jelly.

Philippines

MIXED MEAT ROLL (Morcon)

250 g ham, ground
500 g pork, ground
4 tablespoons grated cheese (gruyere or American, Australian
   or New Zealand)
¼ cup chopped sweet pickles
¼ cup chopped black olives
3 teaspoons soy sauce
2 tablespoons lemon juice
4 teaspoons salt
2 teaspoons pepper
1 egg
1½ kg topside steak, cut 1 cm thick (in one piece if possible)
3 hard-boiled eggs, quartered
2 cups water
¼ cup vinegar
½ cup tomato sauce
1 onion, sliced
3 cloves garlic, minced
1 bay leaf
2 tablespoons flour

Combine ham, pork, cheese, pickles, olives, 1 teaspoon of the
soy sauce, lemon juice, 2 teaspoons of the salt, 1 teaspoon of
the pepper, and the egg. Mix well. Place the steak on a flat
surface and spread with the mixture. If several steaks are
used, divide the mixture evenly. Arrange the quartered eggs
on the mixture. Roll up the steak carefully and fasten in
several places with thread. Place the meat roll in a deep
saucepan. Add the water, vinegar, tomato sauce, onion, garlic,
bay leaf, remaining soy sauce, salt and pepper. Cover and
cook over medium heat for 1 hour, or until tender. Mix the
flour with an equal amount of cold water and add to the gravy,
stirring until smooth. Cook over low heat for 5 minutes.
Remove the meat roll carefully from the gravy and place on a
platter. Cut the threads and remove them. Slice the meat at an
angle and serve with the gravy.

FILIPINO CUSTARD (Leche Flan)

2 cups fresh or dried grated coconut
2 cups light cream
1 cup dark brown sugar
3 tablespoons water
4 eggs
2 egg yolks
1 cup white sugar
2 teaspoons grated lemon rind

Combine the coconut and cream in a saucepan. Bring to a boil, remove from the heat, and soak for 30 minutes. Press all the liquid from the coconut and discard the pulp.

Combine the brown sugar and water in a saucepan. Cook over medium heat until a thick syrup is formed. Spread three-fourths of the mixture on the bottom of a buttered mould, souffle dish, or cake tin. Mix the remaining syrup with the coconut cream. Cook over low heat, stirring constantly, until the syrup is dissolved. Beat the eggs and egg yolks in a bowl. Add the sugar and lemon rind, beating well. Gradually add the cream mixture, beating constantly. Pour into the mould. Place the mould in a pan of water. Cook over very low heat 1½ hours, or until the custard is firm. Do not allow the water in the pan to boil. Place the custard under the griller for 1 minute to brown the top. Serve hot or cold.

Poland

SAUERKRAUT WITH PORK (Kapusta z Wieprzowina)

2 tablespoons salad oil or butter
6 large shoulder or leg pork chops cut into pieces
2 onions, coarsely chopped
2 cloves garlic, minced
1 teaspoon salt
½ teaspoon pepper
1 bay leaf
1½ cups boiling water
2 cups sauerkraut
1 apple, peeled and chopped
2 tablespoons barley
1 teaspoon caraway seeds

Heat oil in a large saucepan and add pork. Cook over high heat, turning the meat frequently until it is brown on all sides. Add onions and garlic, and cook over medium heat until onions and garlic are browned. Add salt, pepper, bay leaf and water and cook for 30 minutes, stirring occasionally. Add sauerkraut and its liquid, apple, barley and caraway seeds, and mix well. Continue cooking for 1 hour or until meat is tender. Correct seasoning. Remove the bay leaf. Serve the pork and sauerkraut together.

CHICKEN CUTLETS (Cotletki Pojarski)

4 slices white bread
½ cup light cream
1 kg uncooked chicken meat, minced
1½ teaspoons salt
¼ teaspoon white pepper
500 g butter
½ cup breadcrumbs
250 g mushrooms, sliced
1 tablespoon flour

¼ cup stock or ½ bouillon cube dissolved in ¼ cup boiling
  water
1½ tablespoons lemon juice
3 egg yolks, beaten
Dash cayenne pepper

Soak bread in cream. Remove meat from the chickens
(uncooked) and grind in a food mincer as fine as possible. Add
1 teaspoon of the salt and the pepper. Melt 2 tablespoons of
the butter and add with the bread. Blend the mixture until very
smooth. Shape into six large or twelve small cutlets. Dip in the
beaten egg and then in breadcrumbs. Melt 4 tablespoons butter
in a pan and fry the cutlets in it over low heat, until brown on
both sides. Add more butter as necessary. Remove and keep
warm. Melt 2 tablespoons butter in the same pan. Add
mushrooms and saute for 5 minutes. Sprinkle flour on top,
stirring until smooth. Gradually add the stock, stirring until
the boiling point is reached. Cook over low heat for 5 minutes,
stirring frequently. Set aside. Divide remaining butter into
three pieces. Place one piece in the top of a double boiler, add
the lemon juice and egg yolks. Place over hot, *not* boiling,
water. Beat constantly with a wire whisk or wooden spoon.
When the first piece of butter melts, add the second. When
the mixture thickens, add the third piece, still beating
constantly. Continue cooking and beating for 2 minutes after
the last piece of butter melts. Remove from the heat. Add
remaining salt and the cayenne pepper. If the mixture curdles,
add 1 tablespoon heavy cream and beat vigorously. Add the
mushroom mixture. Serve the sauce on top of the cutlets.

Portugal and Spain

FRIED BREAD DESSERT (Rabanadas)

3 cups milk
1/3 cup honey
1/3 cup sugar
2 tablespoons grated lemon rind
½ cinnamon stick (optional)
⅛ teaspoon salt
12 slices French bread (15 mm thick) or 6 slices white bread
 cut in half
4 eggs, beaten
1 cup salad oil
¼ cup castor sugar
¼ cup cinnamon

Combine milk, honey, sugar, lemon rind, cinnamon stick and salt in a saucepan. Bring to a boil and cook over low heat for 1 hour. Remove from the heat. Dip bread slices in this mixture and then in beaten eggs. Heat half cup of the oil in a frying pan. Fry the bread in it until light brown on both sides. Add additional oil as required. Cool the fried bread for 30 minutes. Serve with castor sugar and cinnamon.

SWEETBREADS IN SHERRY (Mollejas de Ternera al Oloroso)

3 pairs or sets sweetbreads (brains may be used)
1½ teaspoons salt
1 tablespoon vinegar
2 cups water
4 tablespoons butter
3 onions, chopped
1 cup sweet sherry
6 shallots, chopped

Wash the sweetbreads. Combine in a saucepan with the salt, vinegar and water. Bring to a boil, cover, and cook over low heat for 10 minutes. Drain. Cover with cold water. Allow to cool for 30 minutes. Drain and remove the membranes. Dice coarsely. Melt the butter in a saucepan. Add the sweetbreads and saute for 5 minutes, stirring frequently. Add the onions and saute for 10 minutes, stirring frequently. Add the sherry. Cook over low heat for 5 minutes, then add the shallots. Cook over low heat 5 minutes longer. Correct seasoning. Serve with buttered green peas. If served as a main course, double the number of sweetbreads.

Puerto Rico

ALMOND PUDDING (Pudin de Almendras)

½ cup seedless raisins
½ cup white wine
2 eggs
1 cup sugar
1 cup milk
1 cup heavy cream
1 cup breadcrumbs
1 cup finely ground almonds
2 teaspoons cinnamon
1 teaspoon nutmeg
Whipped cream for garnish (optional)

Soak raisins in wine for 15 minutes. Drain. Beat eggs in a bowl. Add sugar, beating well. Add milk and cream and mix well. Add breadcrumbs, almonds, cinnamon, nutmeg and raisins and mix well. Preheat oven to 177°C. Butter six individual custard cups or other individual dishes. Pour the mixture into them. Place the dishes in a pan of water. Bake in a 177°C oven for 25 minutes, or until delicately browned on top and moderately firm. Serve hot or cold. Whipped cream may be served as accompaniment or garnish.

Russia

MEAT PASTRY (Piroshki)

1 cup flour
⅛ teaspoon salt
125 g butter
3 tablespoons sour cream

Filling:

4 tablespoons melted butter
4 chicken livers or 1 slice calf's liver
½ cup sliced mushrooms
½ teaspoon salt
⅛ teaspoon pepper

Sift flour and salt into a bowl. Add butter and work together with the hands until well blended. Add sour cream and mix again until smooth. Wrap in waxed paper and chill at least 2 hours, overnight if possible. Place the 4 tablespoons melted butter in a saucepan and add livers, mushrooms, salt and pepper. Cook over low heat for 10 minutes. Chop fine and cool for 15 minutes. Roll out the dough 3 mm thick on a lightly floured board. Cut rounds with a pastry cutter. Place a heaped teaspoon of the liver mixture on each and fold over the dough, sealing the edges carefully. Place on a baking sheet. Bake in 190°C oven 20 minutes. Serve hot.

Note: Piroshki are usually served with cabbage soup. However, they may be served as hot hors d'oeuvres.

Scandinavia

CABBAGE SOUP WITH DUMPLINGS (Vitkalsoppa med Kroppkakor)

4 tablespoons butter
1 medium cabbage, coarsely shredded
2 tablespoons dark brown sugar

3 cans consomme and 5 cups water
2 teaspoons salt
½ teaspoon pepper

Melt butter in a saucepan. Add cabbage and saute until brown, stirring frequently. Add sugar and cook over medium heat for 3 minutes, stirring constantly. Add stock, salt and pepper. Cover and cook over low heat for 45 minutes. Correct seasoning. Serve with dumplings.

Dumplings:

4 tablespoons butter
2 onions, chopped
375 g ham, diced
6 boiled potatoes, peeled
¾ cup sifted flour
1½ teaspoons salt
2 egg yolks, beaten

Melt butter in a saucepan. Add onions and saute 5 minutes, stirring frequently. Add ham and saute 10 minutes. Set aside. Mash potatoes. Add flour, salt and egg yolks and mix together. Knead into a dough and shape into a long roll about 2 cm in diameter. Break off pieces of dough about the size of a golf ball and flatten with the hand on a lightly floured surface. Place a heaped teaspoon of the ham mixture on each and shape into dumplings, sealing the edges carefully. Drop into boiling, salted water and cook for 15 minutes. Drain. The dumplings may be placed in the cabbage soup or they may be served in a separate dish.

SALMON WITH LEMON SAUCE (Lax med Citronsas)

3 onions, sliced
2 carrots, sliced
2 teaspoons salt
1 teaspoon white pepper
1 bay leaf
2 tablespoons white vinegar
4 tablespoons chopped dill
4 cups water
4 pounds fresh salmon (in one piece) or 6 slices

Combine onions, carrots, salt, pepper, bay leaf, vinegar, 2 tablespoons of the dill and the water in a saucepan. Bring to a boil and add salmon. Cover and cook over low heat for 20 minutes. Remove cover and cook for 20 minutes. Remove the fish carefully and strain the stock. Sprinkle the fish with the remaining dill. Keep the salmon warm and prepare the sauce.

Lemon Sauce:

3 tablespoons butter
2 tablespoons flour
¾ cup heavy cream, scalded
1 teaspoon salt
¼ teaspoon pepper
1 teaspoon sugar
3 tablespoons lemon juice
2 egg yolks

Melt butter in a saucepan. Add flour and mix to a smooth paste. Gradually add cream and 1 cup of the reserved fish stock, stirring constantly until boiling point is reached. Cook over low heat for 5 minutes. Add salt, pepper, sugar and lemon juice, and mix well. Beat egg yolks in a bowl. Gradually add 1 cup of the sauce, beating constantly. Return this mixture to the saucepan and cook over low heat for 1 minute, stirring constantly. Do not allow to boil. Serve the fish and the sauce separately. Tiny boiled and buttered potatoes are often served with the salmon. If desired, the salmon and sauce may be served cold.

FISH SALAD WITH HORSERADISH SAUCE (Fiskesalat med Pepperrotsaus)

750 g cod fillets or haddock
2 tablespoons prepared horseradish
½ cup sour cream
1 level teaspoon salt
½ level teaspoon pepper
2 level tablespoons finely chopped white onion
1 teaspoon white vinegar

3 tablespoons finely chopped fresh dill or parsley
Lettuce cups
2 hard-boiled eggs, sliced
2 tomatoes, cut into wedges

Poach fish in unsalted water until cooked. Remove bones and skin. Separate flesh. In a large mixing bowl combine horseradish, cream, seasonings, onion, vinegar and two-thirds of the dill or parsley. Fold fish into the sauce. Marinate for at least 30 minutes in the refrigerator before serving. Spoon into lettuce cups. Garnish with the sliced eggs and tomato wedges, and just before serving sprinkle the remainder of the chopped dill or parsley over the salad.

TRADITIONAL SWEDISH CHRISTMAS DRINK (Glogg)

2 cups red wine (burgundy or claret)
2 cups port wine
1 tablespoon finely chopped orange or lemon peel
5 cardamom seeds
1 cinnamon stick or 2 teaspoons powdered cinnamon
5 cloves
½ cup almonds, blanched
½ cup seedless raisins
12 cubes sugar
2 cups brandy

A large copper kettle is the proper utensil for preparing glogg, but a large enamel or glass saucepan may be used. Combine the red wine and port in the saucepan over low heat. Take a small piece of cheesecloth and tie up securely orange peel, cardamom seeds, cinnamon and cloves, and place it in the wine mixture. Simmer slowly for 20 minutes. Add almonds and raisins and simmer for 10 minutes. Remove from heat and discard spices. Place the cubes of sugar in a metal strainer and rest it on top of the saucepan if possible. Set the brandy aflame and pour it very gradually over the sugar. If there is any difficulty in lighting the brandy, warm it briefly. As the lighted brandy is poured over the sugar, it will caramelize. As an alternative, ½ cup of granulated sugar may be dissolved in the wine and the brandy set aflame and poured into the wine. Serve hot in mugs.

Singapore

SINGAPORE LOBSTER CURRY

3 cups milk
2 cups fresh or dried grated coconut
125 g butter
5 onions, chopped
2 cloves garlic, minced
⅛ teaspoon cumin seed
2 teaspoons powdered ginger
Dash of cayenne pepper
2 teaspoons salt
2 tablespoons curry powder
2 tomatoes, chopped
2 tablespoons flour
1 cucumber, peeled and cubed
Meat from 2 boiled lobsters or 500 g lobster meat, cubed
2 tablespoons lemon juice
1 tablespoon plum jam

Combine milk and coconut in a saucepan. Bring to a boil, remove from the heat, and stand for 30 minutes. Press all the milk from the coconut and discard the pulp. Melt butter in a saucepan and add onions and garlic. Saute for 10 minutes, stirring frequently. Add cumin seed, ginger, cayenne pepper, salt, curry powder and tomatoes. Cover and cook over low heat for 10 minutes, stirring frequently. Add flour, stirring constantly. Add coconut milk slowly, stirring steadily until boiling point is reached. Add cucumber and lobster meat and cook over low heat for 15 minutes. Mix lemon juice and jam together and add to lobster mixture. Correct seasoning. Mix well. Serve hot, with boiled rice.

Note: Singapore is famous for the fieriness of its curries. Additional curry powder may be added if desired.

South Africa

PICKLED FISH

12 thin snapper cutlets
4 teaspoons salt
1 teaspoon pepper
¼ cup olive or salad oil
6 large onions, sliced in thin rings
3 tablespoons curry powder
½ teaspoon dried ground chilies
1 cup seedless raisins
2 tablespoons sugar
1 teaspoon turmeric
3 cups vinegar

Wash and dry fish. Mix 1 teaspoon of the salt with the pepper and sprinkle the fish with it. Heat the oil in a skillet and brown fish in it on both sides. Remove bones from fish and let cool. Add 4 onions to the oil remaining in the pan and fry until brown. Combine 2 tablespoons curry powder, the chilies, raisins, sugar and turmeric. Add 3 tablespoons of the vinegar and mix well. Arrange several layers of fish, fried onions and the spice mixture in a bowl or jar. Combine remaining onions, vinegar, salt and curry powder in a saucepan. Boil for 15 minutes. Pour over the layers of fish and allow to cool for 1 hour. Cover and keep in the refrigerator for at least two days before using. Prepared this way, the fish will keep about two weeks. Serve cold as an appetizer.

Switzerland

HORSEHOOFS (Struzels)

2 cups sifted flour
2 tablespoons sugar
2 tablespoons butter
1 egg, beaten
½ cup milk
2 tablespoons seedless raisins
1½ teaspoons baking powder
Fat for deep frying
Icing sugar for dusting

Sift flour and sugar together into a bowl. Cut in butter with pastry blender or two knives. Add egg and milk, mixing until well blended. Add raisins and baking powder and again mix well. Shape a tablespoon of the mixture into a horseshoe. Heat fat in a deep saucepan to 190°C. Drop the horseshoes into it and fry until golden brown. Drain and dust with icing sugar. These pastries may be eaten either hot or cold.

Ukraine

CHEESE BLINTZES (Blintzi z Syrom)

2 eggs
2 tablespoons salad oil
1 cup milk
¾ cup flour
½ teaspoon salt
4 tablespoons butter
1 small packet cream cheese
1 small carton cottage cheese
2 egg yolks
3 tablespoons sugar
1 teaspoon vanilla

Beat the eggs, oil and milk together. Add the flour and salt and beat until smooth. Chill in the refrigerator for 30 minutes.

The batter should be the consistency of cream. If too thick add a little milk. Melt 1 teaspoon of the butter in a 20 cm frying pan. Pour a tablespoon of the batter into the pan, turning it quickly to cover the bottom of the pan. Fry for 1 minute on one side only. Remove from the pan and continue the process until the batter is used up. Stack the pancakes as they are made with the fried side up.

Beat the cream cheese, cottage cheese, egg yolks, sugar and vanilla until smooth. Place a tablespoon of the mixture on each pancake. Turn the two opposite sides in, then roll up carefully. Melt the remaining butter in a large frying pan and fry all the blintzes until they are lightly browned on both sides. Serve hot with sour cream and a little sugar, if desired. They are also good cold.

United Kingdom

WENSLEYDALE DIP WITH CELERY AND MUSHROOMS

250 g Wensleydale cheese, grated finely
2 sticks celery, chopped finely
1 cup mushrooms, sliced
1 tablespoon butter, melted
150 ml cream
Salt
Black pepper, freshly ground
Few caraway seeds
Watercress to garnish

Place grated cheese in bowl, add celery. Toss sliced mushrooms in melted butter and cook for 2 to 3 minutes. Add 150 ml cream, salt and freshly ground black pepper to cheese mixture, and blend to a soft consistency. Stir in the mushroom slices and a few caraway seeds. Pile into serving dish. Garnish with sprigs of watercress. Serve with cheese biscuits.

TRADITIONAL CHICKEN AND LEEK SOUP
(Cocky-leeky)

2 kg chicken thighs
3 litres water
2 teaspoons salt
½ teaspoon pepper
12 fresh leeks or 18 scallions (green onions), sliced
1½ cups rice, half cooked

Wash chicken carefully. Place in a saucepan with the water.
Cook for 2 hours, or until tender, adding salt and pepper at the
end of the first hour of cooking. Remove the chicken and keep
warm. Add the leeks and rice to the soup and cook for 25
minutes. Remove the chicken from the bones and add to the
soup. Cook 5 minutes longer. This soup makes an excellent
meal in one dish.

TROUT IN CIDER

4 medium-size trout
1 tablespoon butter
2/3 cup cider
Salt and pepper
3 to 4 sprigs mint
Watercress and lemon wedges to garnish

Clean trout, remove eyes but leave on head and tail. Dry well.
Place fish, butter and cider in a shallow, buttered ovenproof
dish. Add salt and pepper and two sprigs mint. Cover and
place in moderate oven for 25 to 30 minutes. Baste once or
twice during cooking. Garnish with sprigs of watercress and
lemon wedges.
   Serve with minted green peas and boiled potatoes.

LIVER CASSEROLE WITH MUSTARD DUMPLINGS

500 g lamb liver
1 tablespoon plain flour
Salt
Pepper
4 small onions
1 cup mushrooms
1 tablespoon lard or cooking fat
5 or 6 rashers streaky bacon
1 cup stock (made from stock cube)

Mustard Dumplings:

1 cup self-raising flour
Pinch salt
½ level teaspoon dry mustard
½ cup shredded suet
4 tablespoons milk to mix

Rinse liver, dry on kitchen paper. Cut into chunky pieces. Toss in seasoned flour. Peel and slice onions and mushrooms thinly. Fry onions in melted lard or cooking fat until transparent. Trim bacon and cut into small pieces. Add to pan and cook 2 to 3 minutes. Add liver and mushrooms. Stir until meat is lightly browned all over. Gradually blend in prepared stock and stir until sauce thickens. Turn into a casserole. Cover and cook in moderate oven (175°C) for 25 minutes. Remove cover, season to taste.

To prepare dumplings, sift self-raising flour, salt and mustard together into bowl. Stir in suet. Mix to a soft but not sticky dough with milk. Knead lightly on floured board until free from cracks. Divide into 6 to 8 even-sized dumplings with floured hands. Add to casserole. Return to oven and cook further 30 minutes.

RABBIT PIE

1 kg rabbit joints
3 rashers bacon
1 tablespoon butter or margarine
1 onion, sliced
1 clove garlic, chopped
2 tomatoes, sliced
1 level teaspoon paprika
Pepper
1 cup chicken stock (made from stock cube)
1 level teaspoon salt
315 g short crust pastry
Beaten egg to glaze

Trim rabbit joints, rinse in cold water, dry well. Trim bacon, cut into small pieces, fry lightly in pan in fat. Peel, slice and chop onion and clove of garlic, slice tomatoes. Add onion and garlic to saucepan and cook gently until tender. Place rabbit joints in pan and brown all over. Sprinkle in paprika. Gradually add prepared stock. Season to taste. Add tomatoes. Bring to boil, then reduce heat, cover pan and simmer gently for 1 to 1½ hours until tender. Transfer to piedish 30 cm x 23 cm. Cool. Roll out pastry to 2 cm larger than dish. Remove a strip width of dish rim. Damp dish rim, place strip in position. Damp strip, lift lid in position. Press edges firmly together. Trim surplus pastry, flute edge. Roll out trimmings, cut leaf shapes, arrange on pie. Brush over with egg. Bake above centre of moderately hot oven 205°C for 45 to 50 minutes or until pastry is golden and cooked through.

BRANDY SNAPS

3 tablespoons butter or margarine
5 tablespoons castor sugar
3 tablespoons golden syrup
¾ cup plain flour

1 rounded teaspoon ground ginger
Little grated lemon rind
1 good teaspoon brandy (optional)
½ cup double cream
½ cup single cream

Place butter or margarine, castor sugar and golden syrup in saucepan over gentle heat, stirring till melted. Remove from heat. Sift flour and ground ginger together. Stir into mixture in saucepan, beat well, then stir in lemon rind and brandy if liked. Drop in teaspoonfuls on to greased baking sheets, setting well apart. Bake in a moderately slow oven (170°C) for 7 to 10 minutes or till golden brown. Remove from oven, leave on baking trays for a few seconds till biscuits are easily removed with knife. Roll each biscuit round handle of a wooden spoon, leave a moment to set. Cool, fill ends with piped whipped cream.

CORNISH PASTIES

4 cups plain flour
¼ teaspoon salt
250 g butter or substitute
Iced water to mix
Beaten egg for glazing

Filling:
1 kg round steak, very finely cubed
2 potatoes, cubed
2 onions, finely chopped
2 small white turnips, cubed
Pinch thyme
Salt and pepper

Sift flour and salt into basin. Rub in butter until mixture resembles breadcrumbs; add sufficient iced water to make firm dough. Refrigerate 1 hour. Roll out thinly on lightly floured board, cut into circles (use saucer). Make 6 circles.
  For the filling, combine very finely cubed meat, cubed

potatoes, finely chopped onions, cubed turnips and seasonings. Place filling in centre of each pastry round, making a rather long-shaped mound. Moisten edges with little beaten egg to seal. Lift up opposite sides of pastry to centre, making a seam. Pinch scallops along seam, cut small gash along each side of pasties. Brush with beaten egg. Bake in hot oven 20 minutes, reduce heat to moderate, bake further 20 minutes.

SCOTTISH HUFF PASTRY

This is the name given to the close, unleavened paste formerly (and still occasionally) used to wrap food before baking. It is generally used for game, such as venison, or leg ham which should be soaked before being wrapped to remove excess salt. It contains less butter and more water than short crust, its use being simply to keep in the juices and the aroma of the food it surrounds. Although not intended to be eaten, it often absorbs enough fat and flavour to make it appetizing, and bits can be cracked off and served to those who like it. The following recipe is an example of its use:

½ cup butter or substitute
4 cups plain flour
1 cup water
1 well-seasoned leg of lamb

Sift flour into bowl, rub in butter. Mix to a pliable dough with water, knead until smooth. Roll out on lightly floured board to 5 mm thickness. Completely cover leg of lamb, leaving no cracks or holes; seal with a little water. Wrap with greased greaseproof paper, tie securely, and bake.

The pastry is fairly thin, so no extra baking time need be allowed for the joint because of the pastry covering.

ROAST BEEF

3 rib wing of beef (3½ kg)
½ to 1 teaspoon salt

Individual Yorkshire Puddings:

1 cup plain flour
¼ teaspoon salt
1 egg
1 cup milk
2 to 3 tablespoons dripping

Horseradish Sauce:

1 cup double cream
2 tablespoons grated horseradish
½ level teaspoon castor sugar
¼ level teaspoon dry mustard
Pinch salt
1 to 2 dessertspoons tarragon vinegar

Wipe the joint with a clean damp cloth. Sprinkle with the salt and then place in large roasting tin, fat side uppermost. Calculate cooking time, allowing 15 minutes per 500 g and 15 minutes over for rare or underdone, and 20 minutes per 500 g and 20 minutes over for medium done. Cook in the centre of moderate oven for the calculated time. Transfer to hot serving dish and serve with prepared accompaniments.

To prepare Yorkshire Puddings, sift flour and salt together into bowl. Make a well in centre. Break in egg plus 2 tablespoons milk. Beat with a wooden spoon, gradually drawing in flour from sides. Add just over half the milk little by little, beating until smooth. Gradually stir in remaining milk. Cover and leave in cool place for 30 minutes. Heat a little dripping in small deep patty tins. When dripping is heated, half-fill patty tins with batter, place on shelf in hottest part of oven for about 15 minutes until well risen and golden.

For Horseradish Sauce, whisk cream until just beginning to thicken, taking care not to overbeat. Mix finely grated horseradish, sugar, mustard, salt and vinegar together until really blended. Fold prepared horseradish into the whipped cream and mix lightly together. Place in sauceboat or small bowl and chill before serving with the roast beef.

Note: When fresh horseradish is not available it is possible to purchase grated horseradish in jars. Dried horseradish is usually hotter so use less and adjust to taste.

BANBURY TARTS

Filling:
2 tablespoons margarine or butter
½ cup sultanas
½ cup currants
¼ cup chopped peel
¼ teaspoon nutmeg
¼ teaspoon cinnamon
2 teaspoons sugar
½ cup cake-crumbs
1 tablespoon sherry or orange juice
375 g puff pastry

Prepare filling before rolling the pastry. Melt the margarine and add all the other ingredients, mixing well. Set aside. Roll pastry thinly and cut into six or eight squares. Divide the filling into six or eight portions, pressing each into an oval shape. Place a portion of filling diagonally across each square of pastry. Brush the edges of the pastry with water and mould them over the filling to make an oval shape. Turn so that the join is underneath and press gently with a rolling pin to flatten. Brush with egg white and sprinkle with sugar. Make three cuts with scissors or a sharp knife across the widest part to allow for expansion of the filling and the escape of steam. Cook on an ungreased slide in a hot oven 10 minutes, then reduce to moderate heat for a further 10-15 minutes or until pastry is evenly browned and cooked through.

Note: Eccles Tarts are made by the same method but are round, not oval.

SYLLABUB

Rind and juice 2 large lemons
1 cup castor sugar
½ cup sherry
¼ cup brandy
600 ml double cream
125 g macaroons

Place grated rind and lemon juice in bowl. Stir in sugar till dissolved, then add sherry and brandy. Gradually add cream. Cover base of serving dish with half the crushed macaroons. Whisk the cream mixture till it gains in bulk and is thick and creamy. Spoon it over the macaroons. Place in refrigerator to chill. Decorate with remaining macaroons and sprinkle lightly with nutmeg before serving.

United States

GUMBO FILE (New Orleans)

2 No. 14 (1.4 kg) chickens, jointed
2½ teaspoons salt
1 teaspoon pepper
1 clove garlic, minced
3 tablespoons butter
2 onions, chopped
250 g boiled ham, cut into strips
3½ litres water
½ teaspoon thyme
½ teaspoon rosemary
¼ teaspoon dried ground chilies
1 cup canned tomatoes
1 cup okra
24 oysters
1 tablespoon file powder (powdered sassafras)

Clean chicken carefully. Combine salt, pepper and garlic and rub into chicken. Melt butter in a large saucepan. Add onions and chicken. Brown well. Add ham, water, thyme, rosemary, chilies and tomatoes. Cover and cook over low heat for 1½ hours. Add okra and cook for 1 hour. Add oysters. Bring the mixture to a boil and cook 3 minutes. Remove the saucepan from the heat and immediately add file powder. Mix well. Serve at once. Do not return the gumbo to the heat once file powder is added, or it will become stringy. Serve in soup bowls with boiled rice.

CAFE BRULOT (New Orleans)

1 tablespoon allspice
1 lemon rind, cut into thin strips
1 orange rind, cut into thin strips
1 whole stick cinnamon
4 lumps sugar
¼ cup brandy
3 cups extra-strength coffee, hot

In the top of a chafing dish place allspice, lemon rind, orange rind and cinnamon. Place sugar and brandy in a ladle or bowl and heat. Set the brandy afire and pour it over the spice mixture. Light the flame under the chafing dish and, using the ladle or a large spoon, keep pouring the brandy over the other ingredients until the sugar dissolves. When dissolved, immediately add the coffee, which should be freshly made and about fifty per cent stronger than usual. Keep ladling for a few moments to mix coffee, then serve in demi-tasse cups.

BARBECUED SPARERIBS (Southwestern USA)

3 tablespoons butter
1 cup vinegar
1 cup water
2 tablespoons worcestershire sauce
1 teaspoon tabasco sauce
¼ teaspoon cayenne pepper
½ teaspoon dry mustard
2 teaspoons sugar
1 teaspoon paprika
½ cup chili sauce
2 cloves garlic, minced
2 onions, chopped fine
3 racks of small pork spareribs, cracked

Combine in a saucepan butter, vinegar, water, worcestershire sauce, tabasco sauce, cayenne pepper, mustard, sugar, paprika, chili sauce, garlic and onions. Bring the mixture to a boil. Place the spareribs in a bowl and pour the vinegar mixture over them. Marinate at room temperature for at least 2 hours, basting frequently. Place the spareribs on a baking sheet and roast in a 177°C oven for 1 hour. Baste frequently with 1 cup of the marinade. Serve with potatoes baked in foil topped with sour cream and a tossed salad.

SWEET POTATO PIE (Southwestern USA)

1 cup sifted flour
⅛ teaspoon baking powder
¼ teaspoon salt
1/3 cup butter
3 tablespoons iced water
¾ cup butter
¾ cup sugar
1½ cups grated sweet potatoes
1/3 cup milk
¾ teaspoon ground ginger
2 tablespoons grated orange rind

Sift flour, baking powder and salt into a bowl. Add butter and cut it into the flour with a pastry blender or two knives, until the consistency of coarse sand. Add the water, drop by drop, tossing lightly with a fork until a ball of dough is formed. Chill for at least 1 hour. Roll out the dough on a lightly floured surface and line an unbuttered 27 cm pie plate with it. Place the pie plate in the refrigerator while preparing the filling. Preheat oven to 149°C. Cream the butter, add the sugar, and continue creaming until light and fluffy. Gradually add the sweet potatoes and milk alternately, beating well. Add the ginger and orange rind and again beat well. Pour into the prepared pie plate. Bake in a 149°C oven until delicately browned, about 45 minutes. Serve hot, with whipped cream on the side.

Yugoslavia

PRIEST'S LUNCH (Popina Janja Yanje)

1½ kg brisket of beef cut into 3 cm cubes
4 potatoes, peeled and diced
1 cup diced celery
8 sma'l white onions
3 tomatoes, quartered
4 tablespoons chopped parsley
3 cloves garlic, minced
1 teaspoon salt
2 teaspoons paprika
4 bay leaves
12 whole peppercorns
6 cups stock or 2 cans consomme and 2½ cans water

Combine beef, potatoes, celery, onions, tomatoes, parsley, garlic, salt, paprika, bay leaves, peppercorns and stock in a deep casserole. Mix gently. Cover the casserole with a large piece of parchment paper or aluminium foil so that it slightly overhangs the outside edges of the casserole. Tie the paper with a string to make a tight seal. Place the casserole cover over the paper. Bake in a 175°C oven 2½ hours. Correct seasoning and serve directly from the casserole.

INDEX

pickled red cabbage, 234
pickled shrimps, 279
spiced vinegar, 235
Pies
  fruit, 141
  lemon chiffon, 196
  meat, 133
  passionfruit chiffon, 148
  pastry for, 188
  pork, 245
  potato, 98
  pumpkin, 142
  rabbit, 304
  small pies and tartlets, 136
  sweet potato, 311
Pilau
  green pea, 108
  lamb and fruit, 285
  yellow, 106
Pineapple crunch, 197
Pineapple fruit cake, 184
Piroshki, 196
Pizza, 135
Plum pudding, 212
Pork
  Arabian pork chops, 80
  barbecued spare ribs, 312
  lima bean casserole, 281
  pepper, 243
  suckling pig, 85
  with sauerkraut, 290
Pork pie, 245
Potato balls, 273
Potato soup, 59
  vichyssoise, 61
Potatoes
  bechamel, 98
  pie, 98
  ring, 96
  stuffed baked, 97
  sweet, 311
Poulet au porto, 252
Prawn dill cream, 69
Prawns
  avocado with, 69
  in ramekins, 54
  island prawn curry, 70
  prawn dill cream, 69
Priest's lunch, 312
Prune whip tart, 142